CHILD SEX ABUSE
POWER, PROFIT, PERVERSION

Beverley Chalmers (DSc (Med); PhD)

Edited by Dana Solomon (PhD), D-Editions

Grosvenor House
Publishing Limited

This book is published by
Grosvenor House Publishing Ltd
Link House
140 The Broadway, Tolworth, Surrey, KT6 7HT.
www.grosvenorhousepublishing.co.uk

A CIP record for this book
is available from the British Library

ISBN 978-1-83975-956-7

Abuse, Birth & Children Series: Historical & Contemporary

Other books by Beverley Chalmers in the ABC Series.

Historical

- *Birth, Sex and Abuse: Women's Voices under Nazi Rule*
- *Betrayed: Child Sex Abuse in the Holocaust*
- *African Birth: Childbirth in Cultural Transition*

Contemporary

- *Birth Abuse or Respectful Care?* (Forthcoming)
- *Family Centred Care: Improving Pregnancy, Birth and Postpartum Care*
- *Humane Perinatal Care* (With Adik Levin)
- *Pregnancy and Parenthood: Heaven or Hell*
- *Female Genital Mutilation and Obstetric Care* (With Kowser Omer-Hashi)

Learn more or contact Dr. Chalmers at www.bevchalmers.com.

Dedication

To children everywhere, and especially, those who are abused.

To Bernie, my husband of fifty years, with immense love, and respect for his caring, respectful, wise, and wonderful parenting of our three daughters. Thank you for keeping your promise to me all those years ago and for holding me safe.

Acknowledgements

I would like to thank:

My husband Bernie who patiently read and reread multiple drafts of this book, providing me with valuable and challenging critical insights that made me re-think and re-write multiple times.

My editor and daughter, Dr. Dana Solomon, who had the courage to tell me to start again after years of work, and who always gave me invaluable, although often harshly critical feedback. My thanks too, for her remarkable insights, editing and publications skills.

Dr Sandra Cowan for sharing some important texts on child sex abuse with me.

My reviewers: Dr. Jan Burzlaff, the William A Ackman Fellow for Holocaust Studies at Harvard University, a Former fellow at the *École Normale Superieure*, Paris, and the Jane Eliza Procter Fellow at Princeton University, who read the penultimate draft of the text and gave me valuable thoughts on sections that could be strengthened.

Also, Dr. Stephen Thomas, Executive Director, Analytics and AI Ecosystems, and Distinguished Professor of Management Analytics, Queen's University, Kingston, Canada, who confirmed my representation of internet related issues to ensure I did not make an internet fool of myself. Both these reviewers provided valuable insights, thoughts, and suggestions for the text. I trust I have done justice to their ideas.

Table of Contents

Introducing Child Sex Abuse

Our world provides a climate that enables the sexual abuse of children. Child sex abuse is rampant today with approximately 120 million children under the age of twenty reporting sexual abuse – about one in every ten.[1] Such abuse is not limited to any one society, culture, group, religion, institution, or situation. It is sanctioned by some societies both overtly and covertly with few willing to confront this scourge. It occurs in multiple settings including at home, in educational institutions, religious organizations, sporting bodies, community organizations, in high- middle- and low-income countries, among rich and poor.[2] It affects all children – girls, boys and those with sexual and gender diversity – and is perpetrated on infants, toddlers, children, adolescents, and youth. It occurs at an individual, institutional, societal, and global level. At present, we have few means of preventing it, minimal ability to monitor its prevalence, cannot deter most perpetrators from committing such crimes either in person or digitally, and can barely assist survivors. We choose to ignore sexual abuse of children by hiding behind the taboo discussion of sex as well as by obfuscating the issue behind religious, political, social, or ideological screens. More egregiously, we justify child sex abuse – and sometimes facilitate child sex abuse – allowing it to continue, not only in hidden places, but even in the open. Nor do we punish it with due regard for its impact on the lives of children. In fact, we do not listen to the voices of the children but often blame them for their own abuse instead of holding the perpetrators responsible for their crimes. This book exposes these allegations in all their nuances, and gives voice to the children who endure such horrific abuse and exploitation. It is a wake-up call to us all.

Both perpetrators and victims of child sex abuse are influenced by individual, institutional, societal and global practices. Child sex abuse is not isolated to physical abuse but has severe emotional, cognitive, social and economic consequences for survivors. Its impact is often devastating. Child sex abuse is not just a physical or sexual crime. It is an act of betrayal, humiliation, and degradation that creates enormous challenges for the children's self perception of their worth, intellectual understanding, and trust in the world. They may have to continue with activities that are associated with their abuse and that may even involve their abusers. Perpetrators do not necessarily recognize such outcomes and may believe their actions are harmless, or even beneficial for both themselves and the children they abuse.

Societal, political and global reactions to child sex abuse appear to be inadequate to prevent, monitor, or eliminate much of its occurrence. Our unwillingness to discuss sexual activity, consider that this is affecting children, confront authority figures who endorse or at least cover-up sexual abuse of children, consider values and worldviews that facilitate such abuse, blame the survivors rather than the perpetrators, and understand the rapid spread of abuse using digital media, contributes to the problem. Awareness of sexual abuse distinct from, although related to, other forms of child abuse has only been the focus of research for the past forty years or so. Far too many children are victims of sexual assault; far too many perpetrators exist and escape adverse outcomes, and there are far too many bystanders who choose not to intervene or even to speak out. Few are able to prevent child sex abuse. Many who are aware of ongoing child sex abuse do not speak out about it, or are themselves intimidated into not reporting these crimes. They, by omission, enable the perpetrators. We like to convince ourselves that child abuse is something that happens elsewhere...in other countries, other times, to other people. We do not want to accept that not only is it present in our own communities, homes and schools, but that we ourselves are contributing to it through our willful blindness,

2

our silence, and our ideological certainty that we are virtuous.[3] Child sex abuse is both persistent and pervasive despite legislative, policy and practice initiatives opposing it.[4]

Justify, Hide and Facilitate

This book examines the many facets of child sex abuse in our world, and how we justify, ignore and even facilitate it today, in the hope that if we face up to the problem and its extensive and intrusive prevalence then we might choose to take stronger action to counter it. Part 1 reveals how child sexual abuse within family or family-like settings is often justified by society. Families sometimes support paedophilia, formally endorse child sex abuse through child marriage and facilitate abuse through socially discriminatory practices. Part 2 of this book reveals how child sexual abuse is ignored at the institutional level, particularly within multiple religious organizations such as schools, in mental health institutions, and in social organizations such as sports teams and scouting movements. Child sex abuse in The Canadian Residential Schools, implemented as part of a cultural genocide, in the Irish Catholic School system under the guise of religious fervour, and opportunistically, in Judaic educational programs, is exposed. The Canadian Duplessis children reveal that even mental institutions have been seconded to implement child sex abuse for financial gain. Part 3 examines how child sex abuse on a global level is facilitated by our digital technology, by our military expansion, and by economic incentives that fuel an enormous global trade in sex trafficking. Part 4 reflects on some of the attempts we make to prevent child sexual abuse and what we still need to do.

Wherever possible, the voices of the children themselves are included in the hope that their cries for help can be heard. Creating awareness of the severity and extensiveness of this crime is needed as a significant first step towards countering this growing pandemic in our world. It is hoped that this book contributes to such knowledge and serves as a wake-up call to governments, politicians, lawyers, doctors, caregivers, religious leaders, educational ministries and societal governance authorities to take a stand and take action against perpetrators, while recognizing that the children are not to blame for their own abuse. Only perpetrators and those who stand by and do nothing are.

The remainder of this introduction examines how child sex abuse is defined, types of child sex abuse, who abuses children, where, and factors contributing to child sex abuse at individual, institutional, societal and global levels in relation to both perpetrators' experiences as well as those of victims.

What is Child Sexual Abuse?

Definitions of child sexual assault, sexual harassment, and rape differ, but all agree that any sexual act with a child is the responsibility of the adult involved, regardless of the child's role – or consent – in the event. All definitions involve the use of a child by a person for sexual arousal or sexual gratification of that person or another person.[5] In some countries, such as Canada, the legal definition of rape and sexual assault – and one that guides its use in this book – has moved from one that focuses on the sexual nature of the event to one that emphasizes the power, control and violence associated with the crime. The level of seriousness of the assault is determined by the amount of force used and the degree of injury sustained by the victim. The term sexual assault is used to include unwanted touching, oral, anal, and vaginal intercourse, and sexual violence. A silent or ambiguous response to sexual initiation, or tacit approval given while intoxicated, drugged or unconscious is not a satisfactory indicator of consent. The child must also be older than sixteen years of age to consent to sex. Close-in-age exceptions can be made, granting the ability to have consensual sex among young people under sixteen, although not when one person is in a position of trust or has authority over the other.[6] Some countries have lower age restrictions such as France, which in 2021, adopted legislation that regards sex with a child under the age of fifteen, with or without apparent consent, as rape, punishable by up to twenty years in jail.[7]

Language

The language used to describe child sex abuse often denigrates the children involved or the severity of the crime. For example, the term "pornography" is commonly used for images depicting adults engaging in consensual acts distributed legally to the general public for their sexual pleasure. When children's images are involved, it is not "porn" but abuse, and a criminal act. The Luxembourg Guidelines outlined by Interpol, and developed by an international group of eighteen partners, provide an appropriate list of terminology that should be used to protect children from further, linguistic sexual exploitation and sexual abuse.[8] These guidelines recommend, for example, that "child sexual abuse" be used in preference to "child pornography." These guidelines have been adhered to in this book.

Prevalence

Child sex abuse today is a global phenomenon. The lifetime prevalence of childhood sexual abuse is high for all children but particularly for girls and for children with gender diverse identities.[9] Recent decades have seen a rapid increase in the number of journal publications on child sex abuse in its various forms. Yet, such publications are inadequate to comprehensively cover the subject. Studies vary by country, the definitions used, the types of abuse examined, the ages of children included, the extent of coverage, and the quality of data.[10] Studies are not all comparable, in that some report the number of children abused in any one year, others the number ever abused in their lifetime, and a few report recollections by adults of their childhood abuse.[11]

Much sexual abuse of children is not reported. Police records or hospital admission databases likely underestimate the extent of the problem by a factor of nine.[12] For example, crimes of rape and incest go unreported throughout the world. Girls and women may, often rightly, believe that the trauma of reporting the crime will likely lead

5

to the trauma of not being believed; of being attacked and blamed; and the crime never being punished. Victims also face the negative judgement of the press, community members, family members, and others. Children, in particular, hesitate to report abuse often because they are groomed not to do so by their abuser with threats to themselves or their families. They are not believed when they do, families may prefer to cover-up the "disgrace," or fear the perpetrator, reporting leads to psychological re-assault, as does facing repeated accounting of the abuse in multiple court appearances. Laws may require witnesses for confirmation – an impossibility given the private nature of most abuse – and evidence may be washed away in an effort to eliminate the shame and horror of the assault. Authorities prefer to downplay the extent of the problem, politicians do not want this type of slander on their governance, and countries are reluctant to admit to such shortcomings. Hence a global culture that fails to condemn child sex abuse emerges, unopposed by any vocal, social, legal or political outcry.

Although prevalence studies are difficult to implement, and estimates vary, a comprehensive meta-analysis of childhood sexual abuse as reported in 217 publications over almost thirty years commencing in 1980, including almost ten million participants, indicated that self-reported child sexual abuse occurred in 18% of girls and 8% of boys.[13] Regional reports of prevalence of overall child sex abuse vary widely ranging from 9% in Europe, 10% in America, 23% in Asia, and 34% in Africa.[14] While percentages give an overall impression of prevalence, the raw numbers are staggering: A 2002 UNICEF global review indicated that 150 million girls and seventy-three million boys under the age of eighteen living at that time had experienced forced sexual intercourse or other forms of sexual violence involving physical contact. Taking into account that this is one of the most under-reported crimes, particularly among communities that are marginalised, and often the targets of sexual abuse, these numbers are staggering.

Defining who is a child is challenging. United Nations Organizations today study children under the age of eighteen in

6

research into child sexual exploitation.[15] We tend to think of children involved in sex trafficking and child marriage as older teenagers, yet this is not always the case and many prepubescent girls are caught up in both marriage and trafficking activities, with even younger children being the targets of abuse in the home, school or community. In most cases the perpetrator is known to the child. The rates of sexual abuse, however, rise after menstruation. Children with physical disabilities such as deafness, blindness and mental, intellectual, or developmental disabilities are at increased risk of sexual abuse. Children from poorer socio-economic groups are more vulnerable. The absence of one or both parents, marital disharmony, and drug or substance abuse in the family or among children themselves, increases their risk. Societal customs such as child marriage as well as children with non-traditional gender and sexual identities or expression are also more vulnerable to exploitation.[16]

The consequences for children are devastating. Survivors experience immediate after-effects[17] as well as remain scarred, and live with long term effects, including adverse psychological, physical, behavioural and interpersonal outcomes.[18] Psychologically, sexually abused children can experience long-term post-traumatic stress disorder, depression, low self-esteem, anxiety and panic disorders, guilt and anger, body-image concerns and eating disorders, substance abuse, suicidal attempts, hopelessness, and disrupted cognitive and emotional development. Physically they might experience vaginal (or anal) bleeding or infection, urinary tract infections, menstrual irregularities, sexually transmitted infections, pregnancy, genital injury and gastrointestinal problems. Behaviourally, they may exhibit lower academic performances, sexualized behaviours, exhibitionism or violence, violation of laws and social conduct, and an increased tendency to become perpetrators themselves. Interpersonally, they may become insecure, exhibit reduced social competence, have difficulty communicating, and lack trust in relationships. There is a close relationship between sexual abuse in childhood and adolescence and later victimization, drug abuse, prostitution, suicide, mental illness, self-mutilation, alcoholism, running away from home, and difficulties in parenting.[19] Childhood sexual abuse is also linked with economic consequences in later life, such as lower incomes and higher rates of unemployment.[20] Despite these generalizations, we need to acknowledge that each individual child who is abused is unique and that their potential for recovery is influenced by a myriad of factors. These include the child's own earlier developmental progress and personal sense of integrity and self respect prior to their abuse as well as the support systems that may surround them offered by family members, social services, educators, legal authorities, and societal supports. Optimal background factors, and current and ongoing supportive systems can play a positive role in assisting any abused child to move forward from their abusive experiences favourably. These are, however, not always in evidence.

Increasing severity of sexual abuse is associated with increasingly adverse effects. Incest in particular leads to relationship difficulties.[21] Therapy and extensive social support may help. While the majority of victims recover from the acute experience of trauma within about five years, nearly a third of victims have substantial difficulties that persist for far longer.   The intergenerational cycle of violence that ensues can cause a legacy of suffering and economic hardship at the individual, family, societal and national level.[22] The socio-economic effects are serious with the average cost for each victim being US $210,000.[23] In consequence, the United Nations National Sustainable Development goals of 2015, for the period 2015-2030, added two new targets aimed at addressing this problem. Target 16.2 aims to end abuse and exploitation of children while Target 5.2 aims to eliminate all forms of violence against women and girls including sexual exploitation. In addition to the UN defined targets, we, as a global community, should develop stronger and more effective ways to assist survivors to recover from and to overcome the challenges facing them after abuse. In addition, every country and every community should take active steps to prevent abuse and prosecute abusers. It is likely that many of the ill consequences of sexual abuse arise not only from the abusive incident/s but also from the inadequate societal understanding, acceptance, and support for survivors that they need and deserve to receive.

8

Sources of Information

Academic Texts and Articles

There are few English language academic texts that are exclusively focused on child sex abuse. Rush's work[24] as well as that of Bass and Thornton[25] are notable, although written some decades ago. Distinguished current comprehensive texts on sexuality such as Pukall's *Human Sexuality* address the issue, but briefly: Only a dozen or so pages of this over 500-page excellent contemporary introduction to sexuality covers child sex or sexual abuse. Multiple books address specific aspects of child sex abuse such as sexual slavery,[26] sex trafficking,[27] sex in Church based institutions,[28] or religious Jewish settings,[29] and in genocidal settings such as the Holocaust.[30] While there are multiple journal articles that mention child sex abuse, the topic has really only been addressed to any great extent for the past few decades, leading to a dearth of comprehensive, integrated material on this subject. Although sexual abuse of children has occurred over centuries, there is little systematic reporting or recognition of this, hitherto, taboo subject. This book focuses on present day sexual abuse of children although events occurring in the past century are discussed as precursors to the current stresses experienced by child survivors today.

Memoirs or Biographies

Memoirs and biographies of victims/survivors of child sexual abuse provide a further source of information. In particular, individual stories of their abuse have been told by many of the children abused in Church run institutions that cared for children *in loco parentis* such as in schools, orphanages, and homes for unmarried mothers, in Ireland, the UK, Australia, and Canada.[31] Indigenous children abused in the Residential Schools of Canada have also given voice to their experiences in memoirs and as testimonies to Commissions of Inquiry into the multiple abuses committed in them.[32] Similarly, a few stories of children abused in their homes or in foster care, or forced into child marriage, or prostitution and the sex trade are also available, some written as autobiographies and others told by their caregivers.[33]

News Reports

Accounts of sexual abuse of children are reported globally in news reports, almost on a daily basis. About 200 of these horrific incidents of child sexual abuse and rape occurring between 2016 and 2021 in the USA, Canada, the UK, Europe, Australia, and in multiple African, Asian and South American countries, and reported in news reports primarily by BBC in the UK, but also by CNN in the USA, CBC in Canada, and Reuters globally are included in this book. Despite this exposure, awareness of child sexual abuse, even in Western countries, remains incomplete.[34] News reports are not reliable academic sources. In a global review of sexual abuse, however, and given the sparsity of English language academic reports regarding sexual abuse of children in multiple cultures and countries, such reports provide an extensive indication of the types of child sex abuse that occur. These reports provide a glimpse into the possible extent and severity of the problem globally and are included in this book, while acknowledging this academic caveat.

The subject matter of child sex abuse is vast. Issues that are encompassed include familial abuse, societal abuse, institutional abuse – such as in schools, athletic organizations, and child help programs – sex trafficking, child marriage, sexual abuse during war, abuse of child soldiers, internet-based child sexual abuse, legislation regarding child sexual abuse, consequences of sexual abuse for children, treatment programs for them, paedophilia and its treatment, cultural differences in attitudes towards child sexual abuse, justifications for such abuse, cover-ups, prevalence studies, UN resolutions and actions and programs to counter such abuse, and multiple others. To date there is no text that integrates these various issues into a single resource and that attempts to integrate and conceptualize the global phenomenon of child sex abuse. This is, indeed, a tall order, but is attempted here, at least as an introduction that others may be able to build upon.

It is hoped that this book will raise awareness of the plight of these children, and the extent of the problems facing them. It places the blame and shame for their abuse, not on the children themselves, as is so often apportioned, but on the cruelty, violence and selfishness of the perpetrators and bystanders – family members, friends, neighbours, teachers, clerics, athletic coaches, professionals, pimps, abusers, traffickers, and ordinary people who facilitate child sex abuse on the internet. Even more so, this book calls on politicians, law enforcement, religious leaders, and economic influencers – those with the power and ability to prevent and/or prosecute child sex abusers – to face their responsibilities and take urgent action to change the climate of child sex abuse that overshadows our world.

Part 1: Justifying Child Sex Abuse in Family Settings

We assume that children are safe in their homes and that families are dedicated to keeping them so. We also assume that this safety includes protection from sexual and other forms of abuse. This is not always the case. Some children are sexually abused in their homes, by family or friends despite societal censure for such acts. More egregiously, such sexual activities are not condemned but are regarded as normative and desirable in many parts of the world justified as male rights, methods of healing, or cleansing traditions. Child marriage, for example, may be viewed as little more than societally approved child sexual abuse incentivised by financial gain for the child's family. Our world can be a difficult and cruel world in which to live, for children.

Abuse at Home and Paedophilia

People, of all genders, ages, and sexual orientations sexually abuse children for a multitude of reasons. While some acts of child sexual abuse may be explained by paedophilia, most are likely to result from opportunity, autocracy, authoritarianism, and power, little fear of exposure, possible sexual frustration, hatred and fear of the destitute, or vulnerable, or "other," feelings of insecurity, and the perception that physical, sexual and emotional abuse of others proves the perpetrators' dominance, prowess, and "machismo." In contrast, sexual abuse of children may also be perceived by abusers as generosity and benevolence that is cloaked in an aura of good intentions – such as the men who believe they are helping sex workers to earn a living to pay for their college funds by selling sex, or the man who pays a pittance for a beggar child in a poor country by giving him food, lodging and friendship in exchange for sex. In addition, in some cases, an overriding religious and/ or national ideological righteousness may provide a halo-shining covering that makes abuse of children acceptable, or even desirable.

Child Sexual Slavery

Incidents of long-term abuse of children kept hidden in captivity are uncommon, although devastating when they are revealed. A number have been exposed in the past two decades alone. Argentinian Domingo Bulacio kept his daughter as a sex slave for over twenty years, starting when she was eleven years old, and fathered eight children with her. Ariel Castro held and abused three women and a girl in captivity in

Cleveland for about a decade. A couple in California, Philip and Nancy Garrido, kidnapped eleven-year-old Jaycee Dugard and held her captive and sexually abused her for eighteen years. Krzystof Bartozuk held his daughter for six years raping her and fathering two children with her. Austria's Josef Fritzl fathered seven children with his daughter whom he kept locked in a cellar for twenty-four years.[35] Even when not confined in secret, repeated and cruel child sexual abuse by a parent can cause extreme psychological distress and mental illness, in addition to severe physical harm, such as in the case of Jeni Haynes in Australia. Repeatedly and violently sexually abused from before she was four years old until the age of eleven, she developed multiple dissociative identities to escape her daily horrors. In a landmark case, her father, and abuser, was sentenced to forty-five years in jail when Jeni, now aged forty-nine, and five of her multiple personalities, gave evidence at his trial.[36]

These cases of long-term extreme child sex abuse are likely a mixture of paedophilia and a need for power and sexual violence. While paedophiles are attracted to, and aroused by children, this attraction does not usually persist once the child reaches puberty, as in the case of Jeni. Abuse that lasts into the teenage and adult years is more likely to be a manifestation of power, authority, and violence rather than, simply, sexual arousal in response to children.

Incest and Abuse by Family Members

Most child sex abuse occurs in a family setting and is perpetrated by someone known to the child.[37] Most abusers focus on a specific child and groom and coerce the child into compliance with their needs.[38] Intra-familial abuse is surrounded by secrecy, fear, and power or powerlessness and occurs across social class, educational background, religious affiliation and professional status. Abusers are most often male, although some are women. Women are more likely to be abusive, or are perpetrators, by denying or failing to act on abuse when they are aware of it, regarded as "Mothers pimping their children."[39] While children may also be sexually victimized by other

16

children, the most common abusers within the home environment are adult men (primarily fathers, stepfathers and mothers' boyfriends). Such abuse may occur only once or twice before being revealed and the child moved out of the home environment (by, for example, the breakup of the marriage or relationship, or the interference by child services) or it may continue for a number of years while the child is still too young to object or escape, or is terrorized into compliance. Child sex abuse may also be perpetrated by other children. In California, for example, an eighteen-year-old confessed to abusing "upwards of fifty children" from the age of ten years old.[40] Children with diverse gender identities are also at particular risk of sexual abuse by those in their social network although research into this aspect of abuse is relatively scarce as gender diversity is only slowly being acknowledged and supported.

Children have immense difficulty reporting or relating their experiences of abuse. Grooming them for sexual abuse includes creating fear in them about reporting their experiences, with threats to hurt them or their siblings/parents if they do. They are also taught to think that they are to blame for the abuse, that they invited it, and that they would be punished if they were ever to reveal the events. It can take decades before children reveal what has happened to them and it is difficult for them to confront their abusers, either in person or through the law. In addition, the justice system is rarely understanding of or sympathetic to their turmoil and may even view the children as responsible for inciting their abusers. Children in abusive situations may also have nobody to turn to and nowhere else to go if the abuse occurs in their homes.

Despite the difficulties of reporting sexual assault in their homes, there are multiple reports of familial child sex abuse. In France, for example, Joël Le Scouamec, a sixty-nine-year-old retired surgeon, was charged with abusing his two nieces, a neighbour's daughter and a patient. According to notebooks in which the retiree recorded his attacks, at least 349 children were victims of his acts between 1989 and 2017. If found guilty he could face up to twenty years in prison.[41] In France, however, there has been a tolerance for sexual violence against children with fewer than 1% of rape cases against minors being taken to court. A poll taken at the end of 2020 suggests that one in ten people have experienced sexual abuse in the family. A #MeTooInceste posting in early 2021 following the publication of a book reporting on incest perpetrated by the French professor and constitutional specialist Olivier Duhamel, led to 80,000 responses within five days indicative of the widespread identification of women with this concern.[42] President Emmanuel Macron, in response, has indicated that he will tighten France's laws against incest and introduce education about incest in primary and secondary schools.[43]

France is not alone in this egregious deficit. A recent UNICEF report reveals that while most of the 155 countries they surveyed have laws prohibiting sexual violence against children, the perceived enforcement of these laws is rated as high by only 57% of countries for statutory rape; 50% of countries for contact sexual violence; and 42% of countries for non-contact sexual violence. Further, in about half of the countries surveyed, rape laws do not apply to sexual abuse of boys.[44]

Lucy Gilbert's experiences of being abused by her father, a paedophile, in their North London, UK, home is, unfortunately not exceptional.[45] Shown pornography, including adult-child sex images and videos, from about ten years old, she was groomed into believing that such activities were normal and a way of showing her love for her father. Cared for by him, showered with treats, and then bathed by him, and later bathed with him, she was increasingly encouraged to touch and engage with him in activities that were pleasurable for him. Eventually he raped her at the age of ten. Continuous encouragement by him led to him sharing her with a friend and later, multiple friends, at parties held in his home. Under the guise and incentive of her becoming a film star, these events were filmed and "guests" charged for admission to the parties. Money flowed in, leading her father to buy a larger, expensive house, cars and other luxuries while she "earned" fifty dollars a night. Although she found these events horrific and wanted to stop "performing" as a film star, she was not allowed to, being encouraged to continue by using valium to get her through the evenings, virtually unaware of what was being done to her. She later reported:

> How is it possible to love someone who treats you so
> badly? All I can tell you is that it is perfectly possible.
> I felt such guilt for wishing my life to be different.

The North American Man-Boy Love Association[68] puts forth several arguments in support of their perceived "right" to have sex with children. Their primary argument is that societal values are too restrictive, and that general attitudes to sexual matters have changed over time, for example, as regards masturbation and same-sex sexual behaviours. This argument largely ignores the issue of consent, or at least the inability of children with their limited life experiences and knowledge, to truly give informed consent to adult sexual interactions. Abusers also note that other paraphilias (for example, homosexuality) have been removed from the Diagnostic and Statistical Manual of Mental Disorders (DSM) and that sex with children has existed throughout history. The group argues that sex with boys in the context of a loving relationship is not harmful and that this is a very different situation from that of individuals who prey on young boys exclusively for their own sexual gratification.[69] The voices of adults who have sex with children such as those belonging to the North American Man-Boy Love Association are well illustrated by two episodes of Dick Wolf's Law and Order Special Victims Unit, *Pandora* and *Angels*. *Angels* – gives voice to how perpetrators justify their actions as a normal aspect of life.[70] In *Pandora* paedophiles emphasize that their practices are widespread, lending apparent support for their actions:

> Society says I'm wrong. Not long ago, society said interracial marriage was wrong and executed homosexuals. Now it's paedophiles. I used to think that I was alone. There are hundreds of thousands of paedophiles just like me. You're the minority. You're the freaks. Go ahead and arrest us and persecute us, we're not going away, we're not going to play by your rules and nothing you can do will ever change that.[71]

Other paedophiles go to countries like Cambodia or Thailand and provide housing and schooling for children in exchange for sex. These men often argue that the children's lives are better because of their generosity.[72] For example, Manfred Gast retired to Cambodia in 1993 and was formally charged with "debauchery" by Cambodia police. He justified his relationship with one young boy by saying that he found him as a street orphan and provided him with "shelter food, games and about one dollar a day in pocket money." He stated, "Did I fondle him? Yes. But you must understand the boy never had a home and no one ever cared for him."[73] He further stated that the boy was too young to ejaculate and, therefore, the relationship was not sexual. He saved oral sex and penetrative activities for the older boys he abused.[74] Like most paedophiles, Manfred Gast did not prey on strangers and was not violent. Rather he groomed and coerced a specific child that he became close to.[75] Similarly, Peter Dalglish, an Order of Canada recipient for his work on behalf of children, who founded Street Kids International and has worked with UN Habitat in Afghanistan, and with WHO and the UN mission for Ebola in Libya, was found guilty of sexually abusing two boys that he had befriended aged eleven and fourteen in Kathmandu, Nepal, where he lives. He faces a nine-year prison sentence.[76] Dalglish denies that he abused the children and Nepalese criminal proceedings make ascertaining the veracity of either his or the children's accounts difficult to assess.

In the USA, a group called the Childhood Sensuality Circle as well as the North American Man-Boy Love Association advocated, unsuccessfully, to legalize paedophilia. Other countries including the Netherlands, Canada and the UK have had similar initiatives. In West Germany, where the Nazi past made left-wing political parties especially sensitive to arguments about individual freedoms, the movement fared better. The idea that sexual freedom was a way to prevent authoritarianism was entertained by many.[77] Some proponents of this approach were well known including a prominent sexual researcher named Helmut Kentler who, in the 1960s, arranged for illiterate young teenagers to move in with three known West Berlin paedophiles in the hope that the children could learn to live "proper, unremarkable lives" because they had a sexual relationship with these adults.[78]

Even Freud (writing around the onset of the 20th Century) and the Kinsey reporters (publishing in the mid 20th Century), two of the most prominent and influential writers on sexuality, have been accused of avoiding condemnation of child-adult sexuality, if not endorsing it. Freud's interpretation of his patients' reports of incest were not taken at

Societal Justifications

Child sex abuse is endorsed in multiple global settings although the nature and types of sexual abuse of children vary by culture and context. Individual acts of child sex abuse occur across the globe, but often for differing reasons. It appears to be more common in male dominant societies where a commonly asserted motivation includes the right of men to have sex, with women and children being regarded as the property of men, to be used as they wish. Some cults, or those with religiously disguised beliefs, include sexual abuse of children as part of their accepted rituals. Additional reasons used to justify child sexual abuse include beliefs that violent sex is acceptable, that sex is a pubertal rite of passage, that fathers have the right to initiate their daughters into sex, and that sex is a cure for HIV/AIDS. Two specific cultural patterns are examined, that of Japan where attitudes towards involving children in sexual behaviour have historically been more lenient than in many other parts of the world, and in India, home to the largest child population of any country, where rape of women and children has become a widespread problem.

Cults

Child sex abuse is sometimes rationalised in cults. For example, the religiously modelled cult calling itself the Children of God espouses a value that God is love and love equals sex, meaning that for all members, including children, sharing one's body is the highest expression of love, leading to extensive sexual abuse of children and adults.[100] In this particular cult, everything done in love is sanctioned in the eyes of God, including adultery, incest, extramarital sex and adult-child sex. These are no longer sins as they are done "in love."[101] Celeste Jones, Kristina Jones and Juliana Buhring were three sisters born into and caught up in the "Children of God." As children they were encouraged to and did engage in sexual relations with their child cohorts and the adults in their family circle, at the same time as being exposed to tight authoritarian controls that demanded absolute obeisance to the beliefs of their cult and its leader. For one of them these demands were too great. They write:

> In January 2005, our sister Davida died from a drug overdose. She was twenty-three. The shock of Davida's death affected us deeply though we understood her pain and despair. Each of us in our own way has struggled with painful memories of abandonment, neglect and abuse as children born and raised under the malign influence of a religious cult, the Children of God.
> We were systematically abused. Physically, mentally, emotionally and sexually, from the earliest age. We were separated from each other, and our parents, and raised communally in this organization, which was also known as the "Family" [...]
> Isolated from society, we were controlled by fear – fear of the government, police, doctors and social workers, and the even greater fear of God's wrath if we ever left the protection of the Family.[102]

Sex cults can take differing forms such as the apparently supportive, mentoring group, primarily directed at adults but also recruiting among young, under-age student populations, NXIVM.[103] This group worked with over 18,000 people, offering so-called Executive Success Programs as well as coercing some female recruits into having sex with the founder, Keith Raniere, and branding them with his initials. NXIVM used so-called training, mentorship, self-help, and career advancement programs to recruit and facilitate trafficking and abuse.[104] Raniere has now been sentenced to 120 years in prison, essentially for the remainder of his life.[105] His collaborators included the Red Cross Children's Hospital in Cape Town each month. The number of child rapes and rapes in SA was so embarrassing that the government placed a moratorium on government crime statistics in 2001 stating that they needed "reassessment."[125]

The situation has not changed much over the past twenty years although it is not known whether the belief in rape as a preventive or curative measure regarding HIV/AIDS is a primary or even still a prevalent contributory factor to such violent acts. South Africa is beset with violence on many levels which alone might contribute to the high incidence of rapes. It is associated with broken family structures, inadequate education levels, poverty, and lack of prosecution or punishment for rape. The rape of children in particular, however, might well point to the continuation of this belief. Reported sexual offences in South Africa increased to 53,293 in 2019/20, most of which were rapes (42,289).[126] Children were victims of over 40% of reported rapes in South Africa in the three years prior to 2018.[127] Recently, a seven-year-old girl was raped in a restaurant toilet by a twenty-year-old man who followed her into the toilet, dragged her to the men's toilet and raped her there: He was arrested at the scene.[128] About 63% of rapists who are caught are not even tried for their crimes and only 7% are jailed.[129] A parliamentary report from the Minister of Police revealed that only 21% of child rape cases result in successful convictions. Zakhele Mbhele, the Democratic Alliance's shadow minister of police commented that the "weapons used [in these child rapes] include firearms, axes, spades, pangas [a sharp, large, lengthy blade], hammers, belts and poison – many of these children were practically butchered to death."[130] As one person has commented on this, "South African has become a living horror movie."[131]

South Africa is not the only country where infant sex abuse occurs. The reasons for this are not always provided in reports although the young age of the victims suggests that similar beliefs might underlie these acts. In Somalia, for example, two girls aged three and four were abducted and raped by men while walking home from school. Both required extensive surgery to repair the damage incurred. The rapes led to an outcry against such crimes in the country.[132] In the Democratic Republic of Congo, eleven militiamen were jailed for life for raping

35

over forty children under the age of twelve, including at least one baby of eighteen months old. The men allegedly believed that the blood of virgins would grant them supernatural protection[133] in much the same way as many in South Africa believed sex with a virgin would protect them from HIV/AIDS.

Rape as a Punishment

In a number of cases in India and Pakistan, rape of a girl has been ordered as a form of punishment. In some cases, in Pakistan, child sexual abuse is used by the widespread and largely accepted, local courts or tribal/village councils, as revenge punishment. For example, twenty people from Multan, Pakistan, were arrested for ordering the rape of a teenage girl, in revenge for a rape her brother allegedly committed. The families of the two girls were related. A *jirga* or village council ordered the rape of the sixteen-year-old girl as punishment, as her brother had raped a twelve-year-old. The girl was forced to appear before the group and raped in front of them and her parents. Medical examination confirmed rape in both cases.[134] In India, a nine-year-old girl was raped, tortured, burned with acid, and then killed with an axe and buried in a forest, on the "orders" of her stepmother. The woman was upset because the child was the favourite child of the father, her husband. She ordered her fourteen-year-old son and three others to rape the girl in her presence.[135]

Traditional Japanese Approaches to Companionship or Prostitution

Cultural practices in various countries may also take on a virtually national attitude towards child sex. For example, *"Enjo-Kousai"* or compensated dating, is an underground industry in Japan where adults pay young schoolgirls, or boys, usually between 12-16 years old, for dates that often lead to sex. About one in ten males and one in twenty-five girls report engaging in *Enjo Kousai*.[136] Among females, a history of sexual abuse, drug use, depression, a parent who there is intense social stigma placed on girls who are raped, attacking a young girl causes hurt – for the whole family – as well as to the girl. It becomes a powerful weapon.

The trend for rape videos to go viral, in India as well as in other countries, has led many to believe that smartphones and easy access to violent porn, coupled with a lack of sex education, fuels sexual violence. The argument proposed is not necessarily that watching erotica stimulates sexual abuse of others, but that watching violent or aggressive sexual acts, without any countering education to indicate that sexual activity can be, and should be, respectful and consensual, will lead some to believe that intercourse without a mutually enjoyable context is acceptable, if not just the way sex is done. Studies suggesting a six-fold increase in sexually aggressive behaviour among youth of ten to fifteen-years-old who watch violently aggressive pornographic material, support these fears.[167] It is believed that watching violent sexual content is desensitising viewers to believe that violence is the only way to get pleasure and that female consent is unimportant. A ban imposed by the Indian Supreme court on websites hosting violent pornography was, however, revoked almost instantly due to multiple protests reflecting the widespread societal approval of, and demand for, such websites.[168] This is a concerning outcome that reflects further on the rape culture that appears to exist in India at present.

Some ascribe the fearful rates of child rape in India to the sex ratio imbalance resulting from sex selection abortions.[169] There are around 108 boys to every 100 girls instead of a standard ratio of 105 to 100. The northern state of Haryana which records the highest number of gang rapes in India also has the worst sex ratio in India.[170] In Haryana there are only 88 women for every 100 men.[171] This argument assumes that all men will become rapists if they don't get married or have regular sex – not a verified assertion. Rape is not a sexual act but rather an act of power, aggression and control.

To some extent the factors at play in India with regard to the rape culture that appears to exist is common to other countries as well. Motivations to commit sexual offences based on religious conflict, such as the Hindu-Muslim conflict, may well generalize to other situations of religious or cultural conflict. Sex ratio imbalances may be prevalent in other regions as well and may influence sexual patterns of behaviour in similar fashion. Exposure to violent or aggressive internet sexual abuse of children or adults applies globally. Apparent societal approval of sexual abuse and even abuse of children is not unique to India. The failure to convict or even to arrest or prosecute sexual predators applies to many other countries, developed and developing, as well. Shaming victims of abuse rather than their perpetrators is also a global reality.

Clearly societies across the globe justify child sex abuse through various traditions, beliefs, practices and conventions. Whether it is for religious reasons, as a maturation ritual, as a mythological cure for HIV, to provide companionship, to punish other offenders, or as a right of men, children are being sexually abused while society approves.

Child Marriage

Child marriage provides a formalized system of child slavery and exploitation of children for sexual abuse. A 2018 UNICEF report states:

> Child marriage is a violation of human rights whether it happens to a girl or a boy, but it represents perhaps the most prevalent form of sexual abuse and exploitation of girls. The harmful consequences include separation from family and friends, lack of freedom to interact with peers and participate in community activities, and decreased opportunities for education. Child marriage can also result in bonded labour or enslavement, commercial sexual exploitation and violence against the victims. Because they cannot abstain from sex or insist on condom use, child brides are often exposed to such serious health risks as premature pregnancy, sexually transmitted infections and, increasingly, HIV/AIDS.
>
> Parents may consent to child marriage out of economic necessity. Marriage might be seen as a way to provide male guardianship for their daughters, protect them from sexual assault, avoid pregnancy outside of marriage, extend their childbearing years or ensure obedience to their husband's household.[172]

About 650 million girls and women alive today were married before they turned eighteen, which, in most countries, is the most common age restriction for marriage without the consent of another, and the currently recommended age at which adulthood is recognized. In a few countries the legal age of marriage is as young as twelve (Venezuela, Equatorial Guinea and Lebanon).[173] Levels of child marriage are highest in sub-Saharan Africa, where nearly four in ten young women are married before eighteen, followed by South Asia, where three in ten are married before this age. Countries with some of the highest rates of child marriage include Niger (76% of all marriages), Central African Republic (68%), Chad (67%), Bangladesh (59%), and Burkina Faso, Guinea, Mali and South Sudan with about 52% each.[174] Lower rates of child marriage occur in Latin America and the Caribbean (25%), the Middle East and North Africa (18%), and in Eastern Europe and Central Asia (11%). Although child marriage is a from of sexual slavery, it is not always viewed in this way. Some conservative, ultra-orthodox, Jewish communities encourage marriage at least before the age of twenty, so that marriages under the age of eighteen are supported, although usually require the permission of parents or a judge. In Malaysia the legal age for marriage is eighteen for both genders. Girls can, however, marry at sixteen with the state's chief minister's permission, while Islamic law allows sixteen-year-old girls to marry, and even younger girls with the permission of the Sharia court. Some countries differentiate between child sexual offences and child marriage, such as Malaysia which has laws against child sexual offences, although these exclude child marriage.[175] Over 9,000 child marriages occurred in Malaysia between 2011 and 2016.[176] Child marriage provides a so-called "legitimate" means of sexually abusing children as well as forcing children into what could be seen as domestic slavery.

Most child marriages occur in middle- to low-income countries.[177] Forty percent of women in these countries are married before eighteen and 12% percent before fifteen. Globally, including high income countries, these figures change to 21% and 5% respectively. Poverty, insecurity, tradition and gender inequality contribute to child marriage, with associated increased sexual violence. Globally it is estimated that about fourteen million girls between fifteen and nineteen years give birth, increasing their chances of complications of childbearing and dying.[178] They are also at increased risk of contracting HIV/AIDS. Because they leave school earlier, they have fewer chances of working outside the home and are more likely to live in poverty.[179]

Child marriages do not always involve willing partners. For example, Sharina was forced to marry when she was fifteen:

> The story begins with my father [...] suddenly one day [he] took me to an old man who was visiting our village. At the time, I did not know this old man was the grandfather of the man who would soon become my husband. I also didn't know that this "meeting" was to showcase me as a potential bride.
> It was my brother's wife who told me what was really going on. I was scared. Me – married? I was desperately sad and began to cry. I had no desire to get married.
> After I was chosen as the bride for the old man's grandson, no one talked to me about what was going to happen. At the same time, I dropped out of school [...]
> The thought that I had to marry and move to a place far away without anyone I knew was awfully painful to me. I did nothing but sit inside and cry.
> My family travelled to meet the man who would become my husband, but I never met him – not until we were married.[180]

At her wedding she was coerced into agreeing to marry the man chosen to be her husband:

> I looked down at all times during the formal session of the ceremony, it would be over when I said "kobul" – a confirmation that I consent to the marriage. But I refused to say it. This made my family angry and everyone shouted that I had to say it. They said I was being disrespectful. I had no choice. I said the words and not once did I look at the man I was forced to go away with.[181]

Sharina ultimately became fond of her partner but their friendship took a long time to develop and resulted from his caring attitude towards her. Not all men are this accommodating.

Nujood's story, of her arranged marriage in Yemen, for example, reflects a very different experience from that of Sharina. At about the age of nine, before she had reached puberty, her parents arranged her marriage to an older man, primarily for their financial benefit. These actions were very much in keeping with local customs as reflected by a tribal proverb that claimed "To guarantee a happy marriage, marry a nine-year-old girl."[182] The groom had promised not to have intercourse with her until she menstruated but very quickly reneged on his commitment and raped her. She writes:

> When night fell, I knew what would begin again. Again and again. The same savagery, the same pain and distress. The door slamming, the oil lamp rolling across the floor, and the sheets getting all twisted up. "Ya beint!" "Hey Girl." That's what he would yell before throwing himself on me.
> He never said my name.
> It was on the third day that he began hitting me. He could not bear my attempts to resist him. When I would try to keep him from lying down on the mat next to me after he'd extinguished the lamp, he would start to hit me, first with his hands, then with a stick. Thunder and lightning, over and over. And his mother egged him on.
> Whenever he would complain about me, she would tell him hoarsely, "Hit her even harder. She must listen to you – she's your wife."[183]

Nujood ultimately managed to run away from her husband and make her way to the law courts where a sympathetic judge assisted her to obtain a divorce at the age of ten. International publicity of her situation, followed by generous donations to assist her, have allowed her to return to school and to live a life of her choosing. This kind of escape is the exception, not the rule, especially in a country where 70% of women are illiterate and without any likely means of seeking judicial assistance.[184] In a similar story, a girl of nine married to a Saudi man died three days after her wedding. Instead of demanding an investigation into her death, her parents apologised to the husband, as if trying to make amends for their daughter's failure as a wife, and offered him, in exchange, her seven-year-old sister.[185]

Child marriage can also occur through abduction and rape rather than following a parental arrangement or a mutual agreement. In some eastern European and central Asian countries, in particular, abduction and rape of young girls is usually followed by marriage as the girl, once "despoiled" becomes less marriageable with few prospects other than to marry her abductor. Even spending a few hours in the man's house following the kidnapping is regarded as sufficient to slander her reputation and 84% of kidnapped girls end up agreeing to the nuptials.[186] Bride kidnapping is endemic in some countries such as Kyrgyzstan,[187] Chechnya,[188] and Kazakhstan[189] but also occurs in other countries such as Armenia, Moldova and Ethiopia.[190] My discussions with women who had experienced this form of inducement to marry as young girls, in Kyrgyzstan, indicated that while they disapproved of the practise they were not all that concerned about it as, they said, "you will get to love the man" anyway. This is not always the case, however, and suicide, unhappiness, domestic violence and divorce may well be the outcome for many.[191]

Abuse of Islamic Laws to Allow Child Marriage

In most cases of child marriage, the intention is for the marriage to be "everlasting." The child is married to a man, frequently for the financial gain of the parents, or for protection of the child from possible sexual assault, or for the purpose of childbearing. In a few settings, child marriages are not intended to be long-lasting but are in essence, temporary marriages, or formalized short-term sexual slavery. This form of abusive "marriage" is known to occur in Iraq and Iran conducted by Shia clerics.[192] Some are grooming vulnerable girls and offering them for sex using a controversial but century long-standing religious practice known as "pleasure marriage" or "Zawaj al-mutaa."[193] The girl may be groomed by a man who offers to marry her. The marriage is performed in a religious ceremony in a Cleric's office and the husband then takes her away for a period of time – hours, days or weeks – as specified in a marriage contract. Due to high rates of illiteracy among women in these countries, she may not be aware of the time limitations in her marriage contract. At the end of the specified time, her "husband" disappears. The object of such marriages is sexual pleasure and not a shared lifetime or procreation. It is subject to a contract that specifies its length and the amount of dowry paid to the temporary wife. Such marriages are not permitted under Sunni Islam but some Sunni clerics sanction alternative forms of marriage such as *misyar* which some experts say perform similar functions to *mutaa* marriages. Such temporary marriages are not recognized under Iraqi civil law. When the girls return to the Cleric, he is likely to suggest that the girl enter into similar *mutaa* marriages as she has no other choices available to her.[194]

The Clerics take pictures of the girls. Prospective men can choose the girl in person or from photographs. The Cleric takes a fee from the client and then pays the girl her dowry. The Clerics provide the girls with contraceptive injections and girls as young as nine are available. Out of ten Clerics approached by the BBC in Kadhimiya, an important pilgrimage site, eight offered *mutaa* marriages. If the girl is a virgin, the Cleric may suggest that anal sex is practiced to preserve her virginity. The legal age for marriage in Iraq is eighteen although judges are allowed to permit girls as young as fifteen to marry in "urgent cases." Sharia law says that girls are allowed to marry once they have menstruated.[195]

What Can be Done?

There is much to be done still to prevent the 21% of marriages before the age of eighteen that occur globally.[196] Most important, is the need to prosecute the men who seek child brides and those family members who promote these marriages, even if these are well-intentioned long-term arrangements. Such marriages are usually based on economic necessity, the desire for a housekeeper, or for a convenient sexual partner. Male dominant societies, inadequate education, particularly of the girl child, resulting illiteracy, corruption, and some religions may all facilitate the practice. At the governmental level, actions should be taken to deter this practice and particularly to address the poverty that fuels such arrangements. The legal age of marriage needs to be established closer to the current frequently adopted recommendations of about eighteen and steps taken to assist parents to resist the economic incentives that encourage earlier marital agreements. Open discussion of marriage instead of some traditional customs of maintaining privacy about such arrangements, as occurred with Sharina, should be encouraged. Education of prospective perpetrators of child marriages as well as both parents and their children is needed, as educated girls or boys are less likely to comply with early marriage plans. Legal and emotional support for children who resist such plans is needed as well as providing physical shelter for them if their resistance angers their family or prospective groom. Socio-economic disparities and poverty need to be reduced, the wealth gap closed, and housing and food insecurity addressed to eliminate the economic hardships that contribute to this problem. Monitoring of child marriage registrations may help to deter such practices but would also assist in assessment of children's and families' needs.[197]

In 2016, UNICEF in collaboration with UNFPA initiated a Global Program to end Child Marriage. Their actions target the most vulnerable countries where child marriage is most prevalent, including Bangladesh, Burkina Faso, Ethiopia, Ghana, India, Mozambique, Nepal, Niger, Sierra Leone, Uganda, Yemen and Zambia. In 2018:

> In Niger, nearly 62,000 adolescent girls participated in life-skills training, covering topics such as reproductive health, personal hygiene, gender-based violence, financial literacy and gender equality. As a result, 11,160 girls were referred to health centres, 853 cases of child marriage were cancelled or postponed, and 189 girls returned to school.
> In Yemen, awareness-raising programmes reached over 70,000 people in an effort to change the norms and practices that perpetuate child marriage.
> In Mozambique, 221,000 girls benefited from mentorship and other forms of support – including information and counselling on sexual and reproductive health, HIV/AIDS and violence – in 1,500 safe spaces.

> In India, initiatives to raise awareness of child marriage reached over 3.5 million people. In some programmes, girls learn storytelling and digital literacy to help them share their stories with wider audiences.[198]

What is stunning in this report of UN activities designed to counter child marriage is the apparent focus on the girls themselves – as potential victims – rather than on the men who seek children as wives and the families that seek this for their daughters: the perpetrators of this child sexual abuse. It is time to stop making girls responsible for preventing their early marriage, rather than re-educating boys and men, and prosecuting those who seek to marry, or to marry off, young girls. We need to alter the societal structures such as lack of education for children and economic hardships that facilitate this form of abuse.

The Global Program aligns key players in education, child protection, communication for development, gender, health and other sectors. It builds on the capacities of both Government and non-Government organizations to engage with communities and partners to increase accountability and to initiate actions to overcome this tragic hardship for young people. Politicians need to be recruited to support such initiatives and should bring to bear the power of sanctions, and conditional granting of aid, to eliminate such practices. Child sexual abuse under the guise of marriage, is in many cases, sexual slavery. It would be beneficial to see these programs directed towards men and parents as a priority in future, in addition to assisting girls who are facing, or forced into, these abusive relationships.

Children who are married off at a young age are being sold by their parents into forced and repeated, sexual abuse. For the most part, with some notable exceptions, our world acknowledges this happens but does not cry out to prevent it.

Part 2: Covering-Up Child Sex Abuse in Institutions

Child sexual abuse also occurs outside the home in institutional settings. Prominent among these settings is the school. Educational institutions care for children for a large segment of their lives, both daily and extending over about a dozen years. For most, their school lives are reasonably happy years, if not fulfilling and exciting times, that many look back on with some degree of satisfaction. For others, however, school life provides a period of horror, fear and unhappiness especially if they are abused, emotionally, physically or sexually. Unfortunately, such abuse occurs and, egregiously, may be ignored, denied, or hidden by perpetrators, bystanders, or those to whom the child turns for help, including other teachers, or family members. Society views child sex abuse, for example, as rare, and such abuse as unbelievable, especially when teachers appear to be people of high status and honour. Religiously inspired schools globally, following an Irish school model, have been exposed as providing opportunities for such abuse to fester and spread, ignored, or hidden by clouds of denial and deceit. Abuse of children, emotional, physical and sexual, has been implemented to save the children's souls, or as a means of instilling discipline, while simultaneously demanding gratitude from the children for their shelter. Religiously inspired schools have also been involved in State sanctioned cultural genocide in order to eradicate the children's indigenous culture of origin and to replace it with the dominant Christian and "western" culture of Canada. Horrifically, child sex abuse has also occurred in hospitals, again run by religious orders, but

51

this time simply for financial incentives, such as occurred with the Canadian Duplessis orphans committed to psychiatric institutions. In addition, other societal institutions that provide caregiving and educational opportunities for children have also proved to provide shelter for child sex abusers, such as sports associations, and child scouting activities.

Part 2 of this book explores many of these, including the Duplessis orphans, the Irish religiously based schools that were predominantly Catholic run schools, the Canadian Residential School system that forced children to be removed from their homes and indoctrinated them to discard their Indigenous ancestry under the guise of an educational institution, Jewish religious educational institutions, and community child activity programs. Societies, and sometimes the countries in which these institutions were situated, have ignored, denied or actively perpetrated these abusive occurrences for decades and have only recently been forced to confront them.

The Duplessis Orphans

The "Duplessis orphans" were over 20,000 Canadian children who were deliberately, falsely diagnosed as mentally unfit and sent to psychiatric hospitals in the 1940s and 1950s, in order to misappropriate federal funding, which, at the time, was more generous for hospitals than for orphanages. They are named after Maurice Duplessis, Premier of Quebec for five terms between 1936 and 1959. Under his authority the laws regarding the funding of orphanages and mental institutions that led to the experiences of the Duplessis children were implemented. Pure financial greed motivated this criminal abuse of tens of thousands of children. The Catholic church was complicit in this scheme. In some instances, whole orphanages were reclassified as psychiatric institutions. When this occurred, the Nuns and Brothers running the hospitals stopped educating the children and treated them as "mentally deficient."[199] Seven religious orders participated in this program: The Sisters of Providence, the Sisters of Mercy, the Gray Nuns of Montreal, the Sisters of Charity of Quebec, the Little Franciscans of Mary, the Brothers of Notre-Dame-de-la-Misericordia, and the Brothers of Charity.[200]

Long term incarceration in the orphanages/hospitals, with little if any education, encouragement, or attention to their development, resulted in aberrant behaviour justifying more extreme clinical treatments. The children were medicated to subdue them and to control them. An unknown number of those who were institutionalized and wrongfully diagnosed as mentally ill underwent treatments designed for the genuinely ill, including electroshock therapy, lobotomies, prolonged solitary confinement, ice baths, chaining, force-feeding, and straightjackets. With the advent of neuroleptics, these "treatments" were replaced by medication i.e. "chemical restraint."[201]

Because of the neglectful treatment provided for the children and the lack of educational programs offered to them, the majority of the children spoke only in sounds until the ages of four to six, and were incapable of telling time, eating with utensils, getting around, washing themselves, etc., until much later. In one trade school, up to 25% of the children between nine and sixteen were found to be bedwetters.[202] Most children could neither read nor write when they left the institutions at age sixteen.[203]

An estimated two to four thousand of these children were physically, mentally, and sexually abused.[204] Common allegations include:

> years of recurrent beating and slapping, being tied to the bedspring for bed wetting, unjustified confinement to a cell-sometimes for months or even years, ice baths, regular subjection to restraining measures (straightjackets, neuroleptics ...), electroshock treatment, etc. Allegations of sexual abuse include sodomy, sexual interference, forced sexual favours. From orphans, the children went on to become mentally deficient, i.e., 'not adoptable.' They were subsequently classified-and in some cases became-mentally ill, a label of legal and social inferiority that has remained with them long into adulthood. Everything was set in place to maintain a long period of institutional dependence. Today, many of them have yet to find their place in the society that rejected them years ago. For some who still bear the scars, the physical harm and developmental lags led to a variety of medical problems that have since become chronic or irreversible. For others, mistreatment and sexual abuse have caused sexual dysfunction and relational difficulties.[205]

In 1989, the Duplessis Orphans Committee conducted a questionnaire survey of 90 surviving "Children of Duplessis." Of these, 79% were in psychiatric institutions with 16% having received no education at all and few receiving more than 4th grade. Almost all respondents, 87%, said that violence was omnipresent and cruel with 62% confined to cells during their period of incarceration.

Boys were the most frequently targeted for sexual abuse with 25% experiencing sodomy and 26% molestation. In all, 55.5% of the children were sexually abused or raped.[206]

Legal Compensation

Following various attempts to obtain legal compensation, children and youth who were victims of violence and/or sexual abuse while in these institutions received indemnities ranging from $14,000 to $41,000.[207] The legal system cannot meet the needs of the Children of Duplessis. Technical and legal obstacles, delays, the time elapsed, coupled with the fact that those involved have all refused to accept responsibility, blaming either the other parties or the prevailing values of the day, have all made the legal system problematic for the survivors. In addition, neither the media coverage nor the petitions, criminal accusations, legal proceedings or lobbying of the National Assembly and various departments have been sufficient to reconcile the different viewpoints. The Children of Duplessis now believe themselves to be the victims of a hostile and inaccessible legal system that will not allow them to expose and prove the injustices they have suffered.[208]

In 1999, the government finally apologized and offered $3 million in compensation, which was rejected. The Catholic Church refused to apologize or provide compensation. Following extensive publicity and public pressure, the Quebec government extended another apology in 2001 as well as individual compensation of $10,000 plus $1,000 for each year spent in an asylum amounting to approximately $15,000 per orphan (1,500 qualified for compensation). Legal counsel, however, likely were paid in excess of $1,000 per day.[209] The Duplessis Orphans'

Committee accepted the offer, and the government provided an additional twenty-six million dollars compensation in 2006.

In the case of the Duplessis orphans the primary motivation underlying these acts of abuse was financial. Religiously based institutions, in which child sex abuse has been prevalent, have, however, been driven by an equally or even more difficult-to-overcome motivation, that of spiritual justification. Religiously based schools have, in the past few decades, been exposed as implementing widescale sexual abuse of children in their care. These schools are explored further in the following chapter.

The Irish School System

Child abuse – physical, emotional and sexual – has been perpetrated by thousands of people to whom tens of thousands of children have been entrusted for care, education, and, often, religious guidance. Ideologically and religiously endorsed sexual abuse of children occurred throughout the 20th century and continues today. Usually occurring in highly authoritarian and autocratic settings, and often justified as religiously or spiritually sanctioned if not encouraged, this remains one of the gravest harms that has ever been inflicted on children. In the name of God, and to cleanse their evil spirit and save their souls, children have been horrifically abused by so-called "well-meaning," although clearly misguided, members of religious orders. Given the almost blind respect and adulation given to all kinds of clergy throughout the world, these criminal acts have, until recently, been ignored, or intentionally hidden from societal awareness, escaping exposure, challenge, censure, condemnation or legal action and enabling and facilitating child sex abuse.

The origins of much of the institutionalized sexual, physical and emotional abuse of children in Catholic and other religious institutional care appears to stem from the orders involved in child education and care in Ireland, from the late 19th century and enduring for – in most cases – a hundred years or even more. Children were beaten and treated with extraordinarily cruel levels of emotional, physical and sometimes sexual abuse in almost every one of the industrial and reformatory schools that existed in Ireland, or in orphanages, or homes for unmarried mothers, and among child migrants sent to populate foreign lands. A large proportion of boys were sexually abused and raped by male members of the religious orders who cared for them. Girls too were similarly abused, although it appears that boys took the brunt of this offensive.[210] Children with disabilities were also abused. As the Irish Commission of Inquiry reports, these included children with learning disabilities, physical and sensory impairments and children who had no known family contact. Like all children, they were powerless against their abusers, especially when those were in positions of authority and trust. Impaired mobility and communication challenges made it even more difficult to inform others of their abuse or to resist it, although all children who were abused faced such obstacles. Children who were unable to hear, see, speak, move or adequately express themselves were at a physical as well as psychological disadvantage.[211]

Not all the Nuns, Brothers or Priests caring for these children abused them. It appears, however, that those who did not abuse the children themselves, did not prevent the abuse being perpetrated by others in their communities. Physical and emotional abuse was usually clear for all to see. Even the instances of sexual abuse were sometimes public or, at least, well acknowledged to be part of the community life. Such abuses, while occurring openly within the schools, were kept from public awareness including when complaints against the teachers or school were registered by parents or pupils. Most organizations, whether they were religious institutions, governments, or schools, maintained an often unspoken, unofficial policy of hiding evidence of child sex abuse thus enabling it to continue. Even on the individual level, many parents and children preferred to hide these events rather than confront or report them. As a result, child survivors were often denied the support they needed.[212] Facilitating child sex abuse through silence deserves as much condemnation as that bestowed on perpetrators.

The Christian Brother's Manual of School Government, published in 1832, laid great stress on "the use of 'mildness, affection and kindness, describing 'blows' as a 'servile form of punishment' which 'degrades the soul.' […] They ordinarily harden rather than correct […] and blunt those fine feelings which render a rational creature sensible to shame.'"[213] This insightful approach seems to have been abandoned and the Brothers became known for their harsh disciplinary methods. Complaints of sexual abuse made to the schools either by the children, their parents or through judicial or law enforcement agencies were usually silenced, with the offending member of the clergy being sent to an alternative community. Sometimes the perpetrator was ordered to undergo "treatment" in – usually – Catholic-run remedial institutions before being reintegrated into alternate religious settings, often to again work in close contact with young children. Their abusive history was seldom disclosed to their new communities. In 1982, a frank discussion took place regarding how the Christian Brothers had dealt with members who had "problems." In papers prepared from the Christian Brothers International Spirituality Conference in Dublin, it was acknowledged that "in the past, a common practice was to shift men who had problems – alcoholic, social, psychological – from community to community as a substitute for dealing with the issues."[214] Sometimes these abusers were moved repeatedly, each time continuing to abuse children. This phenomenon was not unique to the Christian Brothers – it was the accepted way in which the Catholic Church dealt with child sexual abusers among their clergy internationally. Such actions were in keeping with Cannon Law that said that Bishops who report serious crimes to the civil authorities would be punished.[215] Pope Francis has only recently contradicted this ruling and endorses that such crimes should be reported to civil authorities[216] although such advice may still be controversial. Avoiding litigation rather than caring for the victims appears to still be a primary concern of the Church in relation to child sex abuse crimes. For example, despite recommendations by the Pope, the Catholic Church in Philadelphia has recently lobbied to prevent changes to the statute of limitations that would allow sex abuse crimes to be prosecuted even after thirty years and up until fifty years after their occurrence.[217] Whether this will change in light of the Bishops' conference on child sex abuse in the Church, convened by Pope Francis in February 2019, and his recent ruling regarding reporting of child sex abuse crimes to both the Church and civil authorities, is still to be seen.

Religious Historical Context

We do not have a history of prohibiting the sexual abuse of children. To the contrary, violence against women and children is part of an ancient and pervasive worldwide phenomenon.[218] Even in Biblical times sex between men and young girls was sanctioned. Under Talmudic law, the sexual use of girls over the age of three was allowed if her father consented and appropriate payment was made.[219] Women and girls were owned, rented, bought and sold as sexual commodities and Rabbis and lawmakers approved as long as the appropriate payments were transferred. Sexual intercourse was an acceptable means of establishing betrothal.[220] Intercourse with a child younger than three years was not a crime but was invalid as a form of ownership. If the prospective groom would penetrate the child just once more after her third birthday, he could legitimately claim his bride.[221] The sexual use of girls under three years of age was not regulated or restricted, while boys under the age of nine were open to abuse. Although sex between men was not acceptable and was punished, men could and did use young boys.[222]

Christianity, built on this Talmudic origin, did not change these rules substantially. Canon law considered that sexual intercourse proved possession, and Popes through the centuries upheld rape as an indissoluble means of contracting a marriage. However, Christian law raised the age for legally valid sex from three to seven, making intercourse with girls over seven, rather than over three, binding. Although the concept of statutory rape was introduced in the 13th century, it was not enforced and the clergy themselves exploited girls in convents and confessionals.[223] In Europe, between the late 1400's and late 1800's approximately nine million people were murdered as witches, most of them women and girls. With the full support of the Christian church, they were gang-raped, tortured, forced to confess to sexual crimes, maimed and burned alive. Commonly women and girls as young as five were accused of copulation with the devil.[224]

The earliest reports of sexual offences committed by clergy in Church literature go back to the end of the first century and include sex with adult women, homosexuality and sexual abuse of boys.[225] The Didache, which set out structures and rules for the newly emerging Church, condemns many sexual practices and includes a specific ban on "corrupting youth."[226] Canon 71 of the Council of Elvira (CE 309) condemns clergy who sexually abused young boys and sets out the penalty for such crimes.[227] In 1051, St Peters Damian, a cardinal, wrote extensively about the sexual crimes and immorality of the clergy of his day. He was critical of homosexual activity by the clergy, but particularly of clergy who abused young boys.[228] Clerical abuse of children is noted, and condemned in reports from the 10th and 11th centuries. In 1568, in his papal order *Horrendum*, Pope Pius V said that Priests who abused minors were to be stripped of the Priesthood, deprived of all income and privileges and handed over to the secular authorities.[229] A 1570 document, nevertheless, reports clerical abuse of a choir boy.[230] In the mid 19th century a German Priest was imprisoned for exposing himself to small girls and for masturbating boys.[231] Most cases were, and may still be, however, sealed and retained in the Vatican archives as Catholic Priests were customarily judged only in ecclesiastic courts.[232] Despite the Church knowing that Priests could and did abuse children, it has, until recently, not dealt with the issue to any good effect. In fact, in 1962 Pope John XXIII issued a new law to deal with cases of Priests who solicited sex in the confessional. This document entitled *Crimens Sollicitationis,* "specifically dealt with how Priests who abused children were to be handled and imposed a high degree of secrecy on all Church officials involved in such cases."[233] The supreme Catholic Church penalty – automatic excommunication – would be imposed on any person who broke the oath of secrecy required by the policy. Even witnesses and survivors could be excommunicated if they broke the oath. Since 2001, this injunction is no longer formally in force.[234]

Child sexual abuse compounded the horrific physical and emotional abuse that occurred in multiple institutions and schools throughout most of the 20th century in many countries. The Catholic Church, and many of its subsidiary orders of Nuns, Brothers and Priests, despite its good work in other instances, must carry the largest burden of guilt for this abuse. Today, although the Catholic Church has been at the forefront of often very public and widespread allegations of sexual abuse of children, other religious clerics, including Protestant, Anglican and – more recently – Jewish Rabbis and Muslim clerics, are also implicated.

Religious Institutions

Irish Catholic institutions varied in nature from schools, to orphanages, homes for unmarried mothers, to health care services and even commercial services such as the Magdalene Laundries. Some provided care for orphans or children abandoned by their families, or released to the care of the Church as their parents were simply not able to look after them. Poverty, large families, and crime that removed one or both parents from society contributed to the number of children in care. The industrial school system was introduced into Ireland in 1868, designed to prepare children for meaningful work, following on the reformatory school legislation introduced to deal with young offenders. Industrial schools were to meet the needs of orphaned, destitute and abandoned children but were commonly linked in the public eye with reformatories and criminal activity.[235]

The system of schools run by various religious and predominantly Catholic orders, was established in Ireland in the mid 19th century with the express aim of "saving children's and women's souls."[236] A total of over 105,000 children were committed to schools by the courts between 1868 and 1969. At its peak the system had seventy-one schools in Ireland detaining up to 8,000 children at any one time. Five of these schools were for Protestants and fifty-six for Roman Catholics.[237] The state funded these institutions and had responsibility for their inspection. A key element to the massive number of children retained in Irish schools, compared to fewer children in schools in the remainder of the UK, was the retention of the per capita system of funding the homes that was abolished by the British Home Office in 1919, while being retained in Ireland for some decades afterward. In the UK, the system was replaced by an annual budget to be met by both local authorities and central government, leading to tighter controls and greater accountability in UK schools, while Irish schools remained self-governing and self-monitoring.[238]

The Christian Brothers were the major providers of schools for boys, although the Fathers of Charity (Rosminians), the Oblates of Mary Immaculate and the Presentation Brothers were also involved.

62

More allegations of abuse have been made against the Christian Brothers than all other male orders combined.[239] The Sisters of Mercy ran the vast majority of schools for girls and also ran most of the facilities for boys under ten. Other orders involved in girls' schools were the Sisters of the Good Shephard, the Irish Sisters of Charity, the Daughters of Charity of St Vincent de Paul, the Sisters of St Clare (Poor Clares), the Sisters of Our Lady of Charity or Refuge, the Presentation Sisters, and the Sisters of St Louis.[240] The Magdalene Laundries in Ireland, run primarily by the Sisters of Mercy and the Sisters of Our Lady of Charity of Refuge, as well as by the Sisters of the Good Shephard, provided horrific working conditions for girls from 1765 until 1996.[241]

A Climate of Abuse

Sexual abuse of children did not occur in a vacuum. It was embedded in a system of generalized child abuse including physical and emotional abuse. Neglect, cold, inadequate education and nutritional deficiencies provided a standard background against which sexual abuse occurred. Some schools had particularly bad reputations, for example, the Artane Industrial school, the largest school, which was almost four times the size of any other school.[242] It incarcerated about 16,000 boys during its existence.[243] There is probably more testimony from survivors of Artane than from any other single school. The evidence of a sustained policy of routine and savage beatings combined with sexual abuse and rape of the boys from this school is compelling.[244] This evidence emerges consistently from the 1930s up until the school closed in 1969 following a fire on the premises.[245] For example, Barney, who attended the school from 1949-1958 writes:

> They were vicious, vicious beyond any reason [...] they'd beat you until they were literally spent. Some of the boys were so badly beaten they used to suffer from what they call head staggers, like when boxers get punch drunk. I remember one boy used to stand there banging his head against walls for hours. Some boys

lost an eye or a finger. One Brother had a hurly stick and he used to fire a sliothar [a hard leather covered ball used in the game of hurling] at you, and that really hurt. They were some of the cruellest, most sadistic, unbridled people I have ever met.[246]

In 2009, a Commission of Inquiry into the Irish institutional care of children heard evidence from 1,090 men and women who reported being abused as children in 216 Irish care institutions. In all, 791 witnesses reported abuse in Industrial and Reformatory Schools and 259 reported abuse in other institutions.[247] The 1,090 witness reports relate to the period between 1914 and 2000, of which twenty-three refer to abuse experienced prior to 1930 or after 1990. Over 800 perpetrators of physical and/or sexual abuse were identified by witnesses. Neglect or emotional abuse were described as endemic within these institutions. Abuse in these schools included physical, emotional and sexual events with fluid and overlapping boundaries between these categories.

Nuns were just as likely to abuse children as Brothers and Priests, although often in different ways. For example, at least 400 children are currently thought to be buried in a section of St Mary's Cemetery in Lanarck, Lanarkshire, southern Scotland.[248] The home was run by Nuns of the Catholic order "Daughters of St Vincent de Paul." It opened in 1864 and provided care for orphans and children of broken or incomplete homes. It closed in 1981 having looked after 11,600 children. A third of the children who died were aged five or under. Very few deaths were registered in children after the age of fifteen, probably because children in such homes were released into the world at around sixteen years of age. Many allegations of abuse in these schools describe beatings, punches, public humiliation and psychological abuse.

Emotional Abuse in Schools

Education was not a priority in the schools although exploiting the children for their physical labour was. Many of the girls were kept out of school to work in the convent, and particularly in the laundries, or to look after the babies during the day and night. Most children who eventually left the schools were illiterate. Few girls from orphanages were ever sent to secondary schools.[249] The children's work saved the considerable expense of hiring outside help. Work in the Magdalene Laundries was particularly hard. In some cases, such as that of Kathleen Legg, the manual lifting of heavy, wet, laundry loads even resulted in uterine prolapse.[250] In institutions catering for a hundred or more people, and providing commercial laundry services for neighbouring institutions, this was hard physical labour.[251] Doing domestic chores in religious institutions was offered as justification for this use of the girls as providing them with good preparation for their lives (perceived of, at best, as domestic servants) once they left the institution.

Witnesses described emotional abuse to the Commission into Irish Care Institutions as an absence of affection, the loss of contact with their family outside the schools or even with siblings within the homes, the loss of their identity, humiliation, criticism, personal denigration, and powerless observation of, or forced participation in, the abuse of their friends or, sometimes, siblings. This emotional abuse affected their social, psychological and physical health at the time and throughout their lives.[252]

Emotional abuse started at a young age. On her first day at St Grace's industrial school, aged about six, Irene recalls:

> I [...] tried to follow Mrs Lawley's instructions. We
> were copying the letters of the alphabet [...]
> "That's not right," she snapped. "Do it again."
> So I tried harder [...]
> "No" she said in a stern voice. "No, Irene. That's not
> good at all. No wonder you're here. You're stupid."[253]

Humiliation of children appears to have been regarded as a clever form of emotional abuse for the Brothers. Tom, who attended the Sisters of Mercy, St Kyran's Industrial School, in Rathdrum, from 1951 to 1959 and the Christian Brothers' Artane Industrial School from 1959 to 1965 recalls:

> I was about twelve, and I'd grown out of my shoes.
> When I asked for a new pair, the Brother wanted to
> know why. The old ones looked perfectly okay, he said.

I told him they were too small, and he hit me with a belt across the face. Sent me flying. "Now tell me the truth," he said. I told him again, "Because they're too small for me." He hit me again, and asked me again, and this went on and on and he kept hitting me. "You're telling me lies," he said at last, "Your shoes are not too small, you're too big for your shoes."[254]

Derek Craig, an illegitimate child born on 14 May 1939, and given to the Foundling Home in London, for care[255] and Deidre Ryan from Caven School tell similar stories.[256]

Not surprisingly, bed-wetting was a constant indicator of emotional distress in the children. Many were afraid to get out of bed at night to go to the toilet. Others were stressed, afraid and homesick. Religious caregivers, on the other hand, regarded bed-wetting as a deliberate challenge to their authority and it was dealt with severely. Children who wet their beds were beaten and flogged each morning at breakfast, sometimes in front of other children. Terry, at St Joseph's Industrial School, Ferryhouse, Clonmel (run by the Rosminians, 1952-1959) said that his five-year-old brother did wet his bed and sometimes soiled himself as well. Terry was forced to beat his brother for soiling the bed.[257] Other children were forced to queue up outside the manager's office to await their beating. Sometimes they were made to wear their wet sheets on their heads and to parade around the school with them on.[258] Children had their faces rubbed in their urine soiled sheets, as recalled by Ann Thomson in a Sisters of Good Shepherd home in New Zealand:

When I wet my bed – which I did most nights – she would hold my hands behind my back, force me down on my knees and rub my face in the wet smelly sheets. The worst punishment was when she shoved my head down the toilet and held it to the bottom of the bowl while she flushed the chain. She didn't care how dirty the toilet was.

…when Sister Blandina's bedwetting punishments failed – as they always did – she would throw me over a chair, pull my pants down, thrash me with her belt and plunge me into a cold bath of strong Jeyes Fluid. I was so nervous about these punishments and what new thing she'd do to me that I kept wetting myself.[259]

Neglect

Witnesses heard by the Irish Commission of Inquiry into the school system described neglect as occurring together with physical, sexual and emotional abuse. Neglect involved cold, inadequate nutrition, lack of appropriate clothing or opportunities for personal care. Failure to provide education and a safe environment had consequences for the children's health, employment and economic status as adults. Untreated injuries and neglected medical care led to permanent impairment.[260]

The clergy who ran the schools neglected the children in almost every way imaginable. Many described facing intense cold without even remotely adequate clothing. Ann-Marie, a child at the Poor Clares School described some of the ways children would find to keep warm in the absence of any actual care from those running the schools. "It was cold, always cold. We used to get dreadful chilblains. There was a pipe in the yard where the hot air used to come out from the laundry. We used to huddle in by the pipes and one girl would be warming her hands while another sat on the pipes to dry her knickers."[261] Despite expectations that such conditions could not have been known by the broader population, that somehow the society would not tolerate such blatant cruelty, this kind of abuse was not only well known, but observed by outsiders on a regular basis. One woman recalled, "I used to go to early mass [...] The orphans used to be there in the freezing cold without any socks on, just sandals and short-sleeved frocks, shivering and yawning with being tired. Sometimes they'd be kept waiting for half an hour if the Priest was late. Sometimes you'd see them faint."[262]

Just as their supposed caregivers withheld basic necessities required to stay warm, their provision of food was equally neglectful. Insufficient and inadequate food, and certainly lack of healthy, nutritious food, that was withheld in order to save money, was the norm. Hannah, a child at the Poor Clares orphanage writes that:

> ...breakfast was shell cocoa made on water and a round of bread and margarine. There would be wriggling things on top of the cocoa but the boiling water would have killed them. [...] For dinner we had vegetables and potatoes, or a bowl of greasy soup with bits of bad potato. We had no meat except on Christmas day or when the inspector came. [...] We were always hungry. [...] at school the children used to go through the waste baskets to find lumps of bread left from the other children's sandwiches.[263]

It is, perhaps, tempting to assume that such an account was unique to one particular school or, in even fainter hope, one particular student. Other children, however, provide equally graphic descriptions of the inadequate, one might even say inedible, excuse for nutrition that was provided in these schools. Kelly, who was in St Grace's orphanage in Ireland, shares her memory of encounters with inedible food.

> I think it was porridge. It looked like lumps of raw oats in dirty water. I [...] took a big mouthful [...] it was disgusting!
> I tried to chew but most of it was raw [...] I chewed and chewed and chewed and finally I managed to swallow it all down. I took another spoonful and then a third. I felt ill but I carried on until I'd nearly finished it all.
> A second later [...] the whole lot came back up again into my bowl [...] Ow! I felt a hard slap across the back of my head.
> Sister Beatrice was behind me. "Eat it!" she ordered. "I'm not moving till you eat it [...] "EAT IT!" she barked [....] "Or else – there'll be consequences."[264]

Stories of children being forced to eat food they had previously vomited up are common, even in children as young as six months old. Tessie, a student at St. Augustine's Industrial School, Templemore, run by the Sisters of Mercy, later learned that a nun had attempted to feed her food that she did not like, when she was six-months-old. She would vomit, and the nun would then feed the vomit and the remainder of the food back to her. When this proved too frustrating, the nun apparently "walloped me on the face, sent me flying across the room. Maybe that was when my jaw was broken."[265]

Bridget Rooney at the Poor Clares orphanage revealed that starvation and lack of food was used as a punishment, with children being forced to go days without any food.[266] Rather unsurprisingly, the disgusting food provided for the children was dramatically different from the culinary provisions enjoyed by the Nuns and Brothers and likely a means of saving money.

Menstruation and the Facts of Life

Menstruation provided a particular source of hardship for the girls as it was a subject avoided by the Nuns, probably because of its associations with reproductive life and the Nuns' own ignorance and embarrassment about puberty, sexuality and nudity. Margaret Stofry's story of her first experience of menstruation while at the Poor Clares School (St Joseph's Industrial School, Cavan, 1950-1967) is illustrative of this:

> No one ever talked to us about sex, or even about periods. The first time I got them [...] I climbed into a little cupboard [...] and I locked myself in [...] We were always being told that the devil would come and get you. And this was it – I had done something wrong and the devil was coming to get me [...] I stayed in the cupboard for hours and hours and hours and I prayed and I prayed and I prayed, but it didn't stop. [...]
> It was just unbelievable terror, and thank God it only lasted for three days the first time. [...] But then it happened again.
> I mentioned it to one of the older girls, because she knew everything, and she said, "That happens

everyone" [*sic*] Just like that. I couldn't believe it. The relief of knowing that they had it as well – because the fear came from the time one morning when we got up and one of the girls has blood on her nightdress. [...] That girl was taken out of the room by the nuns and murdered. Physically beaten, and this was going to happen to me, I was going to get beaten, and I was hiding.[267]

Ann-Marie[268] and Mary,[269] both at the Poor Clares school, tell similar tales of ignorance, punishment and confusion about menstruation. In addition, Elizabeth at St Brigid's Industrial School, Co Galway from 1951-1960,[270] and Anne at St Joseph's orphanage in Dublin from 1954-1963, run by the Irish Sisters of Charity[271] both recalled similarly embarrassing and cruel responses to their first menstruation.

Preparation for life and education about the facts of life was equally inadequate and confusing for the girls. Ann-Marie, Hannah, Ellen and Loretta at the Poor Clares, all confirm that little information was given about sex. As Ann writes,

> And the facts of life, that was a joke. One of the nuns brought me into a room and she said "Say the Hail Mary."
> And I went down to 'Blessed is the fruit of thy womb...'
> "Stop. Where's your womb?" "I don't know Mother,"
> "Do you know the part of the body where you go to the toilet?"
> "Yes, Mother."
> "Do you know the part of the body where the man goes to the toilet?"
> I said "Yes, Mother" even though I didn't know. I mean, where was I ever going to see anything like that? I'd seen a baby boy alright but not a man.
> And she said, "Well you join those two together and you make babies, and if a man ever puts his hand on your leg, slap his face." And that was it, she told me I could go [...] It made no sense to me.[272]

In keeping with such limited education about menstruation and sexuality, modesty about one's body was instilled into children from an early age. Looking at one's body was regarded as sinful and girls were taught how to dress and undress without doing so.[273]

Physical Abuse

More than 90% of all witnesses who gave evidence to the Confidential Inquiry into Irish Institutions reported being physically abused while in schools or out-of-home care. Casual, random acts of cruelty were part of the children's daily lives. In addition to being hit and beaten, children were flogged, kicked or physically assaulted, scalded, burned and held under water. They were abused in front of staff, residents in homes, and pupils, and in private. They were physically abused by both religious and lay staff, older residents and others who were associated with the institutions. Many were injured as a result of the abuse including broken bones, lacerations and bruising.[274]

Beatings were a daily event at many schools. Ellen Neary at the Poor Clares orphanage recalls the cruelty of Mother Carmel. "If the children didn't get up at 6.00 am, the minute she rang the bell [...] she'd pull back the bedclothes and flog them with a bamboo cane."[275] Ellen also recalls Mother Carmel beating the little ones because, on a particularly hot night, they had got out of bed to get a drink of water.[276] Christine Buckley who grew up in Goldenbridge Industrial School in Dublin in the 1950s reported "Children being routinely and savagely beaten, having boiling water poured over them, being locked in a furnace room, being forced to stand all night in a corridor as punishment, and very young children being made to sit on potties so long that in some cases their rectums collapsed."[277]

A variety of weapons were used to beat children including "whips, cat-o-nine-tails, leathers, belts, straps, canes, sticks, tree branches, chair legs, hose pipes, rubber tires and hurley sticks."[278] Some brothers froze their leather straps to make them harder, and consequently more painful when used. Children were kicked and punched on any parts of their bodies and many had their heads shaved for punishment. Margaret, who lived at St Joseph's Industrial School, Cavan, (The Poor Clares) from 1950 to 1967, recalled that beatings combined with emotional terrors were not unusual: "You'd be beaten for everything and often for nothing [...] they'd often make you wait for a long time for your punishment, threatened you with it for ages. And you'd wait in terrible fear."[279] Betty, at Pembroke Alms House Industrial School, Tralee (Sisters of Mercy) from 1951 to 1964 reported that "Things were so bad there that I set fire to myself [...] she whipped me almost every day [...] Every day she'd say to me: 'You're an imbecile, a nobody.'"[280]

Mary at St Francis Xavier Industrial School, Ballaghaderreen, Co Roscommon (Irish Sisters of Charity, 1949-1961),[281] Orty, at St Brigid's Industrial School, Loughrea, Co Galway (Sisters of Mercy, 1951 to 1960),[282] and Irene (at St Grace's orphanage)[283] tell similar horrific stories of physical abuse. Many of the children at the schools, came from poor families. For some this made them particularly vulnerable to abuse. Mary, at the Poor Clares School noted that "The nuns treated us according to our background. I got treated the worst because of my mother having all those children [nine] and because she was poor. The nuns picked on me a lot. They said I'd the devil in me."[284]

Whether they were targeted because their mothers had fallen into difficult circumstances or because they were less likely to have parents who would or could criticize the actions of the Nuns or Brothers is open to debate. Some have tried to defend the schools by arguing that such physical punishment was commonplace in Ireland at this time. It is true that society did appear to accept a level of violence against its most vulnerable that is horrifying today. Raftery writes, however, that the excessive violence in the schools was shocking despite a certain level of acceptance of physical punishment of children in school being standard pedagogic practice at the time.[285]

Sexually Directed Abuse

The Irish model of education, including its climate of sexual abuse that appeared to be tolerated and protected by the orders, spread across the UK as well as to all Commonwealth countries to which Irish Brothers and Nuns went. In excess of 200 survivors have spoken to an ongoing inquiry into over sixty schools and church bodies in Scotland.[286] Most of the testimonies collected were reported by past victims who were in their fifties or older, although some reported recent abuse. Several interviewees reported that physical, sexual and emotional abuse happened on a regular basis, often linked to specific abusing individuals. Many of the children were in these residential schools because of physical or sexual abuse experienced in their own homes. Accepting any form of affection from an adult – which they would have sorely craved – made them particularly susceptible to sexual abuse.[287] Elsewhere in the UK, in Wales, the Waterhouse inquiry into horrific sexual and physical abuse of children in schools in northern Wales revealed that similar widespread abuse of children occurred between 1974 and 1990.[288] Sexual abuse of the children took place in children's residential establishments, private residential places, and in psychiatric hospitals.[289] Sexual abuse of boys occurred in a London home for orphans. The vicar at the hospital became sexually involved with one of the boys and absconded with him. After the scandal was reported in the press, the vicar did not return.[290]

Sexual abuse of children in schools was not confined to the UK. For instance, the USA has also had allegations of sex abuse in schools although there are not many instances made public.[291] An elite, non-denominational, boarding school – Choate Rosemary Hall in Connecticut – has been accused of sexual abuse of children by at least twelve members of staff over four decades from 1960-2010. Sexual misconduct issues were handled internally and quietly. Teaching faculty knew little or sometimes nothing about a teacher's departure and when told, were cautioned to say nothing about the situation if asked. This is yet another example of facilitating sexual abuse of children by those supposedly caring for them.

In Canada, the Mount Cashel orphanage and school in Newfoundland (a Catholic-run and publicly funded orphanage and school under the management of the Christian Brothers) housed approximately ninety residents, many of whom were emotionally, physically and sexually abused during its existence, from the 1970s until 1990.[292] In 1975, following a parent's reports of abuse of his child – who had run away from the school – Newfoundland police instigated an investigation. The reaction of the Christian Brothers was swift. The police and justice system were assured that the self-confessed, offending Brothers were being moved from the community immediately and sent out of the province, never to return. The investigation was terminated and the Church authorities attempted to get all mention of sexual abuse removed from the police report, leaving only mention of physical abuse. Three other Brothers, including the superintendent of the orphanage, who had been implicated in the sexual and physical offences, were left undisturbed and were not even interviewed before the inquiry was terminated. It was not until fourteen years later, in 1989, when a Royal Commission was established to examine Mount Cashel's activities that the full extent of the horrific abuse inflicted on the boys became public. In these intervening years, at least eighty-seven people in positions of authority had learned about the atrocities occurring in 1975, but none took action to expose these crimes.

Child migrants sent from the UK to Australia and New Zealand, were also sexually abused. Between 7,000 and 10,000 children were moved, primarily after WWII. Such child exports continued until the 1970s. They were recruited by religious institutions from both the Anglican and Catholic churches or charities with the aim of "giving them a better life" – and of populating the Empire with "good, white, British stock."[293] Exporting them also gave some relief to the overcrowded child care institutions in the UK. Many of these boys were, however, sexually abused both before leaving the UK and after arriving in Australia. Available documentation indicates that the Christian Brothers in Dublin knew of this sexual abuse although there is no record of how the leadership in Ireland responded to the numerous letters they received informing them of this abuse. As Raftery writes, "These responses are now locked away in the order's archives in Rome, assiduously concealed from public view."[294]

A House of Commons report into the child migration scheme was published in 1998. It noted that "the worst cases of criminal abuse in Australia appear to have occurred in institutions run by agencies of the

Catholic Church, in particular the Christian Brothers and the Sisters of Mercy."[295] The Committee, as reported in the House of Commons Select Committee on Health, Third Report of 1998 into the welfare of former British child migrants, went on to say that:

> It is hard to convey the sheer weight of the testimony that we have received. It is impossible to resist the conclusion that some of what was done there was of a quite exceptional depravity, so that terms like 'sexual abuse' are too weak to convey it. For example, those of us who heard the account of a man who as a boy was a particular favourite of some Christian Brothers at Tardun who competed as to who could rape him 100 times first, his account of being in terrible pain, bleeding and bewildered, trying to beat his own eyes so they would cease to be blue as the Brothers liked his blue eyes, or being forced to masturbate animals, or being held upside down over a well and threatened in case he ever told, will never forget it. [296]

Perpetrators

Ann Thompson's story of her life from the age of about two until she was nineteen, initially in the Sisters of Good Shepherd home in Christchurch, New Zealand, and then, from the age of ten, in Nazareth House, is heartbreaking and illustrative of some children's fates. It was not only one nun who abused her physically. There were many. Sometimes the nuns' brutal beatings consisted of numerous punches with a clenched fist to the face. Ann had her eardrum burst by Mother Euphrasia as a consequence and her nose broken five times. She was never taken to a doctor as a result of those injuries.[297] She was ritually beaten: It was thrashed into her – literally – that because she was illegitimate her mother was sinful and she would be too unless the devil was beaten from her soul:

> When it was my turn to enter the room, all my clothes were taken off me. Naked, I was laid on the bed on my

75

stomach while my hands and feet were tied to the ends of the bed. Three nuns undertook the beating that would become the grisly evening ritual. From the age of ten until I was nineteen I was tied up most nights while they hit me with their belts, hula hoops or whip like canes. My legs would be wide apart while they beat me around my buttocks and thighs.

It was worse when they turned me over so that they could do the same across the lower part of my front as I lay helpless on my back. Their lashings were always around my vagina, hips and thighs [...]

"What on earth have I done now?" I dared to ask at the height of the beatings.

"You are like your mother. We have to get the devil out of you." The nuns' words were always the same as the belt came down on me.[298]

The sexual innuendos of abuse, as evident in Ann Thompson's[299] and many other girls' stories of being repeatedly beaten naked, were not uncommon. A fine line separated physical and sexual abuse in institutions. The beating of naked children was also, often a precursor to sexual abuse.[300] Sexual abuse was reported by approximately half of all the Confidential Committee witnesses. Vaginal and anal rape were reported as well as molestation and voyeurism as both isolated events or occurring over long periods of time. The abuse was mostly implemented in private, although not always. Children were sexually abused by Nuns, Brothers and Priests with some sexual abuse related to religious practices occurring. They also reported being sexually abused by older children in schools, members of the public, such as volunteer workers, visitors, work placement employers, foster parents, and others who had unsupervised contact with them. Abuse occurred when the children were taken on excursions, or on holidays, or to work for others. Those who disclosed sexual abuse were subjected to severe reproach. Girls, in particular, described being told they were responsible for attracting the sexual abuse, by both their abuser, and by those to whom they confided abuse.[301] Sexual abuse of babies, toddlers, children and adolescents occurred, as well as of girls after ending their school years. Some children were particularly vulnerable to abuse including children with disabilities, unmarried teenage mothers, children from poor homes, those in single parent families or with many siblings.

Abuse by Nuns

Multiple types of perpetrators are identified by survivors. Irene, in St Grace's orphanage witnessed sexual abuse by Nuns, even of babies. Both she and her baby brother had open nappy (diaper) pins inserted into her vagina and his anal passage and then rapidly pulled out. She saw the Nuns doing the same thing to multiple babies in the nursery.[302] She decided to run away with her sister and little brother but was caught and returned to the house where she was beaten by the Mother Superior: "You, Irene. You are a very wicked little girl: A bad girl from a bad family […] There is evil in a child that runs away from goodness. Now you'll have the evil beaten out of you. Bend over."[303]

Sexual abuse was also part of Ann Thomson's life from her earliest years in a Sisters of Good Shepherd Home in New Zealand:

> It started when I was no more than a toddler and continued until I left the nursery at the age of five. […] they used to pick me up and walk around with their fingers inside my vagina […] and made me bleed […]
> The three women would come to my bed and strip me, then one of them would sit on my face while the other pushed my legs apart and touched my vagina. They would put things up me, then they would make me lick their vaginas. I could not make any noise or they would sit on me harder.
> This was very painful and I hated it. I knew it was dirty but I did not know it was wrong because it was being done by the three older ladies who looked after us. It wasn't only me they sexually abused in the nursery. Three other women have since told me they were violated when they were little too. In their case,

however, a fourth woman abused them. [...] I believe the nursery women did different things to each of us, though the pattern was similar.[304]

There is one reported account of sexual abuse of a boy by a nun. Paddy Doyle describes the physical and sexual abuse he suffered as a very young boy at the hands of a Sister of Mercy in their industrial school in Cappoquin, CO Waterford. In the 1950s, he entered the school at four years old, when both his parents died. He describes the sexual abuse as "Causing me to squirm and writhe involuntarily. When it had passed, I sobbed uncontrollably, frightened at what had happened."[305]

Abuse by Lay Teachers

Sexual abuse of children also occurred in the classroom setting perpetrated by lay teachers. Irene at St Grace's Orphanage in Ireland reports:

> I jumped when I heard her call out "Irene Coogan! Come to the front!"
> [...] "No, come around here," [...] behind the desk [...] she grabbed my hand and put it under her skirt and between her legs. She wasn't wearing any knickers and I felt her ... her ... urgh!
> I [...] grabbed my hand away [...] Mrs Lawley grabbed my hand again and [...] put my hand right back there. [...] I pulled my hand away again and whimpered. "No, I don't want to do it. I don't want to do it."
> She grabbed my wrist now and held on hard as she pushed my hand down between her legs, but I was crying loudly and a few curious heads bobbed up. She let go and I pulled my hands up to my chest.
> "Get back to your work!" She shouted at the children [...] she picked up her ruler [...]
> "Hands out," she snapped. "Back of the hands facing up"

Getting the ruler on the back of my hands was even more painful than the palms. But it was better that than the other thing she'd tried to make me do.[306]

Elizabeth at St Brigid's Industrial School, Loughrea, Co Galway (Sisters of Mercy) (1951-1969) tells a similar story but adds "there was just no-one you could tell."[307]

Abuse by Brothers

There are multiple reports of boys being sexually abused by Brothers in the schools, including in the Williamstown House Children's Home in north Belfast, the Protestant Kincora Boys Home in east Belfast, the Baltimore Industrial school (known as the Fishing School, 1940s), and St Conleth's Reformatory School, Daingean (Oblates of Mary Immaculate) (1963-1965)[308] and the Catholic Artane Industrial School. Brothers, such as Brother Joseph O'Conner at Artane, were repeatedly mentioned as abusive, both physically and sexually.[309] One report says:

I was in his class once [...] and I had said or done something, and he put me out of the line [...] Then he told me to take off my clothes. And right there in front of the whole class, he sat down on the bench, on the desk, with his foot on the bench where the boys would sit and write, and his other foot on the ground. He opened his cassock and put me across it and put his left hand under my private parts. He was squeezing me and beating the living hell out of my bare backside. He was foaming at the mouth, jumping and bobbing. He was having a sexual orgasm in front of the whole class of boys. And I wasn't the only boy he'd done. It just hurt you to be degraded in such a manner. He didn't even have the goodness to bugger you in private. He was a bastard [...] He was evil. [310]

One man, talks of being tied to a bed and raped at the age of eleven. He testifies to having his head pushed into a drawer, and the

79

drawer closed tight on his neck as he was being raped by Brother O'Conner.[311]

At Mount Cashel in Canada, Brother Ralph used to do his rounds in the dormitory after evening prayers, making the sign of the cross on a boy's forehead and then putting his hands under the blankets and fondling his victim's penis for fifteen to twenty minutes.[312] Brother Waters did the same thing.[313] Christy's experiences at St Patrick's Industrial School, Upton, CO Cork, (run by the Rosminians, 1963-1965) was similar.[314] Brother English, then twenty-seven, in Mount Cashel, liked to have the boys crowd around him and massage his genitals. Billy was one of the boys whose hand Brother English would force down on his penis while the rest of the group was watching television.[315] Brother Kenny tried to "neck" with Billy, grabbing the boy by the face and asking him to bite his neck. Billy later claimed he stumbled on Brother Kenny and an older boy in a compromising situation in the shower room by the pool. "They just had their pants undone together. He [Brother Kenny] was feeling him. They were hauling themselves."[316] A fifteen-year-old boy who had been abused by Father Kelly on at least three occasions told the police that they had performed mutual fellatio in the rectory after which he was given five dollars.[317]

Shane was about eleven years old when he was abused:

> I remember one particular time all of us at St Al's dorm got the measles or chicken pox. Brother Burke used to tell us not to scratch… My chicken pox got really bad from scratching, so Brother Burke got some lotion to put on me […] He told me to take off my pajamas […] He […] had me lay down. He started at my neck and started putting the lotion on. When he got to my penis he told me to spread my legs apart. I did. He started playing with my penis rubbing on the lotion. Then he put his finger up my rectum. He started moving his finger around and asked me if I liked it. I remember saying "Bro, it tickles" He gave me a sucker after he had done this, Shane later told police.[318]

80

The founder of the Irish Christian Brothers was Edmund Ignatius Rice. Leo Gerard Rice was a direct descendant of the family. Both his parents died in 1961 and the three-year old boy lived with his maternal grandmother until her death in August 1968. Eight-year-old Leo and his four brothers were than placed in Mount Cashel where he would stay for the next eleven years. He was sexually molested by both Brother English and Brother Short.[319]

At the notorious Bindoon Orphanage in western Australia, a Brother named Keaney was notorious for abusing children. Alan Gill, in his history of child migration schemes to Australia has argued that "Claims of physical abuse perpetrated by Keaney are so numerous that, even if only ten percent are true, he would be quite unfit for any form of contact with children." Only one account of child rape is criminal, let alone "ten percent."[320]

> I settled into Boys Town, Bindoon, and worked very hard under Brother Keaney but was […] subjected to a Brother taking all his clothes off and all my clothes off and he […] tried to penetrate me for a long time until the lunch bell rang, I was told not to say anything and it won't happen again. The Brother […] took my pants down and belted me with the strap and told I would get the same until I learned to do exactly what he wanted me to do. The climax came on one day when all the boys were to go to the Bindoon show. This Brother was going with them, so I made an excuse to stay behind […] I nearly died when the Brother turned up behind me with no clothes on […] he ordered me to remove my shorts […] I was scared and he grabbed me and threw me onto bales of hay and raped me. I was crying as he kept trying to push his penis into me.[321]

Abuse by Older Children

Given the prevalence of abuse by those in authority at these schools, it is not surprising that older children learned to abuse younger ones. A climate of sexual abuse developed. Lawrence Green reported several times during an interview that there was "a lot of [unwanted] homosexuality on the little boys."[322] Finally, his interviewers asked him if he had experienced this. "Yes, I did. The first time when I was seven. A gang of older boys raped me. Several of the bigger boys would come on to you."[323]

Abuse by Lay Workmen

Lay people were also employed at schools to help care for the children. Ed at St Joseph's School, Kilkenny, (Sisters of Charity 1966-1978) reported stories about one of the carers at this school, David Murray.

> He was a complete pervert. He would bring a group of boys to the cinema and you wouldn't be allowed to wear underpants. He'd put a coat over your knees and he'd play with you right there while the film was going on.
> Then you'd go back to St Joseph's and he'd be in someone's bed. I'd say he abused some boy every night of the week. He'd rub some sort of cream on our ass and then he'd stick his penis in you. There was a group of about six of us in particular that he was raping – we used to talk about it among ourselves but there was nothing we could do. He was in complete charge of us and the head nun didn't want to know.[324]

In 1997, many decades later, David Murray was sentenced to ten years in prison for gross sexual abuse of several boys in St Joseph's. He had also repeatedly raped his two foster sons. He was only one of four staff members against whom allegations of sexual abuse were made at this school. At least three of the four were ultimately, after long delays, convicted in court for abuse.[325]

Sexual abuse of children by workmen was also ignored, and thereby enabled, for a long time. In 1993, in Madonna House (Sisters of Charity), the maintenance man Frank Griffon was sentenced to four years imprisonment for sexually abusing several children in the school during the 1980s and early 1990s. Multiple children were abused. In one case, at least eight years before Frank Griffon was finally removed from the house, thirteen children had been abused and no fewer than seven members of staff had knowledge of some or all of these practices. Sections of the report on Madonna House are missing and have not been published. The house was closed in 1995.[326]

Abuse of Children Sent to Assist Farmers

Sexual abuse occurred when children from the orphanages were sent to nearby farms to help older people with their housework. As the primary training that children in these schools received was to qualify them for domestic service, assisting farmers with their household or farming labour for short periods was regarded as part of their education. For example, Martha, who was at the Poor Clares School, recalled:

> When I was twelve or thirteen, they sent me to an old couple in Ballyjamesduff [...] The old woman was nice enough but [...] the man [...] started fiddling with me. It frightened me and it wasn't till I met my husband that I could bear a man to touch me at all. I still can't bear any other man to even put his arm around me. [...] Then one evening she came into the kitchen and found him interfering with me. She told the nuns I was carrying on with her husband so they brought me back and flogged me. They kept saying "You were letting that man feel you," and I didn't understand what it was all about.[327]

Patricia was raised in St Vincent's Industrial school in County Limerick. When she was fourteen, she was sent to work at a farm where four other girls had been sent before, each one running away for unexplained reasons:

> The farmer made advances to her in the kitchen. She didn't understand what was going on and 'there was this white stuff all over the place' which he told her to clean up. He raped her several times during the following weeks and finally she, too, ran back to the

83

convent. – "Why […] didn't you tell the nuns?" [asked her interviewer]. "Ma'am, you couldn't tell them that kind of thing. They wouldn't understand."[328]

Mary Norris of St Joseph's Industrial School, Killarney, (Sisters of Mercy) (1944-1948) told that one of her sisters was boarded out to a farmer when she was about ten years old. She too was sexually abused by the farmer "although without penetration, just with feeling."[329]

Abuse by Priests

Children sent to assist farmers could not always avoid abuse by Priests, even when away from their school or orphanage. Marie, of St Josephs Industrial School, Clifden (Sisters of Mercy, 1958-1973) experienced sexual abuse, this time by a Priest, when she was sent to stay with a family. "The parish priest was supposed to keep an eye on me. He used to sit me on his knee, and he'd be kissing and hugging me, and touching me down my underpants […] I didn't really know what was happening – at first I thought it was great because no one had ever hugged me before. But then I just decided I didn't want to go there anymore."[330]

Ann Thomson in the Sisters of Good Shepherd Home in New Zealand was vulnerable to further abuse as she matured. On her fifteenth birthday she was sent to Timaru to spend a week with a family named Taylor.

> When a priest called to the Taylor's house and told me to follow him to the bedroom I was really exalted. Convinced he was going to give me a special blessing, I felt sure this would be the best day of my life. […]
> Closing he door behind us, the priest sat down on the chair and called me to him. I approached willingly.
> "Take your pants off," he said.
> He put me on his lap so my legs straddled him and began fondling me. I could feel his fingers inside my vagina first and then I felt the sharp penetration of something else. I couldn't see exactly what the priest was doing because I still had my skirt on. I knew nothing of the male anatomy, nothing about sex – let alone rape – yet I

felt ashamed. I just couldn't look at this man of God who was doing things to me I felt were wrong.

Then, as if to make me feel the whole sordid thing had been my fault, he put me across his lap and spanked me. I assume this was further punishment for something I had done wrong and I was more confused and upset than ever.

On the night of my return to Nazareth house Sister Blandina, Sister Theresa Anthony and Mother Pascal stripped me, threw me across the bed and beat me with cords and belts. This punishment – even more severe than usual – was because the priest had told the nuns I'd been seeing boys while in Timaru. It was a lie, but who was going to believe my claims over those of a priest?

Only recently was the priest's motive for lying to the nuns made clear to me. If I'd been made pregnant, he could have blamed the imaginary boys in Timaru.[331]

Later, many years after leaving the orphanage, Ann met with some of the other children who had been incarcerated with her. She learned that Ella and Lena had also been abused by a Priest shortly after getting to the orphanage:

I must have been about eleven when Father McEeon first told me to come around the other side of the confessional. [...] He put his hand up my leg and touched my private parts. [...] Then Lena told me that same thing had happened to her and it was the same priest.[332]

Similarly, Tina, at the Poor Clares School Reported that Father O'Toole once stood her between his legs and rubbed her up and down and asked her; "didn't I have knickers on?"

Confession

Three crimes are associated with child sex abuse and the confessional. The first relates to the abuse of the child during the process of confession as revealed by both Ella and Lena in New Zealand[333] and Brigid from the Good Shepherd School in Limerick, Ireland.[334] The second is that Priests are forbidden by the Church to break the seal of the confessional, even with regard to reporting crimes of child sex abuse. In 2012, Ireland passed laws overriding the confessional privilege of Church law, and in 2017, an Australian report on child sex abuse recommended a similar move.[335] A third form of abuse occurs when perpetrators confess to sexually abusing children, receive absolution, but then continue to abuse them and to, again, seek forgiveness.[336] The continuing sanctity of the confessional for the Catholic Church makes preventing this type of crime virtually impossible.

Reporting

Abuse was also often ignored by, or concealed from, inspectors. In Williamstown House Children's Home in north Belfast the principal, an Anglican monk, was convicted of sex offences against the boys in 1981. Just a few years earlier, in 1978, an inspector reported an atmosphere of "freedom, friendliness and happiness" there.[337]

No evil could be spoken of the religious. When Colm O'Gorman challenged an Irish Priest who had repeatedly abused him, one of Colm's supporters was injured in a car accident. It was widely believed in his community that it was the inevitable result of "going up against the Priest."[338] As one mother in Canada expressed, the cultural climate of the times revered members of Catholic orders as holy.

> The most eloquent insight into how men of the cloth had been able to perpetuate such monstrous crimes against their parishioners' children and get away with it for so long came from a woman whose cultural eyesight was 20/20. She laid the blame for the tragedy on the traditional role of the priest in Outport, Newfoundland, which she said was as close to God as you could get without playing a harp. Expressing a feeling shared by many of Newfoundland's 215,000 Catholics she told the meeting:

"If a child was born without an arm, people said it was because the mother had said something against a priest. That was nonsense, but a priest with that kind of a shield could get away with anything. We are victims of our own heritage."[339]

Such thinking pervaded Canadian society. For example, Archbishop Alphonsus Penney's resignation for failing to deal with allegations of sexual abuse by the clergy was eventually accepted by Pope John Paul II. Despite the searing indictment of Archbishop Penney in the Winter Report, more than 1,200 Catholics crowded into the Basilica of St John the Baptist to bid farewell to their discredited shepherd at his final Tuesday evening mass.[340]

Children, however, sometimes managed to tell other Priests, or their parents, about their sexual abuse. Reactions of Priests to whom the boys confided were often directed towards protecting the abusing clergy. When he was fifteen, Christy at St Patrick's Industrial School, Upton, CO Cork, (run by the Rosminians, 1963-1965) told another Priest about the abuse. As he reports:

The first thing the priest did was to smack me across the face. Then after a minute or so he went and sat down and called me over and sat me on his knee. [...] I felt him pushing against me and breathing heavily. I think he was trying to do the same thing.
But after a few minutes we both got up, and he went to get some sweets out of the drawer. As he gave me the sweets he told me that I wasn't to tell anyone about what had happened to me, that it would be our little secret [...] And I kept "that little secret" for thirty-four years.[341]

Peter Tyrrell was sometimes stripped naked and beaten for long and was sodomized by one of the Brothers. When he confessed about this to a Priest, the reply was "How dare you speak so of the Brothers. If it wasn't for them you wouldn't have a roof over your head."[342] He was unable to consummate his marriage for over a year after the wedding.

Parents, when told about Priestly abuse, could often not believe it and discounted their children's stories. Barbara, a young child, told of her abuse by a Priest but was not believed by her guardian. As she reported:

> When I was quite young, about six or seven, my sisters who were older than I, and myself used to go to tea at our local priest's house and he would always sit me on his lap and start touching me. He'd touch me between my legs and touch my bottom and put his hand up my skirt. [...] I did tell my guardian when I got home that I didn't want to go there any more. First of all I said I didn't like the smell of his house, any reason but the truth. But she did not believe me and made me tell her the truth.
>
> When I did, I was punished for being so evil and to think this about a priest. I was not given desserts and had to do all the washing and wiping up for about a week. It was never mentioned again but I still had to go to his house. Nobody mentioned it to him at all and he still continued to do it. Since I was told that priests didn't do this kind of thing and I was to blame, I really began to think that perhaps he hadn't done it. I just had a nasty imagination.[343]

Global Prevalence

In the UK, two of the most prestigious Catholic schools Ampleforth College in North Yorkshire and Downside School in Somerset have been exposed for their ongoing child sexual abuse activities. According to a report, the schools "prioritized the monks and their own reputations over the protection of children"[344] and "appalling abuse was inflicted over decades on children as young as seven at Ampleforth and eleven at Downside."[345] In Ireland, a television documentary made in 1996 called *Dear Daughters* reported on events at St. Vincent's Industrial School, Goldenbridge.[346] It was controversial but resulted in the Conference of the Religious of Ireland setting up a hotline for those who had been abused in the school. It received more than 1,000 calls in its first year of operation and by 1999 the number had risen to almost 5,000.[347]

Catholic clerical child sex abuse, primarily of boys, has been reported in multiple countries including the USA, Canada, South America, the UK, France, Spain, Germany, Poland, Spain, Australia, and New Zealand, among others. Similarly, although fewer Anglican schools appear to have been involved in child sex abuse, an Independent Inquiry into Child Sex Abuse in Anglican schools has reported that 390 clergy and other Church of England leaders were convicted of abuse between the 1940s and 2018.[348] In 2021, a Canadian judge found Grenville Christian College in Ontario, an Anglican school, responsible for the systematic abuse of students including excessive, repeated and prolonged verbalized sexual abuse, perpetrated in the 1970's, 80's and 90's. In their defence, the school argued that it was not foreseeable that their actions would or could cause harm despite receiving multiple warnings and complaints about their abusive actions. The school closed in 2007.[349] In all of these situations, a common pattern has emerged: That of enabling abuse. Members of the Irish School community moved to teach in far flung regions of the world, and particularly to Commonwealth countries and to those with large Catholic followings, and took their teaching approaches and philosophy of child care with them.

In the USA, 6,800 clergy members have been credibly accused by their own Church of child sex abuse.[350] Some allegations of child sexual abuse in Canadian religious schools are only now, in the 2020's, becoming public knowledge. Frustrated by the lack of transparency about child sex abusers and their own experiences of abuse, a Canadian group – Survivors Network of those Abused by Priests (SNAP) – collated a list of thirty-five Priests known to have abused minors and in the same Diocese of London (Ontario), who were charged, convicted or linked to victims that successfully sued or settled with the Church for amounts of more than $50,000.[351] The list was made public in 2019 and is a snapshot of fifty to sixty years of allegations that Priests abused children and then moved around after credible accusations emerged.

89

In South America, a predominantly Catholic continent, the Chilean prosecutor's office is investigating accusations of sexual abuse against seventy-eight Bishops, clerics and lay workers of the Roman Catholic Church, involving 104 victims, most of whom were underage at the time of the alleged abuse.[352]

In Germany a 2018 report revealed that over 3,600 children were assaulted by 1,670 Catholic Priests between 1946 and 2014[353] leading at least one German Cardinal, the Archbishop of Munich, to resign for his "shared responsibility for the catastrophe of sex abuse."[354] In France, reports have implicated Priests in child sex abuse. A film called *By the Grace of God* telling the story of a child abused by a Catholic Priest, Bernard Preynat, seventy-three, in France was released in 2019. Three alleged victims of Father Preynat formed an association of eighty-five boys who were all allegedly abused by Father Preynat between the ages of seven and fifteen.[355] An independent commission into sexual abuse perpetrated in the Catholic Church in France, released a report in October 2021, stating that an estimated 200,000 minors had been abused by Catholic Clergy and a further 130,000 by others associated with Church institutions, between 1950 and 2020. Between 2,900 and 3,200 abusers were noted in this report.[356] François Devaux, head of the abuse victims group *La Parole Libérée*, said, in response to this report:

> You must all pay for these crimes [...] there was a betrayal; betrayal of trust, betrayal of morality, betrayal of children, betrayal of innocence of your own people, betrayal of the gospel, betrayal of the original message, betrayal of everything.[357]

Spanish criminal courts have found Priests guilty of sexual assaults on thirty-three occasions involving eighty minors. As appears to be the *modus operandi* of the Church, only three of Spain's seventy Bishoprics routinely passed on information on cases of abuse to the country's criminal justice system.[358] A Polish documentary film – *Tell No One* [359] – reporting on child sexual abuse by Priests in Poland in which victims confront their abusers, was uploaded to YouTube on 11 May 2019. Within a week, it had been viewed over nineteen million times.

Responses from the Church in this staunchly Catholic country have been mixed, with some immediately denying the film's validity, or regarding the film as an attack on the Church and others apologizing outright for harm done. Poland did, however, within weeks of the film's release, announce plans to double jail terms for paedophiles. There was a public outcry in response to the film and demands for the creation of an independent inquiry into Church paedophilia. In March 2019 the Polish Church admitted that over the past forty years, 400 clergy had sexually abused minors, yet none of this had been made public.

A commission of inquiry into abuse in care in New Zealand has revealed similar findings. Up to 256,000 people in faith-based and state-run care were abused including children from as young as nine months old. Most children were between 5 and 17 years-old.[360] A similar formal Royal Commission into Clerical child sexual abuse in Australian institutions was established and its final report published in 2017.[361] The Commission reported that 7% of Catholic Priests working in Australia between 1950 and 2010 have been accused of child sex crimes.[362] Over 4,400 people claim to have been victims between 1980 and 2015 with 1,888 perpetrators from over 1,000 Catholic institutions being accused of sexual abuse. The Royal Commission made more than 400 recommendations including for improved education of members of religious orders, teachers, parents and children regarding child sexual abuse and safer conditions for children in any form of care.[363] Some of the multiple recommendations arising from this commission include the advice for the Catholic Church to consider making celibacy a voluntary component of taking orders, as well as the requirement to expose child sexual abuse events revealed in the confessional as crimes. Both of these recommendations remain controversial and are unlikely to be heeded.

The Church's Response

The Best Picture Oscar winning film *Spotlight* (2015), based on reporting by the Boston Globe Newspaper, revealed how over seventy abusing Priests, were moved around by the Church from diocese to diocese to avoid exposure of their crimes and to avoid the Priests' and Church's accountability. Neither parishioners nor the police were informed of their criminal actions. Cardinal Bernard Law, before his death in 2017, never faced criminal charges for his role in allowing abusing Priests to remain in the church, and his appointment in 2004 until 2011 as Archpriest of the Papal Librarian Basilica of St Mary Major, effectively a second career, was perceived as adding insult to the injuries inflicted on children.[364] While Papal/Vatican responses to such revelations have been filled with expressions of "remorse and shame" – and calls for prayer to overcome such actions – little in the way of criminal prosecution and punishment of offenders, or their protectors, is yet evident.[365] Some abusers and those that covered up these crimes were later elevated to senior roles in the church.[366] Reprimands implemented by the Church appear to be mild, such as removal from public office, and/or directions to undertake a life of prayer, but without criminal prosecution. In 2019, however, the highest-ranking US Catholic official to face charges of sexual abuse, Cardinal Theodore McCarrick, then Archbishop of Washington DC, was defrocked, and now, in 2021, faces charges of sexual assault against a sixteen-year-old perpetrated in the 1970s.[367]

Litigation

Only about one percent of all cases against abusing clergy go to trial.[368] Punishments meted out by law courts also appear to be minimal in many cases. In Canada, in September 1988, fifty-year old Father Jim Hickey, who had twice assured his Archbishop that the charges against him were false, pleaded guilty in court to twenty counts of sexual assault, indecent assault and gross indecency.[369] He was sentenced to only five years in jail despite the knowledge that his crimes probably affected the children for their entire lifetime. Nearly a year later he clarified to Sister Nuala Kenny during a prison visit that he felt no remorse, only a bitter conviction that he had been wronged by the system. In November 1988, a number of Christian bothers at Mount Cashel who were charged with sexual abuse of children were sentenced to prison terms of five to six years including Father John Corrigon (guilty of seven sex-related charges involving boys between the ages of ten and thirteen),[370] Brother Rooney (convicted of eight counts of abusing two eight-year-old boys) and Brother Harold Thorne (convicted on four counts of sexually abusing children including one charge of buggery).[371] Brother Burke (guilty of three counts of indecent assault and one count of assault causing bodily harm) and Brother Edward French (convicted on three counts of indecent assault) were given less: twenty-five months and one year in jail, respectively.[372] Only one brother was given a lengthy sentence: Brother Edward English was found guilty on thirteen counts of sexual and physical abuse and was sentenced to twelve years in prison. One of his victims commented, "If I thought I could get away with it, I would kill the man."[373]

Following the exposure of the Mount Cashel sexual abuse crimes by the Royal Commission, the number of reports of sexual abuse grew from just nine in 1983 to over 600 in 1989.[374] Rev. Andre Guidon of Saint Paul University in Ottawa conducted a survey of Priests finding that one in four Priests needed professional help with sexual problems.[375] As the Globe and Mail newspaper reported there is little intention of making amends for such crimes other than to delay any censure:

> The bishops knew they had to do something about a scandal that has tainted the church's authority and made every priest either a suspect or a laughing stock. What they came up with yesterday, beyond an expression of their personal sorrow, was a committee.[…] Most Canadians […] will not be impressed by a committee.[376]

After the 1989 Royal commission into Mount Cashel, twenty of the abused boys filed suits against the Christian Brothers, the provincial government and the Catholic Church seeking $2 million each for the pain and suffering they had endured as children at Catholic-run orphanages.[377] There are many dozens who could file lawsuits to pay the bills that the Christian Brothers left outstanding when the organization declared bankruptcy in 2012, in consequence leaving them without compensation.[378] Lawsuits against the Catholic Church regarding the sexual abuse of boys at Mount Cashel are still ongoing.

A case recently submitted to the Supreme Court of Canada charging the Church itself, rather than the individual offenders, or only the Christian Brothers, as responsible for the abuses inflicted on the children, was successful.[379] $2.6 million will be shared by the four men who brought these charges against the Church. This judgement is ground-breaking, because until this ruling, only an individual offender or his/her particular religious order, could be held to account for their actions and not the global institution employing them. A declaration of insolvency by each school or institution, in effect put an end to compensation for any victims. Not only the four boys, now men, who are involved in this case will benefit, but hundreds more who are now eligible to sue the Church itself for the crimes committed by its members.

Also in Canada, a former Priest and teacher, William Hodgson Marshall, pleaded guilty in a Windsor, Ontario, court in 2011, to indecent child sexual acts committed against sixteen boys and one woman.[380] His trial, brought against him by one of his victims, Rod MacCleod, has been presented in the film *Prey*. Marshall abused Rod MacCloed, from the age of thirteen, for four years. Some victims of sexual abuse settle their lawsuits against abusing Priests out of court, with $250,000 being a usual settlement.[381] Rod MacCloed refused to accept any offer of settlement and chose to go to trial instead. Midway through the trial, the Church tried to abort the process by offering him $1,000,000 to settle. He refused this too. Ultimately the jury awarded MacLeod almost $2.6 million including a landmark ruling for punitive damages (not usually awarded in Canadian courts) of $500,000.[382]

Punishments allocated by law courts are surprisingly lenient. In France, Father Preynat was stripped of his clerical status in 2019, and has admitted to "caressing" boys in ways which he knew were wrong, and that gave him sexual pleasure. He claims he did not realise his actions were wrong at the time.[383] His trial is still pending. Cardinal Barbarin was recently tried along with five former aides for allegedly covering up Preynat's abuse.[384] He was found guilty of failing to report allegations of assaults of boys by a Priest in the 1980s and 1990s and given a suspended sentence of six months,[385] although this verdict was overturned on appeal.[386]

An Australian Law firm successfully claimed compensation on behalf of 215 former children of Fairbridge Molong, of whom 129 said they had been sexually abused – perhaps 60% of the children there. The Molong Farm School finally closed in 1973. Some of the child migrants claim that they were sent abroad weeks after reporting sexual abuse at their children's homes in the UK. The allegation they make is that they were specially chosen either to get them out of the way, or because they were of interest to paedophiles.[387] The Child Migrants Trust (UK) described the Christian Brothers institutions as "almost the full realization of a paedophile's dream."[388]

Ideological Righteousness

The interpretation that they were doing God's work by beating children unmercifully to eradicate evil thoughts – or even supposedly inherited behavioural or social traits such as "prostitution" or "poverty" – is a blatant corruption of the belief system they purport to protect. Compounding these injuries is the continuing cover-up of such actions by the Church (or Churches) in its efforts to preserve the reputation and existence of the Church itself regardless of its victims. As expressed by the Archbishop of Brisbane, Mark Coleridge, at the conclusion of the Papal summit of February 2019, the Church's moral authority has been "massively damaged" and its credibility "shot to pieces."[389]

Bystanders are Also Perpetrators

As the Irish Commission of Inquiry revealed, many parents, relatives and others knew that the children were being abused. They witnessed evidence of the abuse, either through the children's reports or the marks or injuries that were evident for all to see. Witnesses believed that some awareness existed in society both at official and unofficial levels. Parents and teachers, for example, were sometimes aware that life for children in the schools and institutions was difficult, but many failed to take action to protect them. At the same time, some complaints were made to the school authorities, the *Gardai*, the Department of Education, Health Boards, parish Priests and others, by some of the children, their parents and relatives. At times some protective action was taken. In other instances, complaints were ignored, the children were punished for revealing their abuse, or pressure was brought to bear on the child and family to deny the complaint and/or to remain silent. Child witnesses reported to the Commission that their sense of shame, the power of the abuser, the culture of secrecy and isolation, and the fear of physical punishment inhibited them from disclosing abuse.[390]

The crimes of abuse that were perpetrated against the children were compounded by the neglect of others to take any action to support the children. While perpetrators were clearly in the wrong, so too were those parents or school authorities who stood by and enabled and facilitated such abuse to continue unabated. They were accessories to the crimes and deserve no lesser punishment. It is, however, acknowledged, that members of religious orders would have faced censure and punishment for disobeying the rules of the Church by exposing the abuse perpetrated by others. These clerical bystanders are both perpetrators and victims. The leaders of the Church who imposed rules prohibiting reporting such crimes to secular law enforcement authorities and who turned a blind eye, or covered-up, abuse are clearly also perpetrators. The Catholic Church and other religious groups are currently being forced to confront the reality of child sexual abusers within their ranks. Their failure to acknowledge responsibility for these crimes over decades, coupled with the cover-up of abusers leaves them equally if not more to blame than the abusers themselves for the hardships imposed on thousands of abused children.

The Church's actions over the years follow a pattern of abuse, denial and cover-up. A plan to open a tribunal in the Vatican to judge Bishops accused of covering-up sexual abuse or mishandling cases has been slow to materialize. The commission was marred by the defection of two high-profile lay members who had been victims of abuse. Marie Collins of Ireland who was a child victim of clerical abuse, and Peter Saunders of Britain both quit over lack of progress or cooperation within the Vatican.[391]

In response to increasing pressure on the Church to confront their crimes related to sexual abuse within the Church, Pope Francis convened a four-day conference of 190 Bishops from around the world in February 2019. A senior German Cardinal at this meeting, Cardinal Reinhart Marx, who is a member of the "C9" advisors to the Pope on sexual abuse issues, admitted that files that could have incriminated sexually offending clergy had either never been made or were destroyed, allowing offences to continue. As he said, "It is not transparency which damages the Church but rather the acts of abuse committed, the lack of transparency, or the ensuing cover up."[392]

Repercussions for Survivors

While some survivors reported to the Irish Commission of Inquiry that they, as adults, had managed to enjoy good relationships and successful careers, the majority struggled with the after effects of their early childhood experiences. Some positive experiences were reported by witnesses. These included the kindness of some religious and lay staff, including those who provided support in times of difficulty after they had left the schools. Many spoke of the enormous difference that a kind word or gesture made in their lives. Family contact was greatly valued and friendships and time spent with kind "holiday" families sustained some witnesses. Nevertheless, many reported that their adult lives were harmed by their childhood abuse. They reported troubled relationships or loss of contact with their siblings and families. They described having difficulties parenting their own children. They also described lives marked by poverty, social isolation, alcoholism, sleep disturbance, aggressive behaviour and self-harm. Almost a third (30%) discussed ongoing mental health concerns such as suicidal behaviour, depression, alcohol and substance abuse, and eating disorders, which required treatment including psychiatric admission, medication and counselling.[393]

The outcome of their upbringing in the Irish school system was often sad, and occasionally tragic. Girls, in particular, were vulnerable to sexual abuse when they left their schools, facilitated by their total lack of preparation for consensual sexual encounters. The lack of preparation for their future lives, has been frequently documented by girls, although there is no mention made of the lack of preparation of boys regarding respecting women. For example, the only preparation given to Elizabeth Bright before starting her first job in domestic service at the age of sixteen, was a book that she admitted to the convent Mother that she did not understand. No further explanation was given to her so that when she was assaulted and raped by a young man, she had no idea what was happening.[394]

Irene from St Grace's school was also totally unprepared for her life in the community after leaving school. The lack of legal consequences for her abuser is also stunning. After a local dance she agreed to be walked home by a young man she had met at the dance. He raped her:

> Tom clamped his hand round my mouth and pushed me to the floor. I was stunned. I tried to struggle but he was a big guy and he had his full weight on me. Out of the blue he punched me in the face. Then again in the stomach. For a moment, I was pole-axed and just lay there in shock. Then his hand went to his ankle and the next thing he had a hunting knife and he was holding it at my throat.
> "Now don't you go screaming or nuttin," he hissed in my ear. "Just shut up and don't fucking move or I'll cut your bloody throat open."
> With that he pushed the tip of the knife into my neck and I felt the edge of the blade nicking my skin. I froze and then he pulled down my jeans and ripped off my knickers and forced himself inside me. Oh Jesus, the pain shot up me like a white hot poker. Every time I moved I felt the knife point digging deeper into my neck. Laughing he straddled me, pushing the knife up to my throat.
> "You're going to die." He rasped.[395]

Some days after the assault Irene attempted suicide. She was admitted to a psychiatric hospital where she stayed for five months.

Later she found the courage to testify against the boy when he was arrested and tried. The court, found him not guilty of rape but guilty of grievous bodily harm. He was sentenced to three months although a charge of rape could have earned him seven years.[396] Mary's life after this experience was tragic. She was imprisoned, returned to mental hospitals twice more, tried to commit suicide, turned to alcohol and was unable to maintain steady employment.[397]

Positive reactions of survivors of priestly child sex abuse are rarely heard. James, now a gastric surgeon in his fifties, was abused or tormented for two decades by Father Fernando Karadima, a Chilean parish Priest in Santiago and a renowned sexual predator. He has spent fourteen years in psychotherapy, three times a week, and only managed to break free from Karadima when he began to feel his own children, especially a son, were in danger.[398] Karadima was defrocked in 2018 for sexually abusing minors.[399]

In another account, two months after being removed from school as a young child when his mother discovered some of the abuse he had suffered, James saw a *Star Wars* movie that changed his life. He was able to connect the Brothers who had abused him with Darth Vader, and to value martial arts (embodied in the Jedi) as a means of overcoming and rebelling against his enemies. No longer able to believe in his Catholic faith, he could accept the concept of The Force as a positive life force giving spiritual meaning to his development. His mother, even though she did not understand the extent to which he had been sexually abused, knew he had been struggling, so supported his dreams. He ultimately built an extremely successful career and created a loving family. He attributes this to the values and models provided to him by *Star Wars*. Despite his remarkable achievements, otherwise innocuous daily events remind him of the horrors he experienced, such as the disconcerting meaning that "Father's Day" has for him. "Dad's Day" is, understandably, preferable.[400] While his parents were very supportive, others in his community were far less so.

> When I came out about the abuse in my community my family was chastised for it. I was made fun of. People joked about me being raped as they had their morning

coffee in the local donut shops. My parents lost friends over it. It was a joke to the community. People were more comfortable shunning me than realizing what was happening at the Catholic school. I was the first to publicly come out in my community about abuse. I was mocked for it. I even had an Aunt who made fun of me because I was abused and sent me a letter asking me "how it was working out for me," and that I would "never amount to anything because I was a horrible child and deserved everything that happened." Needless to say, she was not a kind woman.[401]

The Children of Priests

There is yet a further outcome of clerical sex abuse that affects both the survivors of their abuse and the offspring that they may have as a result of their sexual encounters. While much of Priestly sexual activity involves consenting adults, it is also possible that some children and especially adolescent children who are sexually abused by clergy could and do become pregnant and give birth. Multiple examples of this type of sexual abuse among girls within the Irish residential care system, who were sent to assist farmers and who were supposedly under the protection of the local priest reported this type of sexual interaction. For example, Patricia at St Vincent's Industrial school in County Limerick (aged fourteen) and Ann Thomson in the Sisters of Good Shepherd Home in New Zealand (aged fifteen) both recount stories that could have ended with pregnancy but in these instances did not. Such priestly abuse of teenagers could well result in further abuse of the mothers, and the babies they give birth to.

A website, Coping International, is specifically directed towards assisting the children of Priests. It is a voluntary, self-help, mental health organization that promotes the well-being of children of Catholic Priests, or male or female religious clerics, and their parents.[402] For example, at the age of twelve Sarah McDermott found out that her father, whom she'd never known, was a Catholic Priest. She then spent years trying to establish a relationship with him. He was living and working in London, where she lived. Her mother had been in a two-year relationship with her father when he was a trainee Priest. When he learned of the pregnancy, he never spoke to her mother alone again, but only in the presence of another Church representative. Sarah eventually met her father accompanied by a teacher's husband and a Catholic counsellor. The meeting was cold and she was told he would not see her again for another four years. She knows about 100 people who have been fathered by Priests and believes there are thousands more. Coping International helps.[403]

Similarly, in June 2019, Bishops met with members of the French association, Children of Silence. At their request, the sons and daughters of Priests were able to speak out, for the first time, about their fathers, their neglect and suffering.[404] Further meetings are planned as well as promises made to provide access to records regarding their fathers.[405] As with Priestly abuse of children in schools that are covered-up and hidden from the public and from their own communities, the partners of their sexual relationships are discarded emotionally and their offspring discounted and rejected.

Canadian Residential Schools

For most of its 100 years of existence, Canada's residential schools for Indigenous children (First Nations, Métis, and Inuit) was an education system in name only. The schools were created to separate Indigenous children from their families in order to minimize and weaken family ties and cultural linkages, and to indoctrinate children into a new culture, that of the legally dominant Euro-Christian Canadian society.[406] The system was intended to "Kill the Indian" in the child.[407] This experience was hidden for most of Canada's history, until survivors of the system were finally able to access the legal system and bring their experiences to light in several thousand court cases that ultimately led to the largest class-action lawsuit in Canada's history.[408] The Canadian Residential School system also provided an official, government sponsored, and religiously inspired and implemented, forum for widespread and institutionalized child sex abuse.

For over a century, the central goals of Canada's Indigenous people policy were to cause Indigenous peoples to cease to exist as distinct legal, social, cultural, religious, and racial entities in Canada. In 1920, Indian Affairs Deputy Minister Duncan Campbell Scott, directed that all the Native children between the ages of seven and fifteen were to attend Indian residential schools,[409] as had previously been mandated in an amendment to the Indian act of 1884 that required all First Nations children who attained seven years of age to attend residential or day schools.[410] In that year he addressed the House of Commons saying that "our object is to continue until there is not a single Indian in Canada that has not been absorbed into the body politic, and there is no

Indian question, and no Indian Department that is the whole object of this Bill."[411] The establishment and operation of residential schools were a central element of this policy, which can best be described as "cultural genocide."[412] Children were abused, emotionally, physically and sexually and they died in the schools in numbers that would not have been tolerated in any other school system anywhere in the country, or in the world.[413] In the early 1900s, the death rate of children was 75%. Deaths occurred either in the schools or, because the children were severely ill and were sent home before they died, within a few years of returning home. Tuberculosis was a primary cause of death, resulting from extremely poor living conditions in the schools.[414]

At least 150,000 First Nation, Métis, and Inuit students passed through the system. Roman Catholic, Anglican, United, Methodist, and Presbyterian churches were the major denominations involved in the administration of the residential school system.[415] In collaboration with government police forces, children were rounded up from their homes and taken to the schools, by force or coercion. Some were able to return home in some holiday periods while others remained permanent residents in the school until allowed to return to their families years later. Building and managing the system began in 1868 with the establishment of fifty-seven schools.[416] The government's partnership with the churches remained in place until 1969, and, although most of the schools had closed by the 1980s, the last federally supported residential schools remained in operation until the late 1990s when Grollier Hall, the last large hostel in the North, closed in 1997.[417] At the start of 2015, almost 38,000 residential school survivors, who had been physically and/or sexually abused in the residential school system, filed suits against the government for these abuses: Over 30,000 of them, have been awarded damages.[418]

As John Milloy, writes:

> The residential school experience was, beyond question, intolerable... all too often, "wards of the Department" were overworked, underfed, badly clothed, housed in unsanitary quarters, beaten with whips, rods and fists, chained and shackled, bound hand and foot, locked in

closets, basements and bathrooms, and had their heads shaved or hair closely cropped.

There were, moreover, torments which, while not physical, were equally hurtful, ranging from the general loneliness of the children which came from their prolonged separation from their parents and separation from siblings in school to individual acts of profound cruelty. Reverend W Moore, a Methodist missionary on Mistiwassis Reserve, reported in 1903, that at the Regina School where he sent children from his community, one of the teachers, Mr. Gilmour, had handed a revolver to a young girl who announced that she wanted to commit suicide, telling her to go ahead and pull the trigger. She did – but the gun was empty.[419]

On Arrival at the Schools

On their arrival at residential school, students were usually required to exchange the clothes they were wearing for school-supplied clothing. This could mean the loss of homemade clothing that was of particular value and meaning to them.[420] Campbell Papequash was taken, against his will, to residential school in 1946:

> And after I was taken there they took off my clothes and then they deloused me. I didn't know what was happening but I learned about it later, that they were delousing me; "the dirty, no-good-for-nothing savages, lousy." [421]

Gilles Petiquay, who attended the Pointe Bleue school, was shocked by the fact that each student was assigned a number.

> I remember that the first number that I had at the residential school was 95. I had that number—95—for a year. The second number was number 4. I had it for a longer period of time. The third number was 56. I also kept it for a long time. We walked with the numbers on us. Older brothers were separated from younger brothers,

older sisters were separated from younger sisters, and brothers and sisters were separated from each other.[422]

It did not take long for physical abuse to start: Meeka Alivaktuk came to the Pangnirtung school in what is now Nunavut with no knowledge of English. When she failed to obey an instruction because she did not understand it, she was slapped on the hands. On his first day of school in Pangnirtung, the teacher overheard Sam Kautainuk speaking to a friend in Inuktitut. "He took a ruler and grabbed my head like this and then smacked me in the mouth with the ruler four times."[423] Children were not allowed to use their native language. Some children who went to St Mary's said the Priests stuck pins in the tongues of children who spoke their Indigenous language.[424]

Hunger and Nutrition

Hunger was a constant concern for the children.[425] At the inquest into the events at the Williams Lake school, Christine Haines explained why she ran away from the school twice:

> The Sisters didn't treat me good – they gave me rotten food to eat and punished me for not eating it – the meat and the soup were rotten and so bad they made the girls sick sometime. I have been sick from eating it.
> …I used to hide the meat in my pocket and throw it away. I told the Sisters to look at the meat as it was rotten, and they said it was not rotten and we must eat it. The Sisters did not eat the same kind of food as they gave the girls. If we didn't eat our porridge at breakfast, it was given to us for our dinner and even for supper, and we got nothing else until it was eaten.[426]

Similar stories were also told by Ellen Charlie aged sixteen,[427] Louis aged twelve, Mary Sticks, aged eleven, Francois aged ten, and Augustine aged seven.[428]

Mary John, who attended the Fraser Lake, British Columbia, school, recalled that the meals were dull and monotonous, including a regular diet of porridge interspersed with boiled barley and beans, and bread covered with lard. Weeks might go by without any fish or meat; sugar and jam were reserved for special occasions.[429]

In 1965, one of the former students at Brandon School reported that

> They ate food "Prepared in the crudest ways and served in very unsanitary conditions." It included "bread dipped in grease and hardened...green liver...milk that had manure in the bottom of the cans and homemade porridge that had grasshopper legs and bird droppings in it" [430]

A further student described conditions as the Mohawk Institute at Brantford Ontario:

> "90% of children suffered from diet deficiency and this was evident in the number of boils, warts and the general malaise that existed within the school population." He had seen "children eating from the swill barrel, picking out soggy bits of food that was intended for the pigs."[431]

Bernard Catcheway recalled that in the 1960s at the Pine Creek, Manitoba, school, "we had to eat all our food even though we didn't like it. There was a lot of times there I seen other students that threw up and they were forced to eat their own, their own vomit."[432] Bernard Sutherland recalled students at the Fort Albany school being forced to eat food that they had vomited. "I saw in person how the children eat their vomit. When they happened to be sick. And they threw up while eating."[433]

Physical Abuse

Children were abused and beaten.[434] They were sometimes chained to benches or kept in chains.[435] Milloy's national inquiry report states that for her disobedience, Christine Haines claimed that she had been locked in a "cold and dark" room, fed bread and water and beaten "with a strap, sometime on the face. And sometimes [they] took my clothes off and beat me – this is the reason I ran away."[436] Other children made the same charges.[437] The staff who were interviewed denied the children's claims although the sister in charge admitted "sometimes girls [were] shut up in a room for serious faults for periods varying from a few hours to ten or twelve days – this is the longest time. The latter has happened only once."[438] One of the male teachers also admitted that he used a saddle whip on the children guilty of "immorality."[439]

In 1924 children attending the "Spanish" residential school reported home that they were being mistreated as "savages." In one case, the Christian Brothers who ran the school undressed a boy "whipping him naked until he became unconscious."[440] Although this was typical of the severe punishments that were reported regularly in 1924, the Department secretary refused to investigate the school because he was confident that the children were well treated by devoted staff.[441]

Theodore Fontaine reports that

> Most priest and nuns used leather straps that the school's farmer had cut from pieces of tractor belts. They were about six inches long and three inches wide, and they hurt![442]

Bed wetting was a problem for a number of students. A student at the Mohawk Institute at Brantford, Ontario, later reported:

> I have seen Indian children having their faces rubbed in human excrement…the normal punishment for bedwetters was to have his face rubbed in his own urine.[443]

Sexual Abuse

There was pervasive sexual abuse of the children, although the issue is almost completely erased from official files.[444] There were also subtle, and not so subtle, associations between physical and sexual abuse. At one school, for example, the principal chose to beat the girls in private:

> He called me to his room. He says he'll strap me. He told me to take off my jeans and my panty. Instead I pulled it down to the knees. He tells me to kneel down. So I do. He gives me thirteen straps. He also waits a little moment every time I had the strap. [...] I had my body between his legs. That was kneeling down. [...] First thing father wanted me to go to his office so I did. He asked me a few questions, and then he brought me to the other office. He told me to kneel and then he pulled my skirt up and then pulled my pants down. He put my head between his legs and he started to give me the strap. I had the strap at 9.00 pm. I had around 10 straps or over.[445]

Mary Chapman, a Stó:lō grandmother, recalls the shaming punishments meted out by one of the Sisters of St Ann when she was a student in the 1940s and 1950s at Kuper Island Residential School, "When girls were caught doing something like stealing food or talking Halq'eméylem, the Nuns would make then stand in a long line in front of the whole school, then lift their skirts right up. They had to stand there is front of everybody, naked, with their genitals exposed."[446] Chapman also reports another sexualized punishment implemented by the Nuns. "The Nuns would strip the girls naked from the waist down and force them to lie face down on the beds. Then all the rest of us were told to parade by the girls and hit them as hard as we could on their bottoms. The Nuns would just stand there and watch."[447]

In 1990, Rix Rogers, the special advisor to the Minister of National Health and Welfare on Child Sexual Abuse commented at a meeting of the Canadian Psychological Association that the abuse revealed to that date was "just the tip of the iceberg" and that "closer scrutiny of past treatment of native children at Indian residential schools would show that 100% of children at some schools were sexually abused."[448]

Many students spoke of having been raped at school.[449] There was no single pattern of abuse. Students of both sexes reported assaults from staff members of both the opposite sex and the same sex as themselves.[450] Josephine Sutherland was cornered by one of the lay Brothers in the Fort Albany school garage. "I couldn't call for help, I couldn't. And he did awful things to me."[451] Other students were assaulted in the church confessional or in the change room. Some were instructed to report to the shower room in the middle of the night or to take lunch to a staff member's room. An abusive staff person might stalk a student, blocking her or his way, or grope a passing student. Some female students spoke of how some staff members took advantage of their innocence, rubbing against them sexually while they were sitting on their laps. Abuse also took the form of voyeuristic humiliation. Some staff insisted on watching the students shower. Some dormitory supervisors used their authority to institute dormitory-wide systems of abuse. Many students spoke of the fear and anxiety that existed in their dormitories in the evenings. They went to bed fearful that they might be called into the supervisor's room. As Theodore Fontaine writes:

> I am nine years old and resident at the Fort Alexander Indian Residential School [...] The school is run by the Oblates, a religious order of the Roman Catholic Church [...]. Every evening before we go to bed, we are in our classrooms for study periods, and every night it happens. Four or five different boys are called into a room for a weekly ritual exercise known as *ménage* [a French word for "housework"]. [...]
> It's my time for ménage – that weekly ritual, the washing of the genitals by a man in a black robe. [...]
> I shuffle quietly down the hall [...] [I wonder if the shop teacher] sinned when he pulled out his penis in front of me and commanded me to sit on the chair in front of him as he tried to pull it out by its roots. Maybe they're allowed. It looked like a big blood sausage [....]

> This ritual of 'staying clean' happened every week or
> two over the years for many of the younger boys.
> It stopped when we became older and bigger, and our
> determination to threaten, maim, hurt or even kill our
> tormentors gave us the power to refuse the treatment.[452]

Most students came to school with little knowledge or
understanding of sexual activity, let alone the types of sexual abuse to
which they might be subjected.

> A survivor friend remembers drinking with Mr H [the
> shop teacher] and then having Mr H force him to lie on
> top of his wife as he stood aside and masturbated. I don't
> know if he made any other boys do that, but he certainly
> underwent a physical workout in front of me and others.
> This is one of the most belittling, embarrassing and
> hurtful memories I have had since then.[453]

Abuse left them injured, bewildered, and often friendless or
subject to ridicule by other students. Many thought they were the only
children being abused. This made it difficult for them to describe or
report it. Some were told they would face eternal damnation for
speaking of what had been done to them. As they got older and
stronger, some fought back against their far larger and more powerful
assailants with some success. Many others, such as Lawrence
Waquan, concluded that there was "nothing you can do."[454] Some
students ran away from school in an attempt to escape abuse. Others
begged their parents not to return them to school after a break. Some
never reported abuse for fear they would not be believed. Others who
did report their experiences were told that they were to blame. In
some cases, school officials took immediate action when abuse was
reported to them, but such action was rare. Family members often
refused to believe their children's reports of abuse, intensifying their
sense of isolation and pain. This was especially so within families
that had adopted Christianity, and could not believe that the people of
God looking after their children would ever do such things. The
impact of abuse was immediate and long-lasting. It destroyed the
students' ability to function in the school, and led many to turn to

self-destructive behaviours. Staff abuse of children created conditions for the student abuse of other students.[455]

> Sexual abuse at Brannon Lake was common. Certain members of the staff preyed at will on all of us. To get a day trip out of the institution, a boy would have to be a "bum-boy" for certain male supervisors. Many of the older boys were street hardened youth from big cities, used to trading sexual favours for money or privileges, and the staff willingly exploited them. It seemed as though there was no one safe to complain to.
> The older boys could count on school officials turning a blind eye when those boys preyed on smaller, younger boys for sexual favours.[456]

Another account describes the shocking transition into a residential school system.

> Emily Rice's introduction to residential school will be etched on her soul for the rest of her life. [She was] Raised on a lush British Columbia Gulf Island replete with wild deer, gardens and orchards and surrounded by straits that ran silver with salmon and herring. Rice spoke little English at the age of eight when she was told the priest was coming to take her to boarding school. The nightmare began as soon as Emily and her sister Rose, then eleven years old, stepped on the small boat that would bear them away. "I clung to Rose until Father Jackson wrenched her out of my arms." Rice remembers. "I searched all over the boat for Rose. Finally, I climbed up to the wheelhouse and opened the door, and there was Father Jackson, on top of my sister. My sister's dress was pulled up and his pants were down. I was too little to know about sex; but I now know he was raping her. He cursed and came after me, picked up his big, black Bible and slapped me across the face and on the top of the head. I started crying hysterically and he threw me onto the deck. When we

> got to Kuper Island, my sister and I were separated.
> They wouldn't let me comfort her. [Father Jackson's
> name has been changed].[457]

When Emily Rice left Kuper Island in 1959, at eleven years old, she had been repeatedly sexually abused by Father Jackson and three other Priests, one of whom plied her with alcohol before raping her. Sister Margaret, a Nun known for peeping at the girls in the shower and grabbing their breasts, was furious when Emily resisted her. "She took a big stick with bark on it and rapped it right inside my vagina"[458] recalls Rice. "She told me to say that I had fallen on the stick and that she was just trying to get it out."[459] When Emily made her way to the infirmary the next day, she was too afraid to name Sister Margaret. Nevertheless, when she returned to the dorm a few days later, the beatings by Sister Mary Margaret and the other Nuns immediately resumed. Later, Emily would have to undergo reconstructive vaginal surgery twice, and she was left with permanent hearing loss. Father Jackson also wanted to ensure Emily's silence. On the sisters' first trip home at Christmas, he held Rose by her feet over the side of the boat, threatening to drop her into the freezing waves unless Emily promised not to tell.[460]

In the early 1990s, five Shuswap women charged Catholic Bishop Hubert Patrick O'Conner, the former principal of St Joseph's residential school, with sexual abuse. He was a Priest, and, as the only man in the lives of most Shuswap girls when they were at the school, a father figure. His sexual exploitation of the girls to whom he was guardian and a spiritual leader, was a deep betrayal of trust. In September, 1996, after prosecution squabbles, a stay of proceedings and a Supreme Court of Canada decision ordering a new trial, O'Conner was sentenced to two and a half years in jail for raping Marilyn Belleau and sexually assaulting another Shuswap woman.[461]

Willie Blackwater, a survivor of the Alberni Indian Residential School revealed his experiences of not only abuse, but the consequences he faced when he repeatedly tried to report it.

> The abuse began as soon as I got there.[...]
> Arthur Henry Plint was the dorm supervisor for the
> younger boys, boys my age [6-7 years old]. [...] he

woke me up […] told me to come into his office because there was an emergency phone call from my father. […] I went into the office. The phone was off the hook […] he hung it up and said there was no phone call, he just needed to talk to me. […]

He […] dropped his robe, and faced me, naked. He pushed me onto the bed […] told me to take my pajamas off and started to masturbate me. Then he put his mouth on my penis and made me do the same to him, until he ejaculated in my mouth. I started to get sick and tried to puke. He laughed and told me if I puked on his bed I'd get hurt. […]

about a month later, it was the same thing, […] this time he turned me over on my stomach and he penetrated me. After that Plint raped me anally about once a month for the next three years.

I finally got up my nerve to tell Mr Butler what Plint was doing to me. [Mr Butler's name has been changed] Butler gave me a severe strapping and called me a dirty lying Indian. A few days later Plint […] beat the hell out of me. He yelled, "This is nothing compared to what will happen to you if you ever tell anyone again." After that I didn't tell anyone for another whole year.

[…] in the fall, I told my teacher at the public school […] She phoned Mr Butler. I was beaten badly by Butler and I got another severe beating from Plint. The third year I finally got up the courage to tell my father. He phoned Mr Butler, who told him the boys made up stories to stay away from school. I got another beating from Mr Butler. […] When Plint got hold of me, it was the worst beating I ever got. […] punched my head repeatedly. I lost consciousness and I woke up in the infirmary. I was in there two or three weeks.

Plint had his little clique of older students, too, like this guy named Gus and he and Plint took turns raping me after my dad had called the school. I vowed I'd never tell anyone again.[462]

Blackwater laid charges against Plint who was convicted in criminal court in 1995. Plint, then seventy-seven, cursed his accusers as he walked into court, hitting out with his cane in a final act of contempt and violence. He pleaded guilty to sixteen counts of indecent assault of Indigenous boys aged six to thirteen, between 1948 and 1968. He was sentenced to eleven years in prison. Justice [Douglas] Hogarth said that as far as the children were concerned, the Indian residential school system was nothing more than institutionalized paedophilia.[463]

Many reported that their sexual abuse started when they were very young. Barney Williams was five-and-a-half when taken from his grandparent's home to Christie Residential school, two miles from his home. He did not return home until he was a teenager. He was raped by one of the men at the school. The first time he was raped he was so injured he had to go to the infirmary. They didn't send him to the hospital but just dealt with it there.[464] Ted Quewezance was also only five or six when taken to a residential school, Gordon's school in Punnichy, Saskatchewan. He was there for seven years and then moved to St Phillip's in Kamsack for another four. He was sexually and physically abused for all his years at school. "I never knew who I was, or where I came from. I went into alcohol, I went into drugs. I tried to commit suicide."[465] Piita Irniq was eleven when taken to Sir Joseph Brenier residential school in Chesterfield inlet. In his testimony at the Truth and Reconciliation Committee, he summarized the extent of the losses he felt as: "We were sexually abused. We had a loss of culture, loss of language, loss of tradition, loss of Inuit skills."[466]

Danny Watts recalls a confusing blend of sexuality and religion that was forced on him while at the same Alberni residential school as Blackwater. Danny turned to religion to help him cope with the horrors of his school. Even at an early age he could recite the Bible, and tell you all the books and dates of the Bible. His supervisor, who had taught him all this, invited him up to his room one day and, trustingly, Danny went with him.

> Of course, he began by praying to the lord. Then he
> proceeded to take my pants off, and then his own pants,
> and he would have an erection, and he'd lay behind me.

And simulate sex, and have a climax. It was bad enough that this man was doing this to an eleven-year-old boy. What made it even worse was he used to make me kneel and ask forgiveness. We'd do this bullshit about, oh Lord we've sinned, and please forgive us. What did I do? I was just a young boy being manipulated by this old man.[467]

Watts describes the spiritual and sexual abuse as

"violence to your soul, to have this Christianity shit pushed down your throat day in and day out, to have to pray before you eat and pray before you go to bed. And pray after some guy is trying to shove his prick up your ass."[468]

Sexual Abuse in Foster Care

For the most part, residential schools held children for ten months of the year although some federally funded day schools were also established for Indian students such as Prince Edward Island's Rocky Point Day School and another on Lennox Island. Physical, emotional and sexual abuse were also imposed in these schools.[469] At least, however, the children in these schools stayed in an Indigenous peer group; they knew their First Nation of origin and who their parents were, and they knew that eventually, if they survived, they would be going home or could live at home. In the foster and adoptive care system, on the other hand, Indigenous children were placed until they were adults in non-Indigenous homes where their cultural identity, their knowledge of their own First Nation and even their birth names were erased, often forever.[470]

Orphaned children including those parents whom social services, sometimes without good reason but based on prejudicial judgments, deemed were incapable of rearing their own children, were quickly selected for foster care, as were those cared for by an aged grandmother or by parents living in the impoverished conditions of the reserves of the early 1950's.[471] From the 1960s to 1980s tens of thousands of

115

Indigenous children were forcibly removed from their homes by child welfare authorities and placed in non-Indigenous foster homes before they were adopted by white families in Canada, the USA, the UK and Australia – known as the "Sixties Scoop."[472] In 2007 it was estimated that 40% of all Indigenous children were in foster care, effectively continuing the cultural genocide of the residential school era.[473]

Many children were sent to the US to be adopted. As late as the 1980's, the majority of those taken from Manitoba were moved out of Canada by American adoption agencies. In 1981 for example, 55% of the Native children in Manitoba's care were sent out of the province for adoption, compared to only 7% of Caucasian children. The private adoption agencies, often religious, did little screening beyond ascertaining the applicant's ability to pay the five to ten thousand dollars required to adopt an Indigenous child. There are no reports of money ever reaching the relinquishing family.[474] None of the private, public or religious adoption agencies that placed aboriginal children out of province or out of the country monitored the children, and few kept records that would allow adoptees to retrace their roots or find their tribes. There are few government-funded programs in Canada to help adoptees discover who they are.[475]

Children were removed from their loving, supportive families and placed into foster homes in which abuse of all kinds was extremely common. For example, one woman reported that her foster parents physically and sexually abused her.[476] Her Indigenous identity was constantly disparaged. She said, "[My foster parents were] adamant about Aboriginal culture being less than human, living as dirty bush people, eating rats. It made me not want to be one of those people. And for years, I didn't know how to be proud of who I was because I didn't know who I was."[477] Linda Clarke was placed in a foster home with three other children.

> In that foster home there was a pedophile, and I don't [know] what was happening to anybody else, but I became his target. The mother used to always send me to do errands with him. And so every time, he would make me do things to him and then he would give me

candy. Also, in that home there was no hugging of us foster kids or anything like that. And I carried a great guilt for many, many years, because sometimes I didn't want to resist it, I just … But I knew it was very bad.[478]

Inappropriate or excessive selection of Indigenous children from their homes and their transfer to orphanages, foster homes or adoption placements did not only occur during the period of the residential school era. The legacy of this period continues to this day. Sometimes, such child-welfare placements end in tragedy. Where there are province-specific statistics available, the findings suggest that in some parts of the country, Indigenous children who come into contact with child-welfare authorities are significantly more likely to die. These findings are frightening when we consider the proportion of Indigenous children in care across the country: 100% in Nunavut, 95% in the Northwest Territories, 94% in Yukon, between 68% and 87% in the western provinces of British Columbia, Alberta, Saskatchewan and Manitoba, and between 0% and 32% in the eastern provinces of Ontario, Quebec, New Brunswick, Nova Scotia, Prince Edward Island and Newfoundland. Tragic stories still emerge periodically reflecting apparent discrimination against Indigenous parents, such as the newborn baby that was removed from her first-time parents in British Columbia within ninety minutes of a caesarean section, even though there was no apparent cause for concern. The baby, born in 2019, was only returned to the parents two weeks after birth, immediately prior to a court hearing.[479] Also, Indigenous women in Saskatoon have been coerced into being sterilized prior to being allowed to see their newborns.[480] Similar reports of forced sterilizations have emerged from Quebec, Manitoba and British Columbia reflecting an alternate method of eliminating Indian offspring.[481] Research in Alberta has indicated that 78% of children who died in foster care between 1999 and mid-2013 were Indigenous.[482] Indigenous children in Alberta are a minority of the overall population (10%), but represent more than 70% of children under fourteen in care.[483] Across Canada, Indigenous children make up about 4% of all children but 53% of all current foster children are First Nations.[484] The rate of Indigenous child deaths in care is even more concerning with 78% of the children who died in care in Alberta since 1990 being Indigenous. Of the seventy-four recorded deaths of Indigenous children in care, thirteen were due to accidents, twelve children committed suicide, and ten children were the victims of homicide – frightening figures, and a heartbreaking legacy of the residential school era.

Abuse in foster care appears to be an ongoing concern raising questions as to whether foster care facilitates child sex abuse. Certainly, undertaking foster care would allow access to a child within the privacy of a home for someone inclined to such abuse. Foster parents are seen by society as benevolent, virtuous people even though they are paid to care for such children. Foster children, in contrast are often viewed as "problem kids" possibly due to the sometimes many families they have been moved to and the lack of trust in human kindness and human relationships that may result. They may also be groomed to believe that whatever family setting they get, good or abusive, is the best they can hope to get or deserve, leading them to keep quiet about any sexual or other abuse they experience.[485] Reports of sexual and physical abuse of Indigenous children in foster care go back many years. Ernie Crey was taken from Brannon Lake School and placed in a series of foster homes, still under government control:

> A social worker took me to meet Frank, an engaging and handsome young man in his mid-thirties. Frank took me for a drive in his car and bought me an ice-cream. He invited me to come out and live in a group home where he worked, where he promised I'd have lots of freedom and few chores to do. He took me to see the home. There were five teen-aged boys living there. Most of them non-native. I decided to move in. Shortly afterwards, Frank moved in too. He'd split up with his wife, and he appeared to have persuaded his superiors the group home experiment would work best with a resident supervisor.
>
> I soon saw Frank's real motive for living with teen-aged boys. He openly pursued sexual relationships with them. […] I'd hear boys tiptoeing down the hall to join

Frank on the couch of the recreation room where he slept. He had a big collection of kiddie porn, which he left lying around. In one of the magazines we found a picture of a boy we all knew, a child still in the care of the province of British Columbia, whom Frank had taken on a trip to San Francisco.

Frank was a skilled, intelligent pedophile, very exploitative. As foster children they were starved for love, and very vulnerable. [...] Frank even brought another social worker into the house to share the boys' sexual favours.

Looking back, I am angry and amazed that these two pedophiles could have preyed so openly on children in care in a government financed group home.[486]

Ernie Crey reports further:

In the good Christian home in which Bruce [Ernie Crey's brother] grew up, he and Louise [his sister] were kept in the basement on Christmas Day while the foster family gathered upstairs for turkey dinner. Both Bruce and Louise were subjected to bizarre, cruel punishments: they were locked in the closet, threatened with a large hunting knife when grades were poor, and had their heads stuck in the toilet bowl, while it was flushed repeatedly. My brother and sister were told constantly that they were the spawn of the devil. Like most of the aboriginal children who grew up in care, they will battle with self-esteem issues all their lives.[487]

As an adult, Ernie Crey's sister Jane told him, that she had been sexually abused by the son of her foster parents. He was never charged and works as a Christian missionary in Africa.[488]

Many Indigenous adults who grew up in foster care believe they were fortunate to escape the sexual abuse they might have suffered at home, but far more report that they were treated as domestic and sexual slaves in care homes.[489] Donna Lewis and Dianne Marie, two Indigenous sisters, were taken away from their mother, who had a history of alcoholism, when they were seven and four. Their adoptive father, former federal bureaucrat John Lewis, pleaded guilty in a criminal case to sexually abusing them. The girls obtained an out-of-court settlement of between $80,000 and $100,000 after suing the B.C. Ministry of Social Services and Housing.[490]

Cover-ups

The Truth and Reconciliation Commission into Indigenous children's schooling has revealed repeated procedures that covered-up abuses against them. Complaints were often ignored. In some cases, where allegations were made against a school principal, Indian Affairs might contact the principal.[491] Principal McWhitney [at Lejac school] was kept on despite a long-term record of ill treatment of children, including failure to act in 1914, when a farm instructor had sexual intercourse with two girls.[492] In at least one case, Indian Affairs officials worked with school officials to frustrate a police investigation into abuse at a school. When attempting to return some runaway boys to the Kuper Island school in 1939, British Columbia Provincial Police officers concluded that there was good reason to believe the boys had run away because they were being sexually abused at the school. The police launched an investigation and refused to return the boys to the school. When Indian Affairs officials finally investigated, they concluded that the allegations had merit. However, to protect the school's reputation, the local Indian Affairs official advised the suspected abusers to leave the province, allowing them to avoid prosecution.[493] Nothing was done for the students who had been victimized or for their parents. These patterns persisted at least into the late twentieth century. Officials continued to dismiss Indigenous reports of abuse. In some cases, staff members were not fired, even after being convicted of assaulting a student. Complaints were improperly investigated. Church officials failed to report cases of abuse to Indian Affairs, and Indian Affairs failed to report cases of abuse to families. It was not until 1968 that Indian Affairs began to compile and circulate a list of former staff members who were not to be hired at other schools without the approval of officials in Ottawa. The churches and the government remained reluctant to take matters to the police. As a result, prosecutions were rare.

In the documents it has reviewed, the Truth and Reconciliation Commission of Canada has identified over forty successful convictions of former residential school staff members who sexually or physically abused students. Most of these prosecutions were the result of the determination of former students to see justice done rather than investigations initiated by the schools, or government authorities. The full extent of the abuse that occurred in the schools is unlikely to ever come to light as many remain reluctant to speak out. At least some instances are now being exposed. As of January 31, 2015, the Independent Assessment Process (IAP), established under the Indian Residential Schools Settlement Agreement had received 37,951 claims for injuries resulting from physical and sexual abuse at residential schools. The IAP is a mechanism to compensate former students for sexual and physical abuse experienced at the schools and the harms that arose from the assaults. By the end of 2014, the IAP had resolved 30,939 of those claims, awarding $2,690,000,000 in compensation.[494] The number of claims for compensation for abuse is equivalent to approximately 48% of the number of former students. As the numbers indicate, the abuse of children was extensive. For example, from 1958, when it first opened, until 1979, there was never a year in which Grollier Hall in Inuvik did not employ at least one dormitory supervisor who would later be convicted for sexually abusing students at the school.

Children's Reactions

The physical, emotional, and sexual abuse of children was so egregious that many children ran away from the schools and were found either dead or close to death, frozen and starved and with evidence of beatings.[495] At least thirty-three students died, usually due to exposure, after running away from school.[496] In a significant number of cases, parents and Indian Affairs officials concluded that the deaths could have been prevented if school officials had mounted earlier and more effective searches and notified police officials and family members. In the case of Charles and Tom Ombash, two brothers who ran away from the Sioux Lookout school on October 5, 1956, school officials waited until November before informing police or Indian Affairs. The boys were never found—community members continued to search for their remains decades after their disappearance.[497]

The first recorded death of a runaway was that of Duncan Sticks. In 1902, he (nine-years-old) and eight other boys ran away. The other boys were captured and returned to the school, but Duncan disappeared into the forest. His body was found the next day by the roadside, thirteen kilometers away from the school. A second death was that of Augustine Allan from Canim Lake. In 1920, he committed suicide at the school by eating poisonous water hemlock in a suicide pact with eight other boys. He died while the others survived.[498] An inquiry into the death conducted by authorities ignored the children's and their parent's complaints, choosing instead to believe the Sisters and Oblates who reported that the children were "well cared for, well fed and had no reason to run away: It was just their "Indian nature."[499] Such reactions to children's complaints reflect the dominant ideology of the time. As Indian Agent O'Daunt wrote in a letter to the Department of Indian Affairs on 1 August 1920:

> Indians are very much averse to any kind of restraint, and to put it mildly, are not to be believed, as a general thing when they complain about Schools or similar Institutions, as they let their imaginations run riot, if they think that by doing so it will help them to gain what they happen to want at that moment.[500]

At least fifty-three schools were destroyed by fire. In an effort to bring their own residential schooling and abuse to an end, some students attempted to burn their schools down. There were at least thirty-seven such attempts,[501] two of which ended in student and staff deaths. There were at least 170 additional recorded fires. At least forty students died in residential school fires. The harsh discipline, abuse and jail-like nature of life in the schools, meant that many students sought to run away leading to many schools deliberately ignoring government instructions in relation to fire drills and fire escapes.[502] Escape or external doors were locked despite these being fire hazards, resulting in children being burned to death when fires did break out. Fires set in schools were particularly hazardous events.

Complaints were widespread about the health conditions in the schools by the late 19th and early 20th centuries. Parents complained to the Indian Agent about the health of their children, school principals submitted constant reports detailing student deaths, and rumours eventually reached the newspapers. In 1904, The Department of Indian Affairs (DIA) commissioned their chief Medical Officer, Dr. Peter Henderson Bryce, to study the health conditions in thirty-five schools. His report was scathing. He decried the schools for being overcrowded and improperly ventilated. Instead of breathing in fresh air, students were often breathing in foul, contaminated air. Death rates across all thirty-five schools averaged 24%.[503] The File Hills residential school had a death rate of 79%. Tuberculosis had no cure at that time, and Bryce suggested schools were actively taking in children afflicted with it, to secure the government stipend (all children were supposed to have a medical exam prior to their admission, which was to accompany their admission form). He made a series of recommendations to the government on how to improve health; one of the key ones was the government assume direct control over the schools, as none of the church groups were properly maintaining their facilities or discharging their duties. Duncan C. Scott, the Minister in charge of DIA, buried the report. It was Scott's opinion that "Indians" were making up complaints about their treatment in schools.[504] Bryce lamented the indifference of Canadians to the wellness of Indigenous children and emphasized that the mass apprehension of the children was not only a cultural genocide but a biological genocide.[505] In 2007, as part of The Beaver magazine's "Worst Canadians" poll, a panel of historians convened by Canada's National History Society (publisher of the Beaver) named Duncan Campbell Scott one of the worst Canadians of all time in recognition of his actions to "get rid of the Indian problem."[506]

In 1918, the Federal government proposed a National Bill of Health, which included provisions for residential school students. The Bill passed its first reading in Parliament (the first reading is usually a formality). The second reading, which is where debates begin, removed the provisions for residential school students. Bryce was furious. The government of Canada was spending about nine cents a year per Indigenous person to deal with the Tuberculosis problem among 100,000 Indigenous people in Canada, but was simultaneously spending thirty-one cents a year to deal with the Tuberculosis problem in Ottawa alone, which had a population of about 100,000. Owing to his oath of Office, Bryce could not publicly disclose this information until he left office; if he had, he would have been charged and imprisoned. When Bryce retired in 1921, he published what was essentially the report he wrote in 1907.

Longer Term Consequences

The effects of abuse, and particularly sexual abuse, of children in the residential school system as well as in foster care settings, led to long lasting social, economic, and psychological consequences for survivors. The inadequate, one might even go so far as to say, almost nonexistent, preparation for life in their communities provided by residential schools had numerous consequences. These included, poor living conditions, poverty, joblessness, suicidal tendencies, substance abuse, inadequate family life and parenting skills, and even perpetuation of abuse.

Their plight was highlighted in 1993 when television footage from Davis Inlet in Labrador revealed seventeen children huddled in a shack, sniffing gasoline fumes and crying out that they wanted to die. The underlying cause that soon became apparent was that they could see no other way to escape the horrific sexual abuse they were experiencing than to die. The adults of their community, dispossessed of their traditional lands, and of their spirituality, and demoralized, had themselves been sexually abused in church-run schools and were in turn, sexually abusing their own children. Virtually no Innu child was reaching adolescence unmolested. Many had been violently raped by their own relatives or by older children.[507]

Suicide is six times more common for Indigenous youth than for their non-Indigenous peers. They hang themselves, blow their heads off with guns, jump from bridges and step in front of speeding trains. Suicides occur in clusters, each death leading to more suicides.[508] Without societal supports suicide may appear to be a solution to their multiple problems. Adolescents who have been physically and sexually abused are ten times more likely to kill themselves. Alcohol and drug use, facilitated by their inadequate educations, preparation for life, and resulting fewer career opportunities, are also more closely associated with Indigenous suicide than with suicides in the general population.[509] Some apparent suicides may also be murders by policing authorities that are discounted in official reports.[510]

Few Indigenous communities have conducted research into the incidence of child sexual abuse in their communities. Both Canim Lake in B.C. and Hollow Water, in Manitoba, however, found that 75% to 85% of people reported they had endured unwanted sexual contact as a child. In consequence, and not surprisingly, almost 35% of respondents to the 1991 Statistics Canada Aboriginal Peoples' Survey named sexual abuse as the most serious problem in their community; as worrisome as alcohol, drug addiction, and unemployment.[511] Child sexual abuse is a concern in Canada, not only for Indigenous children but for all children. In 1984, Prof Robin Badgely undertook a Royal Inquiry into child sexual abuse in Canada on behalf of the Canadian government. His report concluded that one in four girls, and one in seven boys had been victims of sexual assaults. More recent figures are even more disturbing.[512] A 1992 survey conducted by York University's Institute for Social Research reported that 43% of women respondents had been sexually abused at least once in childhood, with 17% reporting experiences of incest. One in four boys is sexually molested, far more than the Badgely report originally suggested. In 1992, Statistics Canada also reported that 40% of all sexual assaults committed in Canada were on children under eleven years of age.[513] The 75-80% of Indigenous children reporting child sex abuse in the BC and Manitoba surveys is approximately double the rate for children in Canada as a whole. Child sexual abuse appears to be almost normative among Indigenous children.

It has taken generations of Indigenous people to even begin to overcome the dismal outcomes that were a consequence of inadequate schooling, broken familial relationships, shattered cultural identities, loss of spiritual support, and decades of emotional, physical and sexual abuse. Two national inquiries into Indigenous People and the residential school system have been undertaken in the past two decades, with some federal apologies being offered, some compensation being paid, but still insignificant economic and cultural strengthening occurring. In September 2019, the Canadian Human Rights Tribunal found that 40,000 to 80,000 First Nations children were denied public services and removed from their families as recently as between 2006-2017, owing to structural inequities and not inclusive of children who faced physical, psychological, or sexual abuse. The Government was required, by this ruling, to pay CAD$40,000 to each victim of its discriminatory conduct.[514] In October 2019, however, Prime Minister Justin Trudeau announced his decision to appeal the Human Rights Tribunal ruling.[515] In addition, a court order issued by Justice Brenda Brown in the British Columbia Supreme court in May 2020, permits the federal government to begin destroying reports that detail abuse allegations against staff of St Anne's residential school. This, despite these documents being key evidence documents needed in the ongoing legal compensation claims of survivors of St Anne's, one of the most notorious residential schools.[516]

In class-action suits settlements with Indigenous survivors, reached in 2006, Catholic organizations involved in the residential schools pledged, among other things, to "use their best efforts" to raise $25 million (Canadian dollars) to help fund healing and reconciliation efforts.[517] Nine years later, after raising $4 million, the Church declared that it had raised as much as it could and a court absolved them of having to pay the rest. All other Church denominations that were part of the settlement – Anglican, United, Presbyterian – paid their full share many years ago.[518] Until the recent exposure of hundreds, and perhaps thousands of unmarked Indigenous children's graves on residential school sites, the Church's failure to pay this debt went unremarked by news organizations, education systems, and the government. With the recent, and ongoing exposure of children's burial sites, however, many have questioned whether it is appropriate for the Church to be let off the hook so easily, especially given the financial resources at the Church's disposal. Notwithstanding the vast economic wealth of the Vatican, three religious orders that staffed residential schools in Quebec alone, raised $32 million between 2011 and 2021 by selling some of their extensive real estate holdings; the proceeds of these sales were not used to compensate residential school survivors. The orders involved in these sales were the same orders involved in running some residential schools, and obligated to provide compensation to the Indigenous people.[519] Instead, $110 million was spent on refurbishing St Michael's Cathedral in Toronto, and a $29 million cathedral was built in Saskatoon.[520] In addition, a $17 million fundraising campaign is currently underway for renovations to a cathedral and for new construction in the Archdiocese of Regina and a $16 million dollar church opened in 2020 in Alberta.[521] Not surprisingly, feelings about this disgraceful injustice run high. In response to the widespread news reporting of such injustices, the Catholic Bishops of Canada have pledged to give $30 million to survivors of the residential school system over a period of five years. The First Nations, understandably, remain skeptical as to whether this promise will be fulfilled.[522]

Canadian society is still, however, largely unaware of the details of Indigenous peoples' experiences[523] and prejudice against the First Nations peoples remains a concern.

Jewish Religious Communities

As with Christian and predominantly Catholic communities, child sexual abuses have occurred within Jewish communities and many of these have been concealed from both the public and from the police, thus facilitating further abuse.[524] Unlike the sometimes religiously justified sexual abuse of the Irish school system, to "save the souls" of some children, or the cultural genocidal motivation underlying the Residential School abuse, the instances in the Jewish community appear to have not been ideologically motivated, but perpetrated by people in positions of power and authority over the children, allowing for opportunities for sexual abuse. Rabbis and Jewish community leaders have, however, like the Catholic Church, protected abusers rather than victims. Victims and witnesses have been pressured or threatened not to turn to secular law enforcement agencies for help. Jewish "patrols" have displaced the role of police in some extremely religious communities, and collaborate in cover-ups.[525]

Since about 2002, despite these community constraints against exposure, a number of cases of sexual abuse of Jewish teens have been reported in the USA and particularly in Hasidic communities in New York. Some of these include:

- Baruch Lanner – a rabbinic youth leader who was convicted in 2002 of abusing teens.[526]

- Howard Nevison – a cantor at New York's Temple Emanu-El who pleaded guilty to the abuse of his nephew.[527]

- Richard Marcovitz – a Conservative Rabbi of Oklahoma who was convicted of indecent and lewd acts and sexual battery of a child.[528]

- Rabbi Avrohom Mondrowitz: Brooklyn police believe that Mondrowitz's victims (sodomized, fondled or otherwise sexually violated as children) may have numbered in the hundreds, all of them Orthodox Jews, before he fled the country for Israel in December 1984[529] where he was protected from prosecution. On November 16, 2007, twenty-three years later, Mondrowitz was eventually arrested in Jerusalem and extradited to New York to face trial.[530]

As with the Mondrowitz case, Israel is slow to respond to requests for extradition of Jews accused of child sex abuse crimes in other countries. For example, Malka Leifer, a former principal of an ultra-orthodox school in Melbourne, Australia, is wanted on seventy-four sexual assault charges, including rape, involving girls in her former school. She fled to Israel in 2008 with the assistance of the Ultra-Orthodox Jewish Adass Israel School community, after accusations against her were made. She denies wrongdoing. In Israel she falsely claimed mental illness when fighting against her legal extradition to Australia. It took until 2020, twelve years later, for an Israeli court to find her fit to stand trial in Australia enabling her extradition case to continue. Her extradition has now been approved.[531]

A 2007 publication in the American Journal of Psychiatry reported on the past sexual abuse of married, observant, Jewish women: 26% of respondents acknowledged experiencing sexual abuse with 16% reporting that the abuse occurred by age thirteen.[532] In the same year, a series of articles in the Baltimore Jewish Times identified multiple victim reports of sexual abuse at the hands of Rabbis and teachers in Baltimore *yeshivas* (schools of Jewish learning).[533] Sexual abuse of children occurs across all branches of Judaism, but most come from within the Orthodox section of Jewish society, even though these make up only 20% of US Jewry.[534] While most perpetrators are men, there are – more rarely – women in the Jewish community who also perpetrate sexual abuse on children. Those victimized by females feel particularly marginalized as there is little acknowledgement of their experience, and the shame of revealing the abuse may be even more intense.[535]

As has been seen within the Catholic Church, many in the Jewish community would also prefer to avoid public exposure of sexual abuse scandals. Not only is this embarrassing and a *shanda* (a shame) but some fear that such revelations would contribute to antisemitism.[536] Many are vehemently opposed to such exposure. For example, in a large religious enclave outside of London, UK, rabbinic student Eli Cohen (eighteen years old) was convicted of indecently assaulting a young girl. The day after his sentencing, "Between 100-200 people threw missiles at the home of the family of the victim…shouting 'informers.'"[537]

Clearly, those who commit sexual offences would prefer to cover-up or deny their actions. Society too prefers to disbelieve such allegations or to hide these atrocious crimes especially when they occur within one's own community.[538] In addition, stereotypes about Jewish family life deter belief in such acts. As survivor Marcia Spiegel reports:

> I grew up in a world where it was widely accepted that Jews don't drink, use illegal drugs, or commit acts of sexual or domestic violence. I assumed that I must have been the only Jewish woman in the world who had memories of beatings or who lived with an alcoholic.[539]

Halakha (Jewish Law)

Overall, child sex abuse within Jewish communities is almost always covered-up. There are Jewish laws that prevent revealing such crimes to the outside world, although *Halakha* surrounding child sexual abuse is complicated. Some laws appear on face value to encourage covering up abuse while others seem to encourage reporting the crime to, at least, religious authorities. *Lashon Ha-ra* is a prohibition against speaking ill of others which may be used as an excuse not to name offenders publicly. In contrast, *Pikuah Nefesh*, or saving a life, takes precedence. Exposing an abuser could prevent future assaults. The commandment to honour one's parents also contributes, but this

130

may not apply if the parents have committed abusive acts towards the child. In addition, the stigma of sexual abuse may leave an Orthodox girl with few Jewish prospects for marriage as she has been defiled.[540] Victims of abuse are often told that making their abuse public would be a *shanda* for the Jewish community, their families, and for themselves. More severely, they are told that going public constitutes *Hillul Hashem* or desecration of God's name.[541] These laws generally refer to reporting abuse – if indeed one does so – to Jewish authorities, thus ensuring that the shame is confined to the community. There is no consideration of referring the crime to secular law enforcement agencies.

In addition, exposure about Rabbinic child sex abuse undermines a Rabbi's authority. It destroys the mythical image of infallibility of Rabbinic scholars, that supposes that a man "steeped in the Talmud could not possibly be guilty of an abusive act."[542] Shaiya Brizel, an Israeli Jew, describes an Orthodox upbringing during which he was sexually abused by his father, a Rabbi and teacher, who, according to Brizel, also abused many of his students. Brizel went back to his father's school before his book denouncing his father was published and confronted the Rabbi in charge. "You are right that we covered up for him," the aging Rabbi admitted. But the Rabbi did not apologize: He simply pleaded that Brizel not publish his book. "Shaiya, these things happened a long time ago," said the Rabbi, "Your father is old and can no longer sin."[543]

Mesirah, or "turning over" a fellow Jew to non-Jewish authorities is one of the most severe offenses that a Jew can commit – Jewish courts are the required authority, not secular judiciaries. This prohibition applies whether the fellow Jew is guilty or not.[544] Lesher reports that:

> In 2006 a mother reported to secular authorities that her fifteen-year-old daughter had been raped by a thirty-five-year-old man. Local rabbinic authorities were reportedly "furious" that she went to secular authorities rather than to a rabbinic court […] The law of Misirah, or informing, is extraordinary within Jewish law […] If someone inadvertently announces that he is going to violate the rule and inform on another Jew to Gentiles

(including Gentile government authorities), then every Jew has the obligation to use force, even deadly force if necessary, to prevent the informant from fulfilling his purpose.[545]

This interpretation of *Mesirah* is hotly debated in current Jewish deliberations with some Rabbis endorsing strict adherence to its explicit laws, along with its draconian implications, and others arguing that when the reporting of a Jew to secular authorities will save lives, then it is permitted, as is likely in the case of child sexual abuse.[546] Nevertheless, the prohibition against *Mesirah*, or revealing a Jewish criminal to secular authorities rather than to Jewish law enforcement, remains a severe violation of *Halacha* (Jewish law) and not a move that is taken lightly particularly among more religious Jews.

Open defiance of *Mesirah* is rare among ultra-Orthodox Jews. Until recently, there have been few accusations of child sex abuse against Orthodox Jewish adults[547] suggesting that such activities are usually handled within the community rather than exposed to society in general. In apparent agreement with *Mesirah* is the public backlash that has accompanied exposure of child sexual abuse. In 1991, the "False Memory Syndrome Foundation" was established and saturated the public with stories of families that had been torn apart by false abuse accusations. Some academic sympathizers have also proposed that child sex abuse survivors should not be believed. Harassment, ethics complaints, *ad hominum* attacks, legal challenges, and public vilification have all been used to silence attempts to discuss child sexual abuse.[548]

Resnicoff, a professor at De Paul University's College of Law, summarizes the problem of Jewish law as follows:

> American law imposes a variety of affirmative duties on individuals and organizations to protect prospective victims [...] With respect to child sexual abuse, many, although not all, important Orthodox authorities have rejected the ameliorative steps prescribed by secular law. Even more troublingly, they have permitted, and in at least some cases possibly encouraged, reprisals

against those who have reported abuse, including victims and their families.

I argue that the problem does not lie within Jewish law [...] Jewish law not only permits but actually demands that rigorous measures be taken to eradicate child sexual abuse. However, I also acknowledge that the sociological realities of the Orthodox Jewish community seem to have produced a variety of pressures that help to perpetuate the status quo. Such factors include conscious or subconscious concerns for the financial viability of important communal institutions and for the community members' continued fealty to traditional rabbinic authorities.[549]

As with the Church, protecting the image of Jewish righteousness and especially Rabbinic honour is strongly endorsed within strict Jewish law. Hiding from the truth or at least keeping it within a limited circle within the community is the preferred approach within Orthodox branches of Judaism.

Contributing Factors

As in many settings, there is frequently inappropriate sex education in Orthodox Jewish schools and homes resulting in a failure to incorporate appropriate sexual standards into a child's upbringing.[550] These include when or what sexual contact or activities are abusive, or why consent to sexual behaviour is so important. The examples provided below indicate that confused ideas exist about whether sexual behaviours such as contact with women, boys, or images, are acceptable or not. Mandel and Pelcovitz report:

> In one incident [...] a Chasidic Jew on trial for sodomy and child endangerment with minor girls, the defendant, citing religious beliefs, at his own trial, refused to view the photographic evidence of the pictures he took while perpetrating the abuse. He said the pictures were pornographic.[551]

For this young man, viewing the pictures that he had taken himself while abusing the child, was more unethical than his sexual abuse of the child or his photographing these acts while they were ongoing. Another example of a distorted conceptualization of what is sexual abuse and what is not, is the offender, "who acknowledged that he molested young children but insisted that in rehabilitative treatment he can only have a male therapist. His religious piety did not permit him to interact with a woman or be alone with her in a session room."[552] Being alone with a female therapist was unacceptable to this man, although molesting children seemed to be acceptable to him. Yet a third example of such confused sexual ethics is the adolescent who, "when asked by his therapist why he molested young boys, replied that he was taught that touching girls is prohibited. In his mind, refraining from touching girls is religious piety, while he denied seeing anything wrong with sexually touching much younger boys."[553]

A further example of sexually disrespectful and abusive attitudes towards women is provided by a young Orthodox Jewish woman describing the night of her wedding to a very religious Yeshiva student (whom she later divorced):

> Well we leave the [wedding] hall, we get into the car. The first thing [my new husband] tells me is "I want you to know the reason why I chose a Buick Century. The Buick Century is because I measured among other cars and the Buick is higher." And he told me that I have to understand that sometimes boys have urges, that they can't wait until they get home, so the reason why he picked the Buick is that if ever he had an urge, he'll be able to pull over to the side and just take care of what he needs.[554]

Contributing factors are many. It is difficult to establish a pattern of behaviour that can predict who will abuse. Gavriel Fagin has noted the wide variety of child sex abusers in Jewish communities:

> The male survivors that I continue to work with come from Chassidish, Litvish, Yeshivish and Centrist homes. [strict religious groups] The age of

victimization has ranged from infanthood to late adolescence. The perpetrators of these abuses have been classroom teachers (Hebrew and English studies), school principals, school janitors, camp counselors, division heads, head counselors, people doing work in the child's home (contractor, locksmith, plumber), adolescent neighbours, youth group leaders, tutors, mothers, fathers, sisters, brothers, aunts, uncles, and grandparents.[555]

Sexual offenders can be anyone. The pain of abuse is compounded when the abuse is overtly linked with trusted religious authorities whether through the perpetrator or his enablers.[556] As with all religious clerics, and authority figures including doctors, teachers, social workers, foster parents and parents, Jewish Rabbis serve not only as educators and as spiritual guides, but also as role models for their communities. All people, including such authorities, have a responsibility to promote respectful and non-abusive care of others, including children. Their endorsement of child sex abuse crimes by hiding such abuse from secular authorities or even within *Heredic* [strict] Jewish groups is horrendous.

Consequences for the Child

Steven Resnicoff has documented the results of the sexual abuse of children in Orthodox Jewish communities. He notes that, as with all children who are sexually abused, and not only Jewish children, the consequences can be devastating, and include increased likelihood of suicide, and emotional trauma. Consequences can include nightmares, flashbacks, fear, anxiety, panic-attacks, depression, social withdrawal, anger, hostility, mistrust, poor self-esteem, substance abuse, eating disorders, inappropriate sexual behaviour, criminality, difficulty in developing and maintaining close social relationships, and a greater risk of sexually transmitted diseases, including HIV/AIDS infection.[557]

Leonard Shengold sums this up by describing the effects of child sexual abuse as "Soul murder."[558] Nevertheless, our world, including strictly religious Jewish groups, appears to tolerate, enable, or even to promote such abuse.

Non-Religious Institutions

Child sex abuse occurs in situations where adults have power over children, and particularly in authoritarian or autocratic settings that provide opportunities for abuse, such as in extremely religious communities. Virtually all settings in which children spend time with adults impose a power imbalance between adults and children, including the home, school, religious setting, and recreational activities such as holiday camps.[559] While abuse occurs in the home it is often easier for adults to abuse children when they care for them outside of the home setting. School settings, and particularly boarding schools, provide optimal opportunities for such child sexual abuse, but they are by no means the only place where this occurs.

Sporting Organizations

Sexual abuse of athletes has emerged as yet another avenue for widespread abuse of children and young people. So too have such institutions as scouting movements become havens for child sex abuse.

Sexual abuse of children in sporting teams is an area of long-term, hidden, child sex abuse. In the USA, Larry Nassar was jailed for over 300 years for possessing child sex abuse images and admitted to sexually abusing at least 265 members of the USA gymnastics team, as well as multiple other sports students at Michigan State University. In January 2018, more than 200 women testified to the sexual abuse he perpetrated on them leading to his exceptionally lengthy prison sentence.[560] His close associate John Geddert, and coach of the same gold award-winning Olympic "Fierce Five" gymnastics team, committed suicide in 2021 a few days after being charged with 20 counts of human trafficking and additional counts of sexual assault, thus avoiding facing the survivors of his abuse and a fate similar to that of Larry Nassar.[561]

In 2019, George Tyndall, a former gynaecologist at the University of Southern California was arrested and charged with twenty-nine sexual assault, and battery by fraud felonies, between 2009 and 2016. Over 350 women students have spoken out about their traumatic experiences under his care. He allegedly made lewd comments, photographed them and penetrated them during medical examinations.[562] Similarly, Dr Richard Strauss who died in 2005, is accused of groping and performing unnecessary genital examinations on young men at Ohio State university, while treating athletes in sixteen sports.[563] The University failed to prevent the abuse that was reported to occur in examination rooms, locker rooms, showers and saunas. According to students, his examinations were "an open secret" on campus.

In the UK, a tennis coach was jailed for six years in July 2017 for multiple counts of child sex abuse.[564] Daniel Sanders, Wrexham Tennis Centre's former head coach admitted to eight counts of sexual activity with a player younger than sixteen. Boys as young as twelve were shown pornography by adult coaches, explicit sexual language was used on court and young girls were bullied about their physical appearance. One twelve-year-old was called "a hefty elephant" and told by Sanders that she would "never get a boyfriend because of the way she looked."[565] If coaching methods were questioned or complaints brought about them, children would be ostracised by other members of staff, threatened and bullied. Sexual abuse in sports in the UK is not limited to tennis. Barry Bennell, a former football coach, was found guilty of forty-three offences relating to serious sexual abuse of youngsters usually between about nine and fifteen years of age.[566] For decades, Neil Harris, a dance and gymnastics teacher in Birmingham, sexually abused his students.[567] He would not allow them to wear underwear beneath their leotards and would insert his hands down their clothes to check on this requirement. He taught at his school – originally started by his mother – for fifty years. Charming both parents and pupils alike, he avoided conviction. In 2018 he received a five-year sentence for indecently assaulting four girls in the 1970s and 1980s and in 2020 was jailed for a further eight years for assaulting ten girls and one boy between the 1960s and 1990s.

In another example, Peter Seisenbacher, an Austrian judo trainer and Olympic gold medalist in both 1984 and 1988, was jailed in 2019 for sexually abusing two girls aged nine and thirteen, in the 1990's and early 2000's. At his trial in Vienna, a third woman reported that he had tried to sexually abuse her, at a holiday camp, when she was sixteen.[568]

French prosecutors are investigating the claims of Sarah Abitol, a multiple medal-winning French figure-skating champion, of rape, by her coach, Gilles Beyer. Other team members have also lodged similar claims against coaches. Mr. Beyer has admitted to "intimate" and "unacceptable" relations with her for which he is "extremely sorry."[569] He remained the director of the French national skating teams for many years but, in 2001, following two investigations into misconduct had his contract terminated. In consequence, the head of France's ice sports federation, although not implicated himself, has resigned.[570]

In Canada, Gordon Stuckless was sentenced in 2016 to six and a half years behind bars for more than 100 offences related to the sexual abuse of boys, over three decades. He was a volunteer hockey coach and worked as an equipment manager at the Toronto hockey arena, Maple Leaf Gardens, between 1969 and 1988, where he befriended boys and lured them with gifts and activities. He was released after serving two-thirds of his six-year sentence and died in 2020.[571] At his trial, his victims told of lifelong suffering as a result of his abuse. One victim reported, "I am 52 years old and I'm still broken."[572] Another said, "You are the bogeyman in my dreams. I struggle everyday to get up in the morning."[573] Yet another reported having "constant flashbacks" and being always "on high alert."[574]

Sex offenders target organizations where children and youth are present and controlled, thereby making it easy, or easier, to find victims.[575] Sports organizations offer such opportunities as they involve children of all ages, who are generally taught to listen to, respect, and obey adults in authority. Parents don't always question sports organizers, especially in highly competitive sports, and sports organizations are so grateful for the help of coaches that they don't question their behaviours. Many, if not most, of the people involved, particularly in minor sport activities, are parents who are automatically trusted by children and where a close relationship between leaders and players is encouraged. Many activities require children to dress and undress, and to shower in common shower areas. Coaches may have to touch children to demonstrate or correct a move or to help them if they are hurt, offering opportunities for abuse. Team members may spend a great deal of time alone with coaches, travelling, training, and waiting between games at tournaments, etc. The risk of abuse increases with the number and duration of one-on-one situations – in cars, hotels, locker rooms, or private homes. Overnight trips are common.[576] Some sport related abuse has taken place with parents in the room with the abuser under the guise of a medical examination although it is possible that alone-time offers an easier opportunity for some abusers. Children often join sport programs to enhance self-esteem and self-confidence. Abusers may take advantage of such psychologically vulnerable children.[577] Coaches have enormous power over children, especially those who are exceptionally dedicated to and ambitious about their sporting achievements.

Sexual abusers prey on children as young as infants and toddlers who obviously are unable to protect themselves or to tell of their abuse. Most sport programs are offered to children over four, but there are infant and toddler swimming programs, and activities such as gym classes that expose these smallest of children to abusers. Abusers often make children feel that they are responsible for the abuse they have suffered, that they somehow "invited" it to happen thus preventing them from disclosing. Children who feel uncomfortable about what has happened and who are told that they will be in trouble if they tell anyone may be so afraid of the adults in their world that they keep the "secret" – often for many years. It is not surprising then, that sports activities can provide a breeding ground for child sexual abuse, creating a dilemma for both parents and children regarding their participation in sport. The conclusion to be reached, however, is not that children should avoid sporting activities, but that perpetrators are aggressively sought out and punished. In addition, open lines of communication should be fostered with respect and trust of children being a normal part of their family interactions. Societal taboos about sex and children may make it hard for kids to disclose abuse and for adults to believe them.[578] Sports coaches should be carefully screened, and educated, about respect for the children entrusted to them for coaching.

Hazing in Sports Teams

In addition to abuse by coaches, a climate of child sexual abuse may also emerge within sporting fraternities. A 2017 investigation by the Associated Press found seventy cases of teammate-on-teammate sexual assaults in United States' public schools between 2012-17. The report suggested this was "the tip of the iceberg."[579] These cases are shocking in their violence and their similarity, often featuring some variation of older teammates sodomizing victims with anything from a fist, to a bottle, to the nozzle of a carbon dioxide tank.[580] A survey by Alfred University found that about half of high school students reported participating in activities that qualified as hazing although only 14% reported being hazed. In the United States, forty-four states have banned hazing. Similarly, teenagers in Canada have been hazed with fourteen and fifteen-year-olds being beaten and sexually assaulted with broom handles or fingers as part of hazing rituals. At the prestigious St Michaels school in Toronto, seven fourteen- or fifteen-year-old football players were charged with gang sexual assault in three separate incidents. In one incident a video allegedly showing a team mate being penetrated by a broom was shared online. Similarly, boys in a Calgary minor hockey club have also been exposed online, pushing a young boy up against a wall until he passed out, fell to the floor, and then convulsed.[581]

Hazing has been defined as involving

> traditions or rituals expected of someone joining (or maintaining membership in) a group or organization that humiliate, degrade or harm the person, but that are usually framed as community or team building [...]

140

Regardless of the person's "willingness" to participate, hazing creates a cycle of humiliation, degradation or violence.[582]

It is often associated with groups to which students wish to belong such as fraternities, sports teams, residences, or other organizations. The need to belong, to be accepted by one's peers, ignorance about their new university lifestyle and what is or is not appropriate, the wish to appear adult after years of being a school child, all contribute to the willingness to comply with or submit to hazing experiences. Older students who impose hazing rituals are motivated by their newfound power and control over others combined with disregard for sexual or physical abuse and an inability to respect others' sexual rights and integrity. For example, phrases such as "no means yes, and yes means anal," is totally disrespectful of women and says more about the abusiveness of the perpetrators than the bravado with which such slogans are chanted.

Boy Scouts

Almost 100,000 victims of sexual abuse within the Boy Scouts of America have recently identified themselves claiming compensation from the group.[583] Boy Scouts of America, has, like the Church in many instances, declared bankruptcy, putting an end to any claimants' cases coming to court while settlement issues are negotiated.[584] In their 2020 bankruptcy filing, the Boy Scouts of America reported their estimated worth to be between one and ten billion dollars with liabilities of between $100 and $500 million.[585] Lawyers allege that this is the largest sexual abuse scandal in the USA, dwarfing the complaints alleged against the Catholic Church although details have yet to emerge regarding this abuse.[586] Founded in 1910, there are about 2.2 million youth members and 800,000 volunteers across America. More than 130 million young people have participated in scouting programs and at least 8,000 scout leaders have been accused of sexual misconduct.[587] More than 20,000 documents, initially concealed by the Boy Scouts of America, were released in 2012, naming more than 1,000 banned volunteers, who had been identified as abusers and monitored by the Scouts, without consistently reporting them to parents or the authorities.[588] Like the Catholic Church, the Boy Scouts removed scout masters or troop leaders who had been accused of abuse, without referring them to the police.[589] Both the abusers and the Organization that covered up their abuse, or protected their scout masters, are guilty of crimes against children and deserve condemnation. As with participation in sporting activities, belonging to groups such as Boy Scouts or similar groups is, for most children – a wonderful opportunity both for learning valuable life skills and for having fun adventures and meaningful relationships with peers and adults. It is a crime that so many leaders were allowed to escape exposure and have been able to sully the name of such organizations with their criminal actions. It is a tragedy for the thousands of children abused over about 100 years of the existence of the Boy Scouts, whose lives have been destroyed by their experiences. Stories of abuse within the Boy Scouts have not yet been exposed to the same extent as those within the Church, but are likely to be heard in coming years.

Migrants

Political manipulations can also provide venues for child sex abuse. Increasing tension on the southern USA border has resulted in such opportunities. Between 2014 and 2018 the US Health Department received more than 4,500 complaints of sexual abuse against detained migrant children.[590] The Department of Justice received an additional 1,303 complaints of sex abuse perpetrated against unaccompanied minors during the same period. At least 154 of the latter claims are against staff members employed by the contractors who are paid by the Health and Human Services Office of Refugee Resettlement to run the underage migrant detention facilities. Allegations include having sexual relationships, showing pornographic videos to children, and forcible touching.[591] The current surge of migrants to the USA border under the Biden administration will, in all likelihood, face similar challenges.

Child sex abuse is a pervasive menace that is enabled by a society that appears unwilling to confront perpetrators. The varying lengths of imprisonment for child sex abuse crimes is notable. For example, Larry Nassar in the USA was jailed for 300 years for abusing over 260 athletes, while Gordon Stuckless in Canada received only six and a half years, and served only four of them, after having abused over 100 boys. Most sentences reported appear to be closer to that of Gordon Stuckless than that of Larry Nassar, although those with short prison terms may still have to contend with inclusion on sex offender's lists, reintegration into the world outside jail, and restrictions on the type of work they can undertake. Short sentences may also reflect a society's emphasis on rehabilitation rather than punishment, or could reflect a lack of understanding of the severity of the impact of the crime on a child. Survivors talk about living their entire lives in the shadow of these events, often never fully recovering, while their perpetrators often spend only a few years in prison. Many societies appear to be quick to overlook, excuse, or at least, minimize the importance of these crimes, implementing relatively light sentences, thereby lending a level of support for, or at least, tolerance of child sex abuse.

Part 3: Global Enabling

Not only do we justify child sex abuse, and cover-up, or hide such abuse, but we facilitate it at all levels of society, the individual, the societal and the global. Sexual violence against children, particularly against girls (because girls are most often the target of this type of violence), is a global human rights concern and universally condemned but occurs much more frequently than people realise.[592] The remarkable proliferation of child sex abuse in its various guises – slavery and trafficking, child marriage, sexual abuse facilitated by the internet, and child sex abuse within families, schools, communities and societies – raises questions regarding the sexualization and gendering of children in the modern world. Harassment, touching, incest, rape or exploitation in prostitution or internet-based sexual imagery happens in the home, schools, care and justice institutions, the workplace and within communities at large. It occurs everywhere, in low- middle- and high-income countries, as well as in emergency settings. Much of what we do in our world facilitates child sex abuse although we do not acknowledge this.

Part three of this book covers how we enable sexual abuse of children through the internet, through military activities, and through national and global sex trafficking and trade. Underlying these activities is an attitude often adopted towards girls and their sexuality that arises from the commodification of girls, a victim blaming approach and a lack of adequate or appropriate sex education. Children who have trans or non-binary identities are also targets for abuse, often accompanied by severe bullying, although these experiences are highlighted in the literature less often, not because they occur less often but because issues relating to alternate gender identities have only been emphasized in recent years.

Our attitudes to sex and to sexuality among children and adolescents influence our family life, and our interactions with schools, institutions, and society. One of the primary influences on our sexual knowledge and activity today emerges though internet use. This can be both positive and negative. In addition, for many men and often women, service in a military capacity follows school life. Military activities bridge the gap between home-based institutions, such as school or sports activities, and the global arena, particularly as soldiers, sailors, and pilots serve beyond a country's borders. Military service involves a vast number of young people, some even prior to the age of majority. These service men and women also have a direct or indirect effect on the youth population, and their sexual activities, in foreign countries where they may be stationed. Perhaps the most far-reaching impact on child sex abuse, however, arises from the extensive trafficking and trade in sex that has expanded across the globe and that has become one of the most lucrative industries in the world today. The sections that follow discuss these three sources of child sex abuse: the internet, the military, and the sex trade.

Attitudes

Some of the ways in which we, as individuals, support, promote and facilitate sexual assault against children on a global level are considered here. These include the commodification of girls, victim blaming, and inadequate sex education.

Commodification of Girls

Our world still objectifies girls (more often than boys) as sex objects through such venues as advertisements and various forms of media images that degrade women and girls. Child beauty contests are popular in some countries. In the United States, for example, as many as 100,000 children under twelve years old participate in such pageants every year. It has become a billion-dollar industry.[593] Parents spend thousands of dollars on professional hair stylists and make-up artists in preparation for each competition. The girls are spray-tanned, and groomed to so-called "perfection."[594] Some countries like France and Bolivia, have begun to restrict such events for children under thirteen.[595]

Sexualization of girls affects preadolescents when they are made to feel that their worth is inextricably linked to their beauty and/or their sexual appeal, or when they aspire to look "sexy," or when sexuality is imposed on them.[596] Such sexualization of girls takes place on television, in movies, magazines and music, on the internet, and in consumer products aimed at girls even younger than ten.[597] Authority figures in the child's life such as parents, teachers, siblings and peers can also support the idea that physical attractiveness and sexuality are desirable characteristics for girls. This may lead to anxiety about appearance, depression, and feelings of shame, even in girls as young as eleven to thirteen or even younger.[598] Eating disorders and low self esteem may also emerge.[599] Such consequences are not inevitable, however. Children who enjoy playing with, and experimenting with, their appearance, clothes, makeup, etc. may simply be responding to and enjoying the activities of many women and girls in our modern lives. It is only when their self-worth becomes tied up in and dependent on such so-called "desirable" portrayals of beauty that they become more vulnerable to abuse by others who play on flattery to achieve potentially manipulative goals.

Advertisements, the media, pornography, and magazines facilitate sexual abuse of children.[600] Such images do not distinguish clearly between women and girls giving the impression that girls can also be as sexually accessible as are women. Sex sites frequently label their videos or images as "teens" although it is never clear whether the girls are underage or not. Sometimes women are dressed to look like children wearing socks, holding teddy bears or with their hair in pony tails on each side of their heads – as is a common childish style. Alternatively, children with more developed bodies are appealing for some. Movies have portrayed young girls as sexual objects and audio or video covers may show sexually provocative young girls. Although child sex abuse is not condoned in our society, portrayal of children as sexually provocative is.[601]

Victim Blaming

Women are often blamed for inciting their own sexual harassment through their appearance. More extreme sanctions on women's appearances are imposed through practices such as breast ironing with hot rocks as a child to prevent the development of breasts,[602] and female genital mutilation to reduce promiscuity.[603] However, we simultaneously tell girls to aspire to whatever standard of beauty that is in vogue at any one time, such as to emulate the emaciation of

"Twiggy" in the mid 20th century, or to adopt a range of supposed "beauty" habits from constant dieting through to plastic surgery, skin whitening in communities of colour and tanning in others, makeup, hair dyes, tattoos, and piercings. We shame girls who are larger than society deems appropriate, blaming them as lazy or unable to control their appetites, despite well established knowledge that higher weight is rarely under the control of the individual, and in the case of obesity, is a disease requiring treatments that, thus far, do not exist.[604] Women are taught to view "unattractive" women with warnings such as "you'll never get a husband if you look like that."[605] When they get bullied for the way they look, they are told to make a greater effort to be thinner, prettier, more athletic, wear makeup, do their hair nicely, etc. Simultaneously, women who fit society's current view of beauty are criticized for accomplishing exactly that which we punish others for failing to achieve. They are judged for their choice to undergo plastic surgery, dye their hair, get piercings or tattoos. When they are assaulted, they are blamed for that too – because they chose to dress in a way that accentuates the beauty attributes that society both insists upon and denigrates. Women are given contradictory messages. They are told it is their responsibility to both appear attractive to men and, when they do, they are told it is that behaviour that led to their abuse. Until recently, and still in some societies, men are expected to be "experienced" while girls must be "virgins" at marriage. In other places, pre-marital sex has been normalized although a man who enjoys casual sex may well be regarded as simply a man while a woman who does so is regarded as a slut. Such admonitions are based on a victim blaming philosophy rather than teaching all children to respect others' bodies and their rights to choose whether, when, where and with whom they engage in sexual behaviour. UNFPA's 2019 version of their *State of the World's Population* report indicates that only 57% of women around the world are able to make their own choices in this regard.[606] Women do not have much freedom to make their own choices but are subject to their societal and cultural pressures. As such they are victims of male dominant cultural values regarding sexuality where men are often perceived as having the right to sex whenever they wish and women are often blamed for supposedly inciting them.

Society is to blame for perceptions of no or minimal wrongdoing by perpetrators of child sex abuse. For example, the language used in media reports of child sex abuse activities reflects our attitudes towards victims.[607] Newspaper headings reflect society's condemnation of the child sex victim and respect for their abuse/perpetrator. Examples include:

Heading: Ipswich woman arrested for nude photos of teen prostitute.
The perpetrator in this article is named "Ipswich woman" while the victim is labelled "teen prostitute."
Heading: Alleged pimp, fourteen-year-old prostitute arrested at Holiday Inn.
The man is an "alleged pimp" while the teenager is, definitively, a "prostitute."[608]

Furthermore, we are often duped into blaming the victim for the perpetrator's crime. This is indeed society's standard approach to most if not all abuse. When children are bullied, we often teach the victim to stand up to their bully, not the bully to stop the behaviour. When children are teased about their weight, we talk to the child about their unhappiness, rather than chastising the people stigmatising them. When people in authority abuse a subordinate, we teach the junior person to advocate for themselves. When society is racist, the people affected by that racism are expected to solve the problem – not those perpetrating it. When it comes to child sex abuse, we blame children's home backgrounds as not being adequate, or girls for not dressing modestly, or single parent families for not having adequate – usually male – role models in the home. We do not condemn the perpetrators of child sex abuse for their dastardly acts. Some may even regard them with admiration.[609]

Perpetrators themselves are aware of such societal condemnation of children who end up being recruited into sex work, and use these attitudes to justify their actions. As reportedly said by an Asian, Muslim man accused of abusing young girls in the UK, "You white people train them in sex and drinking, so when they come to us they are already fully trained."[610]

Pimps also use this knowledge to persuade children to co-operate by telling them that the police won't believe them if they report being abused by a pimp. They are likely to be re-abused by police interrogation. Also, the girls are told that their families will no longer want them, and that nobody will treat them nicely if they leave their pimp. This may often be true leading to the girls staying with their pimps.[611] Many girls rescued from sex slavery wish that they had had happier family lives.[612] Adrian (a pseudonym) presents a home background that predisposed her to being vulnerable to sexual slavery, this time in Canada:

> I was sexually abused as a child and abused by many men as a young woman, something that clouded my judgement and ability to make healthy choices. I had no sense of self worth and was being used to being taken against my will, so getting paid for it seemed like a good deal.
> I have known and worked with hundreds of girls in the industry and have not met one girl who did not suffer some form of abuse before entering into the sex trade.[613]

Clearly home backgrounds, as well as inadequate social services, contribute to girls being abused although the real criminal behind their sexual abuse is not the girl, or her home background, or the way she dresses, or any lack of social support. It is the perpetrator of her abuse.

In the UK, there is little help available for children who are sexually abused with few receiving therapeutic, mental health services.[614] Inadequate therapeutic services are likely a global shortfall, which, unless societal attitudes towards the victims of child sex abuse change, so that they are seen as victims and are not blamed for their activities, and unless services are provided to assist them, this shortfall in assistance will probably not improve. Victims have little or no choice. As sixteen-year-old Ulla said, "What's wrong with selling my body when it's the only thing I have to sell?"[615] She was locked up, used and raped ten or twelve times a day. Many children who suffer sexual abuse and are obliged to work as prostitutes believe that "this is how life is, and I was born to do this."[616]

Some of this pressure on how to behave to avoid attracting unwanted sexual advances or assault comes from a series of rape myths that are adhered to in many countries.[617] These include:

- *Women invite sexual assault by the way they look or dress.*
  This is simply not true. Women may be raped or assaulted regardless of what they are wearing.[618]

- *It is not sexual assault if either person is drunk or influenced by drugs.*
  Legal consent cannot be given if a person in drunk, under the influence of drugs, or unconscious. Many perpetrators cite alcohol as an excuse for sexual assault.[619]

- *Sexual assault usually occurs outside and at night.*
  Most assaults against children occur in the morning[620] and not in public.[621] Most (60%) occur in a private home and 38% in the victims' own home. [622]

- *Sexual assault usually occurs between strangers.*
  Most sexual assaults are perpetrated by someone known to the victim.[623]

- *Rapists come from a certain class of people: People of Colour, lower-class, "criminal types."*
  Perpetrators of sexual crimes come from every racial, ethnic, socio-economic, age, and social group although there is a clear male majority of perpetrators (around 97%).[624] Many sexual assaults are not reported and often take place in domestic settings where the perpetrators may not have any other criminal record.[625]

- *You can tell a rapist by the way they look.*
  This is simply not true. Many appear non-threatening, are young, married, have children and are just like any person.[626]

- *Sexual assault is an impulsive act of sexual gratification.*
  Sexual assault is primarily a violent act intended to gain or exhibit power over another person.[627]

- *Victims who don't fight back were not really sexually assaulted.* Some people will fight back vigorously, others freeze. There is no "right" way to respond to a traumatic, life-threatening event. Survival is the most important objective.[628]

- *A person cannot be sexually assaulted by an intimate partner.* Partners must give consent every time they have sex. Forcing one's partner to have sex is assault. Similarly, if a partner changes their mind in the process of having sex, it is also regarded as non-consensual sex if it does not stop.[629] Marital rape is considered a crime and is illegal in fifty-two countries although some, like Afghanistan, India, South Sudan, the Bahamas and Nigeria view sexual intercourse as a conjugal right thus excluding marital rape as a criminal offence.[630]

Many of these rape myths, and particularly the first five listed above, blame the victims for being assaulted and not all apply to young children but may well be relevant to adolescents for the way they dress, if they drink or take drugs, go outside at night, speak to strangers, mix with "unsavoury types," or they don't fight back. Society is self programmed to blame the victims of assault rather than to put the blame on the perpetrators of sexual assault. This blame is clearly unsubstantiated by research. We do not have similar tropes that educate boys and men regarding appropriate, respectful, sexual behaviour. Perhaps it is time to create such tropes as "Rapists are criminals." I am reminded of a pencil case owned by my daughters as young adults that read: "Boys are mean. Throw rocks at them." Perhaps this was not as funny as we all thought at the time. We also need to remember that not all sexual assault is perpetrated by men on women. Sometimes the reverse occurs. Even more importantly we need to recognize that as acceptance of alternate genders and gender identities grows in our current world, the incidence of sexual abuse among these children will be exposed and acknowledged more often in future. Children with non-traditional gender identities are particularly vulnerable to abuse of all kinds.

Criticism is usually directed towards girls when it comes to prevention of sexual abuse such as, dress modestly, don't draw attention to your feminine characteristics.[631] In Egypt, for example, sexual abuse is hidden, blamed on the girls' attire, and is only recently being exposed and protested against by women.[632] Malaysia provides an interesting example of such victim blaming on a national scale. Malaysia recently published an infographic school text book that said girls must protect their modesty and dress appropriately or risk being shamed and ostracised. It was aimed at nine-year-olds and distributed to all national primary schools in Malaysia. Sadly, this message encouraged self/ victim blaming for sexual abuse and reflects the clear need for more appropriate sex education of young people and for those who develop such educational materials. Following complaints, the Ministry of Education distributed a sticker to cover up the original graphics, although whether this was ever done is unknown.[633] Blaming girls for their sexual abuse due to the way they dress occurs elsewhere too. A recent dress-code, warning women not to wear tight fitting clothes including leggings, nothing revealing, no crop tops, hot pants, or very short shorts, on the polar research vessel *Akademik Federov* of the MOSAIC, German led, polar exploration expedition was issued. There had been allegations of sexual harassment aboard the vessel days before the policy was introduced. The resulting resentment expressed by women on board the vessel was expressed by them for having to be responsible for managing the behaviour of the men.[634]

Countries (like Canada) have taken legal action to prevent abuse of children or particularly young girls by targeting men who choose to pay for sex rather than targeting the girls or victims of sexual exploitation. Instituting laws that target the men as perpetrators rather than the girls as criminals, can put the blame for sex trafficking and prostitution where it belongs – on the perpetrators rather than the victims, even though these laws may have also had the unintended consequence of endangering the lives of sex workers. While adult sex work is legal, profiting from such sex workers is not, so that the security, safety and support that was previously available to assist sex workers through brothels, sex worker employed cab drivers and other guards, is no longer legally permitted, leaving the women vulnerable to aggressive predators.

Charging those who traffic girls and children both at home and abroad, is a start, with lengthy prison terms being mandated as a minimum, rather than the minimal sentences that so often seem to be handed down. Prosecuting men who frequent brothels that exploit children as sex workers or who pay for child sex in more sophisticated ways through internet sites, is another important legal step to take to protect children from sexual abuse and slavery.

Sex Education or Sex Suppression?

Religiously inspired actions involving extensive behavioural restrictions for girls in such countries as Saudi Arabia are intended to keep girls pure.[635] Similarly, Female Genital Mutilation is forced on two to three million children and young girls each year in the belief that this will prevent promiscuity and keep them faithful to their husbands.[636] Less draconian, however, are the guidelines for sex education – or sometimes sex suppression – that can be offered to school children. Globally, debates still abound regarding whether sex education in schools (at various stages and for all ages) increases sexual behaviour or decreases it. In America, right wing evangelical movements have grown rapidly in recent decades, leading to such organizations as the Abstinence Clearinghouse that argues that sex education of children encourages sexual activity and that abstinence is blessed by God.[637] Research evidence contradicts this view indicating that abstinence only education is contributing to increasing teenage pregnancy and birth rates, unrelated to such factors as socioeconomic status, educational level, ethnicity, and availability of medical insurance for family planning services.[638] It is not reasonable to think that in this digital age we will be able to keep children from exposure to sex. Rather we needed to determine the best way to manage their understanding and attitudes towards sexuality.

Children need to learn about sex. They must learn how, and when, to enjoy sex, and how to do so safely, respectfully and with consenting partners. Teaching children about the anatomy and function of the reproductive organs is insufficient. Children/adolescents need to learn about how to have sex, how to pleasure others and themselves, with or without intercourse. They need knowledge about contraception, including what methods are available to both men and women and who should take responsibility for providing, and using, these contraceptive methods. Society needs to consider whether providing free condoms for men, as is often done, but not free female contraceptives is equitable. Continuing to financially support male contraception suggests that men can have access to free contraception, and protection from sexually transmitted infections, if they choose to use this, but women can't, without incurring sometimes considerable financial cost. Does this also imply that women must trust men to protect them from pregnancy and from infection?

Sex education also should include knowledge about sex offenders, how to recognize them, in real life or on the internet, who to turn to for help, and how to counter their advances. Ignorance is not sufficient to protect children from harm and will certainly not enhance their sexual fulfilment throughout life. Sex education is needed, although just how this is provided in the most optimal manner is still open to discussion.

Sex and the Internet

Although the internet is sometimes blamed for influencing children's sexual behaviour, this is a multifaceted issue that requires more nuanced examination. The internet is a remarkable tool that has any number of benefits for adults and children alike. This chapter, however, will focus on its more dangerous aspects. The internet does not abuse children, but it may facilitate their abuse by perpetrators. Social networking has, in many ways, contributed to the ease with which children may be groomed by perpetrators through its ability to undermine the self confidence of young people. Social networking perpetuates the myth that everybody else is doing better than you are; they're prettier (thanks to filters and endless hours of playing with camera angles and edits), have better jobs, more friends, more money, better clothes, or nicer food. Whereas before girls used to look at models in magazines and then feel bad about their bodies, now they only have to look at sites such as Instagram. The destruction of self confidence that is a recognized part of social media use makes it that much easier to convince children that they need the help of some predator, or sugar daddy, to be better.

This chapter explores exposure of children to erotica or pornography on the internet and its impact, as well as the misuse of the internet though the "dark web." Sexting offences by children against other children, threats made to children on the internet, including deception and bribery by perpetrators, are also explored. Finally, the sexual abuse of children by taking photographs and videos of them while being forced or coerced to participate in sexual activities that are then shared widely on digital platforms, by commercial entities and even by their own parents, is exposed.

Erotica and Pornography

One of the most significant challenges facing the world today regarding child sex abuse, is the growing use and abuse of the internet with its vast international reach, particularly in relation to its role in sexuality. Often viewed by individuals in the privacy of their own homes, the internet provides an anonymous shield for perpetrators, and is powerful in its ability to shame victims and thereby extort increasingly perverse forms of sexuality from them. Global law enforcement appears to be relatively powerless to take most of these perpetrators down, although some are caught and prosecuted. While the internet is a powerful tool used by predators to abuse children, the internet is also a useful tool that can contribute to sexual enjoyment of many. Institutions such as schools, scouts, and sports teams, are excellent resources that are valuable for most, but that also enable child sex offenders who choose to exploit the opportunities they offer to abuse children. Likewise, the internet is a remarkable development mostly for good, but that can also be abused by those wishing to exploit the opportunities it offers for child sex abuse. Both the abuse of, and the use of, the internet will be examined.

The internet is often considered as a stimulus for child sex abuse although this is only partially true. For the sake of this discussion, sexually explicit material on the internet can be usefully distinguished as erotica or as pornography.[639] Erotica is material that promotes or creates sexual arousal and that shows enjoyment of sexuality in an equal and balanced manner towards all people, regardless of the type of sexual activity, provided this is between willing and consensual participants. Pornography, on the other hand, may be defined as material that promotes or creates sexual arousal but in a non-consensual, unequal, unbalanced, violent or degrading manner.[640] Access to sexually explicit material has grown enormously in recent years especially among adolescents. The rapid expansion of this medium was

158

stimulated by the availability of personal computers in the 1980s, the increasing access to the internet in the 1990s and the development of pay-per-view home movies from the 1990s onwards,[641] followed by downloadable movies, or online viewing platforms. The use of the internet for sexual arousal remains controversial although the industry generates more than $55 billion annually indicating clearly that vast numbers of people use it. Among adults, over 80% of men and over 50% of women access such material with few adverse effects.[642] Most children usually encounter sexually explicit material through the internet at around the age of thirteen. Studies suggest that at age fourteen they are developmentally mature enough to process what they see.[643]

Among adults, studies generally report that viewing erotica has positive effects. Among adolescents and children, the consequences of viewing sexually explicit material, and particularly pornography, are more concerning.[644] Some research suggests that viewing pornography at a young age encourages sexist and unhealthy ideas of sex and relationships and that it increases the likelihood of indulging in sexual assault.[645] Similarly, studies have found that intentionally viewing violent pornographic material leads to a six-fold increase in sexually aggressive behaviour among ten to fifteen-year-olds.[646] Viewing sexually explicit material is also associated with having more recreational attitudes to sex among boys as well as perceptions that the sex they viewed was realistic. Teenage girls are less likely to be affected in the same way or to see the images portrayed as realistic.[647]

Early exposure to sexually explicit internet material may also be related to seeking earlier experiences of sex with partners. Young men – between twelve and seventeen – who watch internet-based, sexually explicit material are more likely to have oral sex earlier than those who don't. Both boys and girls who watch such material have sexual intercourse for the first time at younger ages.[648] Others have noted links between earlier exposure to internet sexual material and earlier onset of sexual activity, pregnancy and sexually transmitted infections.[649] Some studies have also indicated that exposure to sexually explicit internet information results in reduced sexual satisfaction among both men and women.[650] Young women report more negative effects such as lowered body image, and increased pressure to perform acts depicted in films. Young men became more critical of their partner's bodies as well as their own, and less interested in actual sex.[651]

Blaming the internet for child sex activity is, however, not appropriate. Nor is it realistic to believe that society can prevent young people's exposure to sex on the internet. More relevant is to consider the impact of some parents in our society who are so sexually repressed themselves that they refuse to – or do not know how to – discuss sex with their children, refuse to allow schools to teach about sex, and then wonder why the only information their children get about sex is from the internet. The problem is not the internet, and nor is it even pornography on the internet. The problem is a society in which children are never taught about sex in anything more than the most basic mechanical/physiological sense rather than considering its psychological, emotional, and interpersonal levels.[652] Do our sex education programs address how children can manage situations where sexual activity needs to be negotiated? Who wants what and who doesn't? There is no discussion about whether, for example, choking is a good thing, or whether a partner might enjoy spitting, slapping, bondage, or any other variations of sexual behaviour. When *Fifty Shades of Grey*[653] came out, it was shocking for many – and judging from its worldwide success in both book and visual formats – was a desperately wanted and needed source of information, because it was one of the first mainstream conversations about what amounts to relatively minor kinks. A huge part of the book and its sequels, was about consent and power about non-vanilla sex. Why don't we talk to our children, or even to each other, about kinks? Why don't we talk about different desires and sexual interests the same way we talk about one person's desire to run a marathon versus another's desire to swim laps?[654] The sexual practices involved in kink or BDSM (bondage dominance sado-masochism) rarely result in clinically significant psychological impairment, and if they do it is usually a result of societal stigma associated with these practices and not the sexual activity itself.[655] The internet is an accessible, affordable, and safe means of learning about sexual variations, all of which are appreciated by millions. It is not the primary cause of sexual predation. In contrast, embracing it as a tool for education about sexuality would be far more

160

productive than its current use simply as a (secretive) visual depiction of what can be, and is, done. Condemning sexual imagery on the internet makes it exciting "forbidden fruit," especially for young people seeking information, and shrouds it in embarrassment, shame, guilt, and condemnation. Why not utilize it as a means of providing useful knowledge about when, where, how, and whether to explore sexual behaviour safely and with consensual pleasure?

Individual use of the internet as a tool for abuse of another individual, is one level of sexual abuse that can be contrasted with a more serious and far-reaching level of internet-based sexual abuse that may be termed "global" abuse. In the latter form, abusers run large scale sexual exploitation rings or sites that involve thousands, if not millions, of users/abusers. In most cases, at least until recently, this form of abuse has mainly occurred on the "dark web."

The Dark Web Child Sex Marketplaces

Until recently most abusive child sex on the internet was hidden on the dark web, accessible to a select/knowledgeable few. There are multiple examples of this globally, usually exposed when some of these paedophile rings have been infiltrated by law enforcers and taken down. Interpol, with its law enforcement collaborators across 194 countries, maintains an International Child Sexual Exploitation database that allows more than sixty of these countries to exchange information and share data with colleagues across the world, facilitating the location of child sex abuse victims and their abusers. Interpol's resources have helped identify some 23,500 child victims worldwide. Based on their collection of more than 2.7 million images and videos they acknowledge that 84% of them contain explicitly sexual activity. More than 60% of the unidentified victims are pre-pubescent, including infants and toddlers, with 65% of them being girls. Severe abuse images are, however, likely to feature boys, and 92% of the offenders who are visible are male.[656]

A number of child sex abusers utilizing the dark web have been exposed. In the USA, in 2021, an Irish man, Eric Eoin Marques, was jailed for twenty-seven years. He was described by the FBI as the world's largest facilitator of online child sex abuse. His dark web site hosted more than 8.5 million images of child exploitation.[657] In 2018, in the UK, a "warped and sadistic"[658] twenty-nine-year-old paedophile who blackmailed victims and shared abuse tips and images on the dark web, Mathew Folder, was jailed for thirty-two years. In 2019, his sentence was reduced to twenty-five years.[659] He admitted to 137 charges, including rape of forty-six people. He was a former geophysics lecturer at the University of Birmingham whose offending lasted ten years. Four of his victims attempted suicide, a further fifty-one offences remain on file.[660] Investigations into his crimes led to more than 300 people being arrested following the take down of one of the world's largest dark web child sexual marketplaces in 2019.[661] His site, with nearly eight terabytes of data, contained more than 200,000 videos which had been downloaded more than a million times. These videos portrayed sex acts involving children, infants and toddlers and specifically asked users not to upload videos featuring adult-only pornography. About twenty-three children were rescued at the time the site was shut down. In all, however, only 337 suspected users were arrested in thirty-eight countries.

Along similar lines, in 2016, a British court gave Richard Huckle twenty-two life sentences for abusing babies and children, mostly in Malaysia, and sharing images of his crimes on the dark web.[662] He was jailed for sexually abusing as many as 200 children between the ages of six months and twelve years, between 2006-2014, but was stabbed to death in prison in 2019. At the time of his arrest, his computer had more than 20,000 indecent pictures and videos of his assaults which were shared with paedophiles globally.[663]

In Scotland, in 2016, more than 500 children were identified as potential victims of online sexual abuse. Thirty million indecent images were seized and seventy-seven people charged with rape, sharing indecent images of children and grooming for sexual purposes, sexual extortion, indecent communication with children, possession of a firearm, bestiality, and drugs offences. Some of the 523 potential victims were as young as three. In Scotland, there was a 60% increase recorded over a year in the number of indecent communications offences carried out by adults against children aged under thirteen.[664] For example, at least 1,400 children were abused in the South Yorkshire town of Rotherham, Scotland, from 1997 to 2013.[665]

In another case, seven members of a paedophile gang (aged thirty to fifty-one) in the UK were involved in the rape and abuse of babies, toddlers and children in attacks that were streamed on the internet and seen on every continent. The sex ring preyed on the families of the children they targeted, in one case grooming a mother and father before their baby was born. Members would travel long distances to carry out the attacks together, or to watch the abuse on the internet, often using the dark web. Two were tried and convicted while the other five pleaded guilty. They faced more than thirty charges including the rape of a child, conspiracy to rape a child, sexual activity with a child, and administering a substance with intent against three victims – a baby, a toddler and a pre-school age child. They hid behind a veil of respectability with careers and families, to habitually target children under five in Yorkshire and in the southeast and west of England. Their communications referred to "nep," a shortening of "nepophile" that describes those sexually attracted to babies and toddlers.[666]

In 2017, German police uncovered an internet-based child sexual abuse website with 111,000 users. The "Elysium" platform was created around the end of 2016 and was accessible only via the dark web. It was used for the worldwide exchange of child sexual abuse images and to make appointments for the sexual abuse of children. The website had a title "Babies and Toddlers" where members exchanged photos and video recordings of violent sexual abuse of children aged up to four years old. German public prosecutors brought charges against four people aged between forty and sixty-two. One of the four suspects, a sixty-two-year-old man, was charged with serious sexual abuse of two children aged four and six whose father, an Australian citizen, had contacted him through the platform. The father was also prosecuted for child abuse.[667] Also in Germany, a further, extensive, dark web platform containing child sex abuse materials, known as "Boystown," was taken down in 2021, with 400,000 registered users. Four German men between the ages of forty and sixty-four were arrested in this connection.[668]

In Cologne, Germany, a cook has gone on trial for sexually abusing his baby daughter. Jorg L, forty-three years old, posted images on a Swiss secure messaging service Threema. He is alleged to have committed sexual violence, sometimes severe violence, against his daughter in sixty-one cases. Jorg met up with a chat partner, a twenty-seven-year-old former *Bundeswehr* soldier – sentenced to jail for ten years for severe sexual abuse – several times and they sexually abused each other's children. Eighty-seven suspected paedophiles have been identified in all sixteen German states as a result of this case, and fifty children, aged from three months to fifteen years have been removed from their abusive parents. As many as 30,000 people are believed to be linked to the paedophile chat groups under investigation. Some of the online chats had up to 1,800 participants at a time.[669] Recently, a court in Germany found members of another paedophile ring guilty of multiple counts of child sex abuse. A twenty-eight-year-old man identified as Adrian V was sentenced to fourteen years in prison, after which he will be kept in preventative detention to prevent his re-offending. His mother was sentenced to five years for aiding and abetting the abuse. Three other men were given between ten and twelve years each. The men allegedly drugged a group of boys and kept them in a building for a number of days. They uploaded footage of their abuse on the dark web. One of the victims was Adrian's partner's eleven-year-old son.[670]

Also in Germany, Andreas V (fifty-six) and Mario S (thirty-four) abused dozens of children between 1998 and 2018, even using Andreas' six-year-old foster child as bait to lure their victims into Andreas' camper van that served as the headquarters of his paedophile ring. He recorded these encounters and sold the images on the dark web. Investigators discovered fifteen terabytes of data reflecting over 1,000 acts of abuse of about forty children aged four to thirteen, including his foster daughter. Some of the evidence – at least 155 CD's and DVD's confiscated from Andreas V were lost "while in police custody," but this represents only a small part of the data obtained. Reports by children and their parents over many years were not heeded.[671] Andreas V and Mario S were jailed for thirteen and twelve years respectively in 2019 but will be held in protective custody after serving their sentences, effectively locking them up for life.[672] Questions remain as to why Andreas V was allowed to care for a foster child.

In Australia, fourteen men including a former child care worker have been charged with producing and sharing child abuse material on the internet across Australia and abroad: Forty-six victims, including sixteen from a single child care centre were identified.[673]

An international paedophile ring was recently exposed with fifty children saved and nine people arrested in Thailand. The dark website included 63,000 members with at least a further 100 children being abused but not yet identified. The youngest, so far, is fifteen months old.[674] Between January 2012 and July 2016, 12,987 cases of child sexual abuse in Malaysia were reported to police. Charges were filed against 2,189 cases resulting in 140 convictions. Most complaints of child sexual abuse in Malaysia do not lead to successful prosecutions largely due to weaknesses in the nation's criminal justice system. Paedophiles may be targeting Malaysia as the laws are less stringent there. It has become one of South-East Asia's biggest centres for the transmission of child sexual abuse images on the internet. It is the second largest after Thailand: Over a twenty-four-hour period 1,000 child sex transmissions were made in Malaysia. In Bangkok 1,800 were made in this same time frame.[675]

South Korea is known for illicit videos taken in public toilets and change rooms and posted online, using cameras as small as the head of a needle. Known as Molka, the Korean word for secret camera, 6,400 cases were reported in 2017, with the number of incidents increasing each year.[676] For some, the shame of being filmed in this way is too much, leading to their suicide.[677] Secret cameras are not only placed in toilets and change rooms but in public spaces such as in stores, on elevators, escalators, or on beaches, or streets. Upskirting is a recognized sexual variation. Although the prevalence of Molka has been established in Korea, there is no knowledge as to how common this practice is in other countries.

Brazil has arrested 108 people in a major anti-paedophilia operation.[678] They were detained as part of a ring that shared pornographic images of children using the dark web. More than

150,000 files containing disturbing images, including images of babies and young children being abused, were found.

The dark web provides an extensive platform for child sex abuse that appears to be relatively difficult to isolate and disassemble. While a number of websites have been infiltrated and taken down, relatively few perpetrators of the abuse are caught and prosecuted. The clandestine nature of the dark web enables those who like to observe or even participate in child sex abuse to do so mostly hidden from public view. Hundreds of children have been sexually abused to create these images while thousands of abusers have deliberately gained access to them for their pleasure. This is not simply a case of a few wayward perpetrators: it is an excessive proportion of humanity.

Children Abusing Children

Children sharing sex related images on their cell phones or on social media is another increasingly severe cyber crime emerging today.[679] Sexting – texting explicit sexual messages or images – is widespread. Police in England and Wales recorded 6,238 under-age sexting offences in 2016-2017. That amounts to seventeen a day. The number of cases of under eighteen-year-olds sharing, usually without consent, indecent or prohibited images was up by a third on that recorded the previous year. The youngest children involved in sexting images were aged ten. Fourteen-year-olds were the most common offenders. Girls were more likely to be victims, but both boys and girls were equally perpetrators. The British police received almost 30,000 reports of sexual assaults on children by other children in the four years prior to 2018. A child who opens a forwarded "sext" may find themselves on a sex offenders register.

A teenager whose intimate image ends up widely shared online may be driven to despair or suicide.[680] This is not surprising given that such an event frequently leads to public shaming by classmates and random strangers. It may be impossible to ever get the images off the internet. The abuse becomes permanent and may well continue for life. Every stranger encountered, every potential employer, or potential partner, may have seen those images. Any internet posting of sexual abuse, whether resulting from sexting by other children or from exploitative adults who post visual images of their abusive actions, has similar implications and can emotionally destroy the children who are abused.

Children can also abuse and bully other children through manipulation of internet messaging. In Canada, a teenage girl of sixteen callously manipulated a fellow schoolmate of the same age into having a sexual encounter with her by posting about two thousand erotic messages to him inviting him to meet her in the school bathroom, and explicitly describing what she would hope to do with him. Shortly after their meeting, she charged the teen with sexually assaulting her. He was expelled from the school. She had erased all the images from her Instagram account while the boy made his copies available to the police and the courts. The judge in the case found the boy's testimony to be unshakeable, and her manipulation of him to be a callous "set up." The girl and her co-conspirator friends regarded such manipulation as fun.[681]

Internet Threats to Children

Sadly, referrals of child abuse images to the National Crime Agency in the UK have surged by 700% in the last five years. It is estimated that about 80,000 people posed online sexual threats to children in 2018. The Home Office reports that images are becoming more graphic and abuse against children under the age of ten is depicted more and more frequently. For example, Haitch Macklin, thirty-eight, sold sexual torture videos of babies and toddlers to other offenders, and reported a desire to acquire "snuff" films showing real life murders. The National Crime Agency arrested him and jailed him, remarkably, for only twenty months.[682] Around five hundred child sex offenders are arrested each month safeguarding around 700 children a month.[683]

Child sexual exploitation can also occur in a more indirect manner, through the use of technology and without the child's initial recognition that this is sexual manipulation. For example, by being persuaded to post sexual images on the internet/mobile phones without immediate payment or gain, in the belief that they are chatting with a friend. Obviously, having access to the internet facilitates this process. In the USA, in 2015, 61% of children aged three to eighteen had internet access in their rooms at home.[684] In the UK, in 2012, 60% of eleven to sixteen-year-olds had internet access in their own rooms, compared with 30% six years earlier, making them increasingly open to online abuse.

Four out of five sixteen-year-old children in the UK regularly access porn online while one in three ten-year-olds has seen explicit material.[685] Accessing porn sites is a major part of internet use and for some, includes viewing child sex abuse images. For example, Pornhub is a popular porn streaming site that registers anything from 42 billion[686] to 100 billion visits a year,[687] more than Netflix or Amazon.[688] Pornhub, owned by a private Canadian conglomerate called Mindgeek, is based in Montreal, and includes more than 100 websites, production companies and brands. Its sites include Redtube, YouPorn, XTube, Spankwire, ExtrmeTube, Men.com, My Dirty Hobby, Thumbzilla, PornMD, Brazzers and GayTube.[689] It is ranked as having the third greatest impact on society in the 21st century after Facebook and Google but ahead of Microsoft, Apple and Amazon.[690]

Live streaming of abuse is also on the rise facilitated by faster internet speeds, smartphone technology and the growing ease of money transfers across borders. Calls for internet giants such as Google, Facebook, Twitter, Microsoft as well as others to monitor and prevent child sexual abuse online in much the same way as they are beginning to control internet terrorism are being made and, fortunately, starting to be heard.[691] In November 2019, for example, Facebook reported removing 11.6 million child abuse posts made between July and September 2019. From January to March of this same year 5.8 million pieces related to child nudity and sexual exploitation were removed.[692] Twitter closed 264,000 accounts in six months of 2019 for engaging in sexual exploitation of children.[693] Pornhub is changing its rules regarding user uploads and downloads after being publicly accused of facilitating child sex abuse in a New York Times article.[694] Users must now be verified before uploading videos and downloads will be prevented, inhibiting the further spread of digital recordings. The changes were introduced after Visa and Mastercard – prompted by these public accusations – launched their own investigations into the claims.[695] Mastercard, Visa and Discover blocked their customers from making purchases on Pornhub on their credit cards within days of the New York Times investigation.[696] A class action suit against Mindgeek has also been launched by 40 women in California who claim it continues to profit from pornographic videos of them that were published without their consent.[697] Canada is currently pursuing legislation to enforce such porn hubs remove child sex abuse from websites within 24 hours.[698] In contrast, new European Union laws regarding the protection of privacy have forced Facebook to remove some of its child abuse detection tools – particularly from messaging services – thus making it more difficult for Facebook to detect child sex abuse online.[699]

We are also learning that internet sharing of child sex abuse images and videos is no longer confined to the "dark web" but is increasingly being traded in encrypted apps, including Telegram and Discord.[700] Telegram links to these images are buried in public comments sections of YouTube videos. These contain code words that are indexed by search engines and once clicked on lead to the closed group of images. At least one of these groups contains hundreds of indecent child sex images. Videos showing the rape of minors are also posted onto porn websites that are easily accessible, such as that of Rose Kalemba who, raped at fourteen, like dozens of other girls/women with similar experiences, struggled to get the video taken down.[701] Online sexual imagery may also be violent giving rise to viewers' perceptions that disrespectful sex is a norm, wanted by men and women.[702] A BBC Radio Five survey revealed that more than a third of UK women under the age of forty have experienced unwanted slapping, choking, gagging or spitting during consensual sex. While this may or may not have been consensual, or related to watching abusive online pornography, 20% of the women were left upset or frightened.[703]

Some internet sites advertise sexual images that are for sale for $50 for nine gigabytes, $500 for fifty gigabytes and $2,500 for 2.2 terabytes. Nine gigabytes could contain many thousands of images depending on file sizes. Some users also declare that they sell access to child sexual abuse and rape forums. In England and Wales, more children are being groomed on Instagram than on any other platform. Over 5,000 cases of online grooming were recorded between the time when sexual communications with a child became a crime in 2017 and January 2019. Instagram was used in a third of these cases, Facebook in almost a quarter (23%) and Snapchat in 14%. While girls aged twelve to fifteen are most commonly targeted, children as young as five have been approached. A fifth of all victims are eleven or younger.[704] In Canada too, 4,174 cases of making or distributing child sex exploitation images were reported to police in 2019, compared to 850 in 2015. Cybertip.ca, a national tip line for reporting child sex abuse, processed 28,556 cases in 2019.[705]

In 2017, thirty-nine suspects were apprehended in Europe and South America after they shared illegal images on WhatsApp. More than 360,000 files depicting child sexual exploitation were obtained – several terabytes of data.[706]

Deception/Bribery by Perpetrators

Internet child sex crimes that offer incentives for children to indulge in sexting are increasing in frequency and innovation. In Queensland, Australia, a forty-two-year-old man allegedly posed as Canadian singer Justin Bieber on a number of social media platforms to gain indecent images of children. He was charged with more than 900 child sex offences.[707] One mother of an eight-year-old girl said her daughter had downloaded a popular social media site for just two days before being approached by an account impersonating a celebrity. The first message invited her to enter a competition: Winning would get her a five-minute chat with the celebrity. The second massage was "all you need to do is send me a photo of you naked, or your vagina." The third message said "Don't worry about it. All the girls are sending me these photos. Just do it, it'll be our secret." And then the last message: "Do it now." This program was found on platforms from Facebook, Twitter, Instagram and to newer platforms that have large teenage audiences, such as Musically. The message/s had been downloaded by more than fifty million people under the age of twenty-one, with a sizeable number under sixteen.

In South Korea, Cho Ju-Bin, who is accused of leading a group that blackmailed girls into sharing sexual videos which were then posted on pay-to-view chatrooms, has been named after a public outcry. Some seventy-four people including sixteen underage girls were exploited. Police suspect that there are about 260,000 participants in his chat rooms.[708] Cho recruited women by posting fake modeling jobs on line. Women would submit personal information so that they could get paid, along with photographs. Once hired they would be asked to provide increasingly revealing pictures. These were then used to blackmail the girls. Users of his chatrooms paid as much as $1,200 to enter premium rooms. Cho received payment in Bitcoin allowing him greater privacy than standard banking security systems.[709] He was named after five million people signed petitions to have his identity made public. The Minister of Gender Equality, Lee Jung-ok, has vowed to revise the laws governing sex crimes including online grooming and the blackmail of children and teenagers. Since September 2020, eighteen chat room operators, including Cho, have been charged. Some are asking "But will the changes go far enough in a country where being drunk is a defence for rape?[710] Under South Korean laws, possessing images of child sexual abuse is punishable by up to one year in prison or fines up to $16,000 but watching pornographic videos when the viewer does not know the subject is underage is not punishable. That provides a defense where viewers can prove they did not realise the girl was a minor.[711] Cho-Ju-bin has, however, now been jailed for forty years.[712]

In 2018, almost half (47%) the detected internet-based child sex abuse images were hosted by websites in the Netherlands. In all, over 105,000 sites were detected. While other countries have taken steps to curb such sites, the Netherlands has been slower to do so.[713] In Norway, a top psychiatrist has been convicted for downloading child abuse images while serving as a child protection agent. He was sentenced to twenty-two months in jail after admitting that he had downloaded nearly 200,000 images and more than 12,000 videos showing sexual abuse or sexualization of children. Some appeared to show children being raped. He confessed to having viewed such images for twenty years. He played a key role in reviewing child protection reports. The Norwegian process, of which he was a part, has been criticized for being far too quick to put children into care, splitting families unnecessarily.[714]

In Denmark, more than 1,000 young people have been charged with distributing sexually explicit material by sharing indecent video clips of two fifteen-year-olds having sex. Those found guilty face conditional prison sentences of up to twenty days and could be listed for ten years on a register of internet-based child sexual abuse offenders.[715] While these laws impose punishments on sexting or sharing sexual images on internet sites without consent, many other aspects of Denmark's laws against sex crimes are still to be strengthened. Similarly, in Belgium, a fourteen-year-old was gang raped by five teenagers who then shared the images on social media.[716] The girl took her life four days later. About 200 gang rapes are reported in Belgium each year.[717]

Popular internet platforms that are currently used by sex predators include Facebook, Telegram, Discord, Snapchat, Twitter, Musically, OnlyFans, Instagram, TikTok and WhatsApp. In the UK, pimps are using Vivastreet, a classified advertisement website where people can trade cars or household goods, to advertise multiple women under their control.[718] Google and Microsoft are increasingly focusing on the problem, although maintaining the freedom of the internet remains a controversial obstacle to intervention in these sites. Maintaining their sources of income is, not surprisingly, also a priority for such sites.[719] Clearly technology should have better controls but the internet is not the cause of the child sex abuse problem. It is the child predators that need to be targeted. Even if social media can be shut down as a means of child sex predation, these perpetrators will continue to explore alternative ways to achieve their goals.

Voluntary Child Sex Internet Use

While the internet is commonly used by child sex predators to exploit young people by exposing them sexually, some teenagers are voluntarily using the internet to earn large sums of money by uploading sexual images/movies of their own bodies, while masturbating and using sex toys, or having sex with consensual partners, for financial gain.

The OnlyFans platform has over a million creators who share video clips, photos or messages directly with subscribers, for a monthly fee.[720] Although the site is used for monetizing any professional program, such as exercise or fitness programs, it is also used for "adult" themes. It may prove to be financially rewarding for both adults and children who choose to share sexually related videos that subscribers choose to watch. It is also financially beneficial for OnlyFans. The site takes a 20% share of all payments. The Financial Times reported that OnlyFans revenue grew by 553% in the year 2020 to November, with users spending 1.7 billion UK pounds on the site.[721] While adult use of the site is not problematic, voluntary child use is also occurring. In addition, forced child sex abuse images are being screened as well as images of missing children being abused.

Parents Who Sell Their Children for Internet-Based Sexual Abuse

A woman who sold her son to paedophiles on the dark web was jailed for twelve years and six months by a court in southern Germany. Her partner, the boy's stepfather was also jailed for twelve years. They were forty-eight and thirty-nine years old and had sexually abused the boy themselves for at least two years. A Spanish man was jailed for ten years for sexually abusing a boy repeatedly. Five other men have also been prosecuted in connection with the abuse which also involved a three-year-old girl.[722] Few of these crimes are easily resolved, with chance occasionally assisting. For example, one suspect was arrested when a mother identified her four-year-old daughter's picture that had been posted online and on TV. The man was identified as her twenty-four-year-old boyfriend. He was believed to have sexually abused the child nine times, to have filmed the abuse and then distributed the images.[723]

In Jakarta, Indonesian authorities arrested at least seven people including the mother of two of three boys who featured in internet-based child sex abuse videos. One boy was only seven. These videos showed adult women engaging in sexual acts with the boys. The videos were sold to child sex offenders in Canada and Russia while the director was paid $2,307 to make them.[724]

In some cities/villages in the Philippines, families bring their children to houses where they are filmed in sexual acts for internet distribution. This trade is driven by people in the west paying adults to make the films or simply to watch them. Families who facilitate the sex abuse of their children say they need the money to survive. Two-thirds (69%) of children forced into online sex abuse are exploited by their own parent or family member with victims ranging from as young as six months old. About 50% are aged twelve or younger.[725]

In an area of the Philippines visited by the BBC in 2014, eight houses were involved in this trade. In this village in the south of the country, twelve children aged between five and fifteen were rescued. The Philippine government estimated at that time that there were between 60,000 and 100,000 child victims of sexual exploitation, many of them by cybersex.[726] Reports of global on-line child sex abuse from the International Centre for Missing and Exploited Children indicate that the number of instances has now risen. In 2015 the Centre received reports of 6.5 million videos or other files, in 2017, 20.6 million and in 2019, 69.2 million. The Philippines is the epicentre of this problem.[727]

The Extent of the Problem

These multiple reports of internet-based child sex abuse are only the tip of the iceberg of real time and internet facilitated child sexual abuse crimes. Clearly, child sexual abuse is far more prevalent than we would like to believe with over 78,000 websites containing child sex abuse images being detected in 2017.[728] In addition, it appears that countries vary widely in their condemnation of child sexual abuse with many paying lip-service to its unwantedness and others allowing financial interests to overshadow morality. Child sex abuse is big business. As the incidents reported here show, there is huge public demand for it, it is consumed in private, is difficult to trace, and it indulges a taboo desire of thousands, if not millions, of perpetrators. Porn sites and particularly dark web sites are enormous sources of income for their owners who clearly would not like to see any controls on their activities imposed. The extent of the crime is not widely exposed or even acknowledged by society. Families, schools, doctors, teachers, internet giants, lawmakers, government officers, and politicians, are not outspoken enough about these criminal abuses or abusers to be effective in demanding change in this global climate of abuse. Controlling the internet is still in its infancy, with calls for privacy, and freedoms for its use making imposing controls on its access challenging. Interpol, while providing a significant, major, United Nations endorsed, global criminal identification network that addresses all types of crime, primarily acts to identify victims and offenders of child sex abuse but is not directly tasked with prevention of child sex abuse. Their priorities are to "identify and rescue young victims of sexual abuse; block access to child sexual abuse material; [and to] prevent sex offenders from travelling abroad to abuse children or escape justice."[729] While such actions are essential, more direct preventative action targeting potential perpetrators is needed if this pervasive, abusive, sexual exploitation of children is to be curbed.

Military Activities

Militarized zones, established in the name of international security, both in times of war and in peace, also foster a climate of sexual abuse, through the development of sexual trafficking and abuse in their vicinity.[730] After the establishment of a militarized zone, brothels are created to provide sexual outlets for soldiers in which sexually transmitted infections can be monitored and managed. The local community from which girls are drawn to work in these brothels eventually becomes dependent on this form of occupation for their income contributing to a continuing sex trade long after the departure of the military installations.[731] For example, today there are at least 400,000 women working in the Philippines as registered prostitutes. This emerged from the USA army bases in this region during WWII and for four or more decades thereafter. In the 1990s the sex trade in the Philippines grew rapidly with the local community of young girls seeking sex work as a lucrative occupation. This business has grown to the extent that it has now become a popular site for paedophilic sex tours from the USA and Europe.[732] Estimates of the number of children exploited in this sex trade in the Philippines range from 60,000 to 100,000.

Further, at the start of the Vietnam war in 1957, it is estimated that there were 20,000 sex workers in Thailand. The US army opened seven military bases and invested sixteen million dollars in the Thai economy annually. By 1964, the population of women involved in sexual exploitation had grown to 400,000.[733] As Jim, a soldier in the Vietnam war later reported:

When they took us to Thailand for the first time, the general showed us a slide show of the brothels that were army approved. The brothel doors had stickers with a green beret. That meant that the Thai government had recruited their prostitutes with funds provided by the US government to ensure that the girls were virgins upon arrival and that they were healthy. Every time we went to the brothels, we saw very young girls. No soldier questioned them, we simply used them, and that was it. But we were not the only ones doing this; all armies have used prostitution as a source of relaxation therapy for their soldiers. It didn't matter if the girls wanted it or not, or if they had been kidnapped or not; the important thing was that we were enjoying our days of R & R.[734]

It is not known how many of these "girls" were underage, although the fact that they were required to be virgins at recruitment, and were perceived by Jim to be "very young girls" suggests that they might well have included children under eighteen. Military socialization to "make a man out of the boy"[735] may facilitate misogynous heterosexuality in the soldier. "Numerous military stories, songs, and other symbols also link male prowess to violence against – and especially to the sexual use and misuse of – women."[736] It is unclear if/how this has changed in modern military practices, particularly given the increasing number of non-male soldiers. While it is to be hoped that this level of abuse is no longer practiced, the reports of highly prevalent sexual abuse in the military suggest that there is a great deal of progress that has yet to be made.

Rape as a Weapon of War

In addition to women working in brothels serving the military, women also find themselves victims of rape by military who regard this as a justified part of military life. Rape has been used as a weapon of war and as a reward for soldiers in most wars as well as in many genocides. Whether the victim of a single rape, a single incident of

177

gang rape, or prolonged enslaved exploitation, women war victims, including young girls or adolescents, are often ostracized from networks where they might receive protection and care. Such victimization, provides a potential pool of women who have been "despoiled" and are left unable to create lives for themselves other than through sex work. As Farr reports: "Massive rape in war leads to the promotion of a sex trade industry. These populations of women who are raped and therefore disgraced to their families and in their communities, are particularly vulnerable to the procurers of the [sex] industry."[737] Women forced into or used in brothels suffer the same fate.

In some instances, rape in wartime can lead to extreme community actions:

> The importance to men of maintaining ethnic or religious purity is illustrated by the actions of some combatants during the armed conflict over the India-Pakistan partition. Reportedly, the fear that their women would be raped and impregnated by the enemy, resulting in the "pollution and impurity" of their religion, led some men (particularly Sikh village men) to murder their own women. Afterward, these women were described as having been martyred rather than murdered.[738]

Rape as a weapon of war is increasingly being observed. Rape in wartime can also lead to extreme cruelty such as occurred with Japan's "comfort women" during 1932-1945, many of whom were children at the time:

> Tomasa Salinog, a Filipina former comfort woman, told how soldiers broke into her home in the middle of the night, decapitated her father, and dragged her to a military installation, where she was raped by two soldiers and beaten until she was unconscious. Tomasa was 13 years old at the time.[739]

Similarly, thirteen-year-old Julia Porras, also kidnapped from her home in the Philippines by Japanese troops, was enslaved in a tunnel. She was then raped by four to five soldiers every day for eight months during the war. She told no one about her torture for the next forty-eight years.[740] There are no reliable statistics for such "comfort women" – essentially sex slaves – for the Japanese military, but estimates suggest there were 80,000 to 100,000, mostly Korean, and young.[741] The Japanese Tenth army indulged in a sadistic and rampant orgy, burning down every village and small city they encountered and raping most women and female children that they seized.[742] Thousands of men died when they tried to defend their families from rape. Murder of a household's men often served as a prelude to gang rape of its women. A few Japanese even reportedly cut off and ate the penises of Chinese men they killed, believing this would increase their sexual prowess and overall virility.[743] Soldiers raped almost all the women they could capture and not only young ones. They raped the very old and the very young. Many were violated numerous times and sometimes by numerous men at any one time leading to genital rupture and death. One method of killing a rape victim was the insertion of a long sharp object such as a bayonet or a sharpened bamboo cane into a woman's vagina resulting in internal injuries. Another was the insertion of a live grenade or firecracker into the girl's vagina. Sometimes female children or infants were raped. If the act seemed impossible for physical reasons, the child's genital area was simply sliced open with a bayonet before she was raped. Other girls or women became sex slaves for the entire period of the army assault. They could even be turned into "rape furniture," tied naked to posts at the entrance of barracks or inside the barracks themselves, to be used for casual rape by passing Japanese. Some of the most attractive women became "comfort women." When not killed or raped to death, they remained sexual slaves for years. Women who became pregnant sometimes committed suicide, or killed their babies at birth. A few carried their babies to term and raised them, remaining conflicted and tormented by their choice for years.[744]

Rape in Multiple Wars

Rape in war is common.[745] Multiple examples of mass rape of women and girls in wars are provided indicating that sexual abuse

– and often violent sexual abuse – of the "enemy's" women is a fairly common practice, particularly in recent conflicts. In 1991-5 the Serbian paramilitary groups promoted the rape of Bosnian Muslim women as a strategy to expel Muslims from their homes and villages. In Rwanda, between April and July 1994, Hutu troops raped thousands of Tutsi girls and women. In Ciapas, Mexico, in 1994, Mexican soldiers raped Indigenous women in mountainous regions; as many as 700 have been documented. In 1997, dozens of Algerian women accused Islamic Revolution rebels of kidnapping them and making them sex slaves. In the Democratic Republic of Congo, since 1998, more than 500,000 girls and women have been raped and hundreds suffered sexual violence in ongoing conflict. Women were regularly raped and used as sexual slaves by men of opposing ethnicities and religions during the civil conflict between India and Pakistan in 1947. It was estimated that two years after this, 75% of the abducted girls and young women were still being bought and sold from one man to another. In 1970, violence erupted again in east Pakistan's fight for independence and eventual emergence as Bangladesh. During these eleven months, hundreds of thousands of Bengali girls and women were raped by Pakistani soldiers.[746] Rogue soldier groups also kidnap women at random for sexual enslavement and even temporary or permanent "marriage." The Algerian government believes, for example, that between 1991-2002 in their war against Islamic rebel groups, about 1,600 young women and girls were abducted and sexually enslaved by "roving bands from armed Islamic groups."[747]

UNICEF reports that even today, millions of children and women around the globe live with the terrifying threat of sexual violence in conflict. During wars, they are subjected to kidnapping, rape, sexual slavery or trafficking, forced marriage/pregnancy, enforced sterilization, killing, maiming or recruitment into armed groups. Sexual and physical violence may be used to intentionally humiliate a population or to force people from their homes.[748] In 2017, for example, there was a 670% increase in cases of child abduction in Somalia alone. The Al-Shabaab group abducted more than 1,600 children in order to increase their ranks by using boys and girls in combat and support roles.[749] In 2021, rape is being used as a weapon of war in the Ethiopia-Eritrea conflict in

Ethiopia's northern Tigris region.[750] Women are being gang-raped, drugged and held hostage.

Some armed groups, such as Boko Haram in Nigeria, often specifically target girls, who are raped, forced to become wives of fighters or used to perpetrate suicide attacks. In February 2018, for instance, the group abducted 110 girls and one boy from a technical college in Dapchi, Yobe State, the majority of whom have since been released.[751] Such abductions, followed by release after negotiations, have now, in 2020-2021, become regular events. The Chiboc girls and Yazidi women are further examples of such group abductions where young girls have been kidnapped and forced into long lasting sexual slavery by their abductors. Both girls and boys are at risk.[752]

Sexual abuse of children may be facilitated after the conclusion of a war. In 2021, in Afghanistan, the withdrawal of American forces, and the assumption of power by the Taliban, has contributed to economic hardships for the population. This, in turn, has led to an increase in child marriages as a means of providing financial support for other members of the family. Parwana Malik, for example, was sold at the age of nine years to a fifty-five-year-old man to provide some income for her father to enable him to provide for his remaining eight family members. Her twelve-year-old sister was sold a few months earlier for the same reason. Magul, aged ten, was also sold to a seventy-year-old man to settle her family's debts.[753] Although marrying children under fifteen is illegal, it is commonly practiced. With the reluctance of the Taliban to allow female children to return to school, they and their education are no longer regarded by parents as an investment in the future, resulting in an increased likelihood that they will be sold into marriage.

Child Sex Abuse in Genocides

Sex abuse and particularly child sex abuse occurs in war, and in genocides. For example, Jewish children were sexually abused during the Holocaust, although acknowledging this is taboo.[754] Nazi ideology, while advocating killing children, did not promote child sex abuse directly, but facilitated such abuse indirectly through its total destruction of Jewish family life with its normal safeguards for child safety. As a result, children were left vulnerable and unprotected from sexual abuse in homes, villages, ghettos, camps, and hiding places, while those in authority turned a blind eye when Jewish children were sexually assaulted or murdered. Perpetrators were ordinary people who were also Nazis, members of the SS, *Einsatzgruppen* members, *Wehrmacht* soldiers, their allies in occupied countries, Russian soldiers at the end of the war, as well as rescuers of children who were hidden, in Europe, and those who offered homes to children who were sent to "safety" in countries beyond Europe's borders. Few of the perpetrators reported in *Betrayed: Child Sex Abuse in the Holocaust*[755] – unlike most of the perpetrators of child sex abuse of children today – followed the well acknowledged paedophilic pattern of grooming children for sexual abuse. For most perpetrators, sexual assault was a crime of opportunity, authority and violence, often coupled with antisemitic justification, and occasionally, religious vengeance.

In our more recent genocides, children have also been deliberately targeted for sexual abuse and rape, such as in Rwanda[756] and Darfur, Sudan.[757] Women and children were saved as a priority in both World War I and II. In contrast, children were specifically killed to prevent them growing up to avenge their parents' deaths in the Holocaust, as also occurred in the Armenian genocide perpetrated by the Turks,[758] and in the Rwandan genocide against Tutsi.[759] In almost all genocides and wars, however, children become the victims of terror, hardship, starvation and violence, such as in Cambodia[760] and during the Stalinist starvation of Ukraine.[761]

Child Soldiers

The precise extent of use of children as soldiers globally is not known although it is recognized that between 1990-2001 at least, eighty-seven countries included child soldiers in their troops, and in most – all but seventeen – they were sexually abused.[762] Child soldiers were reported during this period in Afghanistan, Angola, Burundi, Cambodia, Colombia, Democratic Republic of Congo, Honduras, Liberia, Mozambique, Myanmar, Peru, Rwanda, Sierra Leone, and Uganda. Countries such as Canada, the United Kingdom and the United States recruit youth under the age of 18 into their armed forces. These are not forcible conscriptions but volunteer recruits who may also benefit from educational opportunities supported by their militaries. Nor are they sent into combat situations until they have completed some years of training. This is qualitatively different from children abducted from their homes, taught to use weapons, and to kill, and forced into active combat.

Monitoring the use and abuse of forced child soldiers is difficult to do. Perpetrators of child sexual abuse among child soldiers tend to be male, often having been forced into child soldiering and abusive settings themselves, while victims of sexual abuse are predominantly, but not only, female.[763] Abusers in these situations are both perpetrators and victims of child sex abuse. The highest incidence of child exploitation occurred in Uganda where, 21% of approximately 11,000 abducted children were female, nearly all of whom were sexually abused. Girls who were forcibly recruited into armies were given to the soldiers as their "wives." Although often referred to as "forced marriages" this is by no means an accurate representation of their sexual slavery. In Sierra Leone, girls who became pregnant and gave birth were expected to continue with their combat duties with their babies on their backs. "I picked up a gun and strapped the baby on my back."[764]

In contrast, girls in Latin America often voluntarily joined armies although they were not aware this would lead to their sexual exploitation. As one girl soldier in Honduras explained:

> At the age of 13, I joined the student movement. I had a dream to contribute to make things change, so that children would not be hungry, later I joined the armed struggle. I had all the inexperience and the fears of a little girl. I found that girls were obliged to have sexual relations "to alleviate the sadness of the combatants." And who alleviated our sadness after going with someone we hardly know?[765]

183

Similarly, in Columbia 40% of girls who joined FARC [the Revolutionary Armed Forces of Columbia] were trying to escape abuse at home and hoped to be treated more equally. Instead, in FARC they were expected to provide sexual services, in addition to combat activities, were treated badly, and punished, sometimes through sexual acts. One girl described:

> They abused women a great deal, they treated them like bitches and so on [...] they passed by and they called them bitches, whores, that's what they shouted at them. And the girls that answered back defiantly, they came and said this broad is in heat, they came and she got "la vaca." What is "la vaca"? That means a gang rape involving twenty, twenty-five guys.[766]

With child soldiers, rape is used against the girls (and boys) within one's own army, potentially to terrify them into compliance. Not only are these children later rejected by their own people – if they are lucky enough to ever be reunited with them – but they are abused by their own senior "officers," who may themselves be children or adolescents, to exact loyalty through fear and intimidation. This difficult situation has led to legal complications as well. While sexual abuse of the enemy is a recognized war crime, sexual abuse of one's own soldiers is not quite so clear cut. After much legal wrangling over this issue the International War Crimes Tribunal, did, in 2014, conclude that the rape and sexual slavery of girl soldiers is a war crime, thus resolving the legal ramifications of this situation.[767]

Sexual Abuse by UN Peacekeepers

The child soldiers in the multiple countries where they are used, do not claim to be honourable role models who respect "western" human rights standards, but claim distinction through their fighting abilities and even their ability to exploit children to achieve their goals. UN peacekeepers, on the other hand, are respected as honourable troops with a mandate to protect and preserve human rights of oppressed peoples. Despite their apparently honourable intentions and mandates, they have also been accused of sexual abuse of the people whom they are supposedly protecting. Blue helmets, as they are called, have enslaved girls in the Congo, purchased sex slaves in Cambodia and Eritrea and became known less for peace than for rape.[768] Recently, WHO aid workers – men and doctors tackling the Ebola outbreak in the DR Congo – have been accused by thirty women of sexual abuse and exploitation.[769] Twenty-one of eighty-three aid workers who were perpetrators of sexual abuse were employed by WHO.[770] Eight additional women have accused men from the DR Congo's Health Ministry. Two other UN Agencies and four international charities were also named in the report on the exploitative events.[771]

In 2006, five American troops raped an Iraqi girl not yet fourteen-years-old in front of her relatives and killed her.[772] Sadly, in 2019, President Trump's Republican administration's increasing opposition to abortion led to a watering down of a UN resolution on ending sexual violence in war. This despite the majority of Americans (61% in 2019) being supportive of legal abortion in all or most cases. The Trump administration removed all reference to sexual and reproductive health from the resolution on the grounds that a phrase implied support for abortion. The removed phrase reads "Recognizing the importance of providing timely assistance to survivors of sexual violence, urges United Nations entities and donors to provide non-discriminatory and comprehensive health services, in line with Resolution 2106."[773] The final version of the resolution that supposedly was intended to prevent sexual violence in war settings, was also pressured into removing reference to a monitoring body that would report acts of sexual violence.[774] Such actions do little to discourage or prevent sexual abuse of women and children during war. Sadly, political interference to bolster a home-based controversial and conservative viewpoint, and potentially to protect abusing US servicemen and women, was allowed to prevent appropriate UN resolutions aimed to reduce or eliminate sexual violence against girls and women among military forces during war or peacetime.

Sex Trafficking and Trade

Sex trafficking is probably the fastest growing aspect of human trafficking occurring at present,[775] and is almost as profitable as the drugs and arms trade if not more so.[776] There is some consensus that sexual exploitation is the most commonly occurring type of human trafficking accounting for about 79% of all human trafficking in the world.[777] Forced labour is the second most frequent form of human trafficking occupying about 18% of the trade. The remaining three percent involves domestic slavery, forced marriage, which amounts to sexual slavery, and organ extraction.[778] Exploitation of children for begging and to serve as soldiers is not yet quantified. Trafficking in people is truly global in scope. It has been documented in 175 nations for sex work or labour.[779] Interpol estimates that 71% of all human trafficking victims are women and girls and three out of four of them are sexually exploited.[780] Four million people are trafficked annually, and about 1 to 1.4 million women and girls (estimates vary) are trafficked into prostitution around the world.[781]

In the USA sex trafficking of minors occurs in every state of the nation, although the exact number of victims is unknown due to the lack of systematic monitoring of this information.[782] A Statistics Canada report indicates that the majority of human trafficking victims in Canada are women and girls under twenty-five, with children under the age of eighteen accounting for more than a quarter of the victims. One-third were trafficked over international borders. There were 340 reported incidents in 2016, up from fifty in 2009, the first year that statistics were recorded. The true rate is probably far higher given that

Statistics Canada does not differentiate the various kinds of human trafficking that occur in their figures. In addition, the fact that most crimes go unreported clouds such estimates.[783]

An estimated twenty-seven to forty million people (estimates vary) are currently living under some form of slavery with the majority being women trafficked for prostitution and being held under some form of debt bondage or contract slavery.[784] In debt bondage, girls and women pledge their services against a debt they owe (for example, to cover travel costs), but the person to whom they owe it does not deduct the value of their services from the debt owed, and does not specify the length or nature of these services.[785] Recruiters may use a variety of methods to entice young children into the sex trafficking trade including grooming them to accept offers of apparently lucrative jobs, offers of friendship and happiness, and abduction.

It is, however, difficult to quantify sex trafficking.[786] International laws on sex crimes differ from place to place making accurate reporting of sex crimes problematic. The result is that authorities do not have definitive knowledge regarding organized sex crimes.[787] Whatever figures we do have are likely a severe underestimate. Such numbers also do not reflect the context of the crimes: What happened, to whom, how, where, what were the reactions to the crimes, how was it dealt with, what were the consequences for the victim/s or the perpetrators/s?

Sex trafficking is defined by the Trafficking Victims Protection Act of 2000 in the USA as "the recruitment, harbouring, transportation, provision, or obtaining of a person for the purpose of a commercial sex act, in which the commercial sex act is induced by force, fraud or coercion, or in which the person induced to perform such act has not attained eighteen years of age."[788] Sex trafficking, forced prostitution, "voluntary" sex work, forced marriage, sexual slavery, sexual exploitation are all terms used to describe the myriad of sexually abusive acts perpetrated on children forced into the sex trade. There are about three million known victims of sexual exploitation under eighteen in the world with this group being those most vulnerable to sex trafficking, especially the homeless or those without legitimate employment.[789] We do not often distinguish between victims that have, for example, been kidnapped and forced into prostitution, compared to those who are enticed into a relationship and voluntarily enter into a sexually exploitative situation from which they feel powerless to escape. Nor do we consider differences between these situations and young women or children who chose – for whatever reason – to enter into a "sugar daddy" (or "sugar mommy") relationship with an older man (or woman) who provides financial benefits for the child in exchange, or those who have no alternative means of supporting themselves other than to sell their sexual services. Or those who simply like sex work.[790] Society tends to condemn all these children regardless of their background, often disparaging such victims rather than their abusers, pimps, or their sexual predators. Terms such as prostitute, sex worker, mistress, escort, porn star, child bride, sex slave, are all used to describe those children who by design, following abduction and/or forced marriage, after trafficking and being pimped by others, or simply in order to survive, are involved in trading sex. Most reports indicate that the majority of sex workers have experienced childhood sexual and/or physical abuse.[791] Our language – and attitudes – do not readily empathise with the predicament of the child, nor condemn the perpetrators or pimps appropriately. In all these instances our language is murky and indistinct. It is abusive of the child victims and lets the perpetrators escape verbal, or other, condemnation.

Where Does it Take Place?

Transactional sexual abuse describes situations in which sex is traded and which exploits the needs, vulnerabilities and emerging sexualities of children and young people. Transactional sex, in contrast to intrafamilial abuse, is sustained by societal values, gender-based poverty, or the promotion of sex as a commodity that can be bought and sold. "Economic sexual exchange," "prostitution," "sex-trade," and "commercial sexual exploitation" all describe the exchange of sex in return for money, goods or favours. Transactional sex usually involves adolescents, while intra-familial sexual abuse begins when the child is young and may continue until puberty or even longer into adolescence.[792] In both types of sexual abuse of children, intrafamilial and transactional, the responsibility for the abuse lies with the perpetrator and/or those who benefit from the interactions.[793]

Transnational sex trade can refer to those who travel to a different jurisdiction and engage in child sex abuse. Or it can describe those who intentionally live abroad permanently or semi-permanently in order to abuse children. A third form of transnational sex offending occurs in internet facilitated sex crimes. Estimating the extent of the problem is almost impossible due to the under-reported nature of the crime,[794] although the US Department of Justice estimates that more than a million children are forced into the sex trade each year.[795] What is known, is that almost all child sex abusers are reportedly male (99%), with a median age of above 40 years.[796] Sexual abuse of children through travel or tourism usually involves a short-term contact with the child/ren. Embedded offenders usually reside for a longer time in the overseas destination and engage in grooming of the child and repeated victimization. Fantasy driven users tend to engage with their victim only online, while contact driven users wish for real life encounters.[797]

At least 250,000 children serve as sex workers in China, 100,000 in India, and the majority of those working in the sex trade in Bangladesh are under eighteen. An estimated 60,000 to 100,000 child victims of sexual exploitation are active in the Philippines, 60,000 in Taiwan, 40,000 in Vietnam, 40,000 in Indonesia, 40,000 in Pakistan, and 30,000 in Sri Lanka.[798] In the Philippines a whole generation of girls between twelve and eighteen assume that women are born to be raped and sold.[799] Thousands of North Korean women and girls, some as young as nine, are being forced to work in the sex trade in China. They are abducted and sold into slavery, or enticed into escape from North Korea by fake marriages to Chinese men. The trade is estimated to be worth $100,000 million a year for the criminal organization behind it. The women and girls are trapped, as if exposed, they would be repatriated to North Korea where they would be tortured.[800] About 20,000 children are prostituted on the streets of Johannesburg to child sex offenders. Some 16,000 children are in prostitution in Mexico.[801] Approximately 10,000 or more children in the UK are estimated to be victims of sexual exploitation at any one time.

The UK provides one example of what may happen to children recruited into the sex trade. In the UK, these children usually end up in the hands of street gangs. Estimates indicate that about 12,500 girls and young women are closely involved with gangs in the UK and a similar additional number live in fear of them. Most are in London. A 2008 study uncovered forty different gangs in just one borough of south-east London.[802] Gang life in the UK is just a microcosm of what is really happening in the sex trafficking world no matter where this occurs.

Where Are Girls Trafficked To and From?

South Africa has a burgeoning sex industry with women and girls being sold to eastern European countries, and to Angola, Mozambique, Tanzania, Zambia, Uganda and Kenya within Africa. More than 20,000 Nigerian girls were forced into prostitution rings in mining camps and hotels in Mali by traffickers who had promised them jobs in Malaysia.[803] The trade has expanded to Latin America, including the Caribbean – and particularly the Dominican Republic – and to some Central and South American resort zones.[804] Child trafficking has also become a major problem in India with the country becoming a centre for prostitution, slavery and forced marriage.[805] Few children are rescued from such prostitution rings. For example, in 2019, only about 150 children, from Benin, Burkina Faso, Niger, Nigeria and Togo, some as young as eleven, were rescued from sex and labour trafficking in west Africa.

Sex trafficking routes involve multiple countries with some being centres for the recruitment of girls, and others being the destination countries to which they are sent to work as prostitutes. Multiple countries are involved in transporting girls from one country to another. For example, forty-seven countries traffic girls to and from Russia. Twenty-nine countries exchange women and girls with Ukraine. Forty-nine countries are involved in USA routes and thirty in Germany's routes. About sixty-six countries are involved in sex trafficking with African countries, fifty-four countries are linked to South East Asian areas, and fifty-two with Middle East countries.[806] Affluent countries such as western Europe, North America, Australia and New Zealand are almost predominantly destination countries for trafficked girls.[807]

Current indications are that sex trafficking of local girls is also occurring throughout Canada, trafficked by, and being raped by Canadian men, although clear indications of just how prevalent this problem is in the country are difficult to obtain.[808] Between 2009-2016 there were 1,320 police reported incidents of human trafficking in the country. Individuals convicted of trafficking another human being can, theoretically, receive a prison term of up to fourteen years, although most perpetrators spend less than three years in custody reflecting a light sentencing policy in this country.[809] One Canadian girl (Elle – a pseudonym) who was rescued from a life of sexual slavery in Canada observed that organized crime groups have permeated social systems including government licensing agencies and police forces that allow them to keep women and girls vulnerable to prostitution and sexual exploitation.[810]

Indigenous women in Canada are particularly vulnerable to sex trafficking. Little research has been done on this issue although it is known that this community is particularly at risk due to poverty, domestic violence, inadequate laws and services, the country's colonial legacy, a high crime rate, and limited education for these women.[811] In addition, post-colonial biases of law enforcement, health care workers, and other social services tend to ignore Indigenous people, disregard them when they report problems, and by so doing, facilitate further abuses against them.[812]

Anti-trafficking activists risk their lives in countries such as India. Five women employed by an NGO who were performing a street play to raise awareness of and discourage sex trafficking were gang-raped at gun point in the eastern state of Jharkhand. The women were forced into cars, taken to a secluded area and raped.[813]

On the border between Malaysia and Singapore, people may buy girls to sell and torture. These torture sessions may be filmed as pornography and uploaded to the web, appealing to those who like sexual violence. One story illustrates this. Lydia Cacho, who has explored international sex trafficking extensively, was able to interview a young woman in a shelter who had deep scars on her body. She had been bought by a young North American for $7,000. The perpetrator kept his face covered by a black mask while he filmed and photographed her. After he abused her, he paid the trafficker to "ensure that she was taken to a private clinic" so that nobody would investigate the lashes, puncture wounds, and cuts. The trafficker did take her to a clinic, and then afterwards gave her $200 and left her on the street in Malaysia. She felt grateful that he had not left her to die of an infection.[814]

How Old Are the Children?

Through trafficking, child sex abuse today has moved beyond institutions such as the family setting or schools into the more loosely organized, global economic trade industry. Three age ranges have emerged for sexual trafficking abuse of children: Toddlers to about four years of age form the youngest group, five to twelve-year-olds being the next age group, and teens being the oldest target age.[815] The average age of women and girls being sold is thirteen: They have a life expectancy of seven years.[816] The average age of these children is decreasing from around fourteen-sixteen, down to around twelve-fourteen.[817] In Nepal, the highest prices paid are for girls between ten and twelve.[818] Their lives are filled with rape, forced drugging, humiliation, degradation, threats, diseases, pregnancies, abortions, miscarriages, torture, pain and constant fear of being killed or having those they love hurt or killed. In more recent years there is an increasing demand for harder core sex and pornography than in the past, driving the thirst for even more cruelty for younger and younger girls.[819]

How Lucrative is the Trafficking Trade?

The sex trafficking business is highly lucrative. Estimates suggest profits range around $7 billion annually if not as high as $12 billion or more.[820] On average, a child is raped by 6,000 men during a five year period of servitude.[821] In North America, girls and women may be pimped to as many as fifty men a day at $25 a time with pimps making $150,000 to $200,000 per child per year.[822] The girls and women are highly mobile, being moved around a country, such as in America where hotels, rest stops, bus stations and truck stops are hubs for the sex trade.[823] Reports indicate that adults purchase sex with children 2.5 million times a day in the USA with 100,000 children being used for sex every year in the USA.[824]

The income earned from selling girls for sex though prostitution is staggering. As Cacho explains:

> 50,000 girls under 18 [have been] trafficked from Vietnam to Cambodia and enslaved, extorted, starved and sexually exploited. A girl under ten years old is given one euro for giving a European oral sex, but the trafficker charges forty euro. According to some girls who were rescued, they have to have oral sex with fifteen to twenty clients each day. A trafficker can earn 600 euros each day from one girl. Supposing they are exploited five days a week, and using the lower number of clients, each minor generates 3,000 euros per week. The sexual exploitation of 50,000 Vietnamese girls in Cambodia provides the traffickers with 150,000,000 euros a week. The money is distributed among the owners and tenants of bars and hotels, taxi drivers and bellhops, mafias that provide protection, and police officers that are paid to alert them to investigations being carried out by organizations defending children's rights. In addition, the profits support banks and local economies.[825]

There are many individuals who have made their fortunes from the sex trafficking trade, in addition to the owners of the thousands of porn websites that exploit children, women, and men sexually and predators financially. Matilde Manukyan's story as a great Turkish madam, epitomizes the wealth that can be gained from sex trafficking.

> Once she was legitimately operating within the legalized system of prostitution, Manukyan began trafficking in minors. Next she invested the profits from trafficking in

women and girls in real estate. Before her death, she owned three five-star hotels, more than 120 apartments in many tourist areas of Turkey, an export company and a business of more than 300 luxury taxis. She had a collection of Rolls-Royces, Mercedes, and BMWs. She built a hotel in Germany and had a luxurious mega-yacht that she used to entertain her powerful friends.[826]

The market is consistent, resisting fluctuations in economic prosperity and extends across clubs and brothels, to mail-order brides, women for rent, and sex tourism.[827] It is expanding rapidly facilitated by the internet. In some countries there is little legal sanction imposed on sex trafficking. As one British police officer noted:

> If you get caught smuggling cocaine, you're looking at 20 years. If you're smuggling women [or children] the profits can be just as high and if you get caught the only thing you're looking at is living off immoral earnings. If you're a criminal, the choice about which to go for is pretty simple.[828]

More stringent laws are gradually being introduced globally as awareness of the rapidly expanding and developing world of global sex trafficking increases. In Canada, for example, the Criminal Code now carries a maximum penalty of life imprisonment where it includes kidnapping, aggravated or sexual assault, or death, and a maximum penalty of fourteen years in all other cases.[829] Knowledge of this trade, how it works, and how to monitor or control it is a relatively new development – only a few decades old – resulting in control measures still lagging behind its worldwide expansion.

Why Buy Child Sex?

The majority of paedophiles who abuse children aged ten or younger are from the United States, France, Norway and Canada.[830] Reasons for the increasing desire for younger and younger children vary from country to country. These may include myths that appear to elevate children as more desirable targets including that children have a natural sexuality, that a young virgin invigorates and restores male libido, that a man can be cured of HIV if he has sex with a virgin – particularly prevalent in South Africa – that children are easier to dominate and they are – erroneously – believed to be less likely to be infected with and transmit HIV/AIDS.[831] In addition, younger children do not know how to defend themselves and it is easier to get them to cooperate and be raped as prostitutes.[832]

Why Use Child Sex Workers?

It is likely easier to use children as sex workers rather than older adolescents or women. Children do not have many rights.[833] It is not uncommon to see adults holding on to children in public places, or to see children angry or upset with the adult they are travelling with. We assume it is just a kid throwing a tantrum, and we ignore them. When an adult says their child likes to make up stories, or is just misbehaving, people are inclined to believe the adult. Children don't carry their own ID, they have no money, they cannot vote to ensure their rights. Society makes children more vulnerable by denying them agency in almost every aspect of their lives. They are always controlled by adults, so we expect that any adult we see with a child is supposed to be controlling them. This extends to the realm of child abuse as well. We do not always believe a child's tale of sexual abuse. Children too, may not be aware of the meaning of what has happened – that the sexual abuse is totally inappropriate – and they may lack the words to describe it or the understanding that this should be reported, or the ability to challenge the adult perpetrator who is supposedly their protector and who may be threatening them with dire consequences should they speak up. Society makes children easier targets for abuse than older victims.

Who Controls Sex Trafficking?

While individuals are no doubt involved in small trafficking circles, multiple people from all walks of life are involved in large, global, organized crime networks including politicians, military officers, business people, journalists, religious leaders, bankers, police officers, judges, priests and ordinary people.[834] Mafias – in a number of countries – are dominant players in the sex trafficking world using corruption as a major source of economic and political power wherever they work. The search for pleasure is the common thread between them all. While some create the market for human sexual slavery, others protect it, promote it, and feed it.[835] Mafias manipulate women in multiple ways including buying, selling, giving, kidnapping, renting, loaning, raping, torturing and killing women and girls.[836] Such activities are evident in organized crime groups worldwide including the Japanese Yakuza, the Chinese Triads, the Italian, Russian, and Albanian Mafias and the Latin American drug cartels.

Attitudes towards women in these groups – based on the stories told by survivors who have escaped and lived to tell their tales – are misogynous and contemptuous. Arely's story is typical.[837] As a Venezuelan teenager she was enticed into becoming a dancer in a Mexican nightclub in Monterrey and, to make her more attractive to clients, was given breast enhancement surgery – the costs for which, of course, were added to her debt. Some time later she was persuaded by her recruiter to move to Cancun and to continue working, now as a sex worker, with the costs of her flight to Cancun now added to her debt and amounting to US $10,000. She learned that a number of other girls had been tricked by the same recruiter with similar promises of rescue and marriage following the move to Cancun. She decided to try to escape.

> They told me, "Look at yourself; you are ungrateful and miserable." They had pulled me out of poverty in Venezuela and this was how I repaid them, with tantrums. And I thought: Am I crazy: I don't like to be forced to have sex. Sometimes they [the men] are disgusting. I'm tired. They smell bad. I don't like drunkards. "This is a job like any others," the mansion housekeeper said to me. All I wanted to do was dance. I don't know if I'm crazy because I don't like to obey.[838]

She ran away and tried to catch a flight home but was caught at the airport without a passport or ticket and no money. She was taken to the local police station and immediately assessed as a prostitute. Four of the officers raped her. The police officer in charge asked her: "Why are you crying? You are a whore, and this is what whores do." When the prison governor was interviewed about this later, he replied, with a smile:

> You don't understand. These girls make a living from this. They provoke the boys and later regret it. She most likely offered sex as a way to get out of jail, but here we comply with the law. Also, my officers tell me that it isn't true that they raped her; she had already been raped before she arrived...She was no virgin.[839]

She was rescued from the local jail by an aid organization where she was found drugged with an overdose of benzodiazepine and tied to a bed. She was, at that stage and after years of control by the sex trafficking gang, nineteen years old. Although Arely's story is representative of many, her rescue is not. Many never escape their bondage and even when they do, they are not always accepted back into their families once they are reunited with them. Arely was fortunate that her family welcomed her home but not all families are willing, or able, to assist the child or young woman with the lengthy and difficult process of recovery that is needed to regain their self esteem after an extended period of sexual abuse.

By the mid 1900s, shortly after the fall of the Soviet Union in 1991, there were over 200 illegal sex businesses in Moscow alone and most were either owned by the mafia or paid protection money to them against police or other raids.[840] By 2002 there were at least 12,000 crime groups in Russia. A sizeable number have global prominence. Their activities are diverse and include not only sex trafficking of women and children, but money laundering, smuggling weapons, cars, fuel, cigarettes and drugs. They also make money by bribing officials, forging documents and racketeering. Russian criminal groups at all levels are involved in the international sex trade.[841] Mafias in other former Soviet states include the Ukrainian and Albanian mafia, in collaboration with Turkish mafia, all of which have close ties to trafficking markets in Hungary, Austria and the Middle East.[842] The Japanese Yakuza has a long history of trade in prostitution of women and children that extends throughout South East Asia and into the former Soviet regions as well as to Africa, the USA, Canada and Latin America. Japanese law enforcement appears to be cooperative in these ventures.[843] One Thai woman who wrote to her father after being trafficked to Japan wrote:

> I live without hope. What I do everyday is just have customers. There are more than ten Yakuza here. This letter must be hidden from them. If they find it, I will be beaten. If I try to run away from here, I will be killed, and my body will be thrown into the sea ... I do not know where I am now. All of us do not speak. There are lots of Thais and Filipinas. I am prohibited to talk to them ... The Yakuza are always watching me carefully. I am forced to stay at the place where the Yakuza live ... The Yakuzas are threatening me ... Living here is like living in hell.[844]

Her father came to find her after receiving this letter, but was unsuccessful.[845]

The Chinese Triads are loosely organized criminal groups. They remain flexible and relatively non-hierarchical. They collaborate with other organizations known as tongs, only some of which are criminal groups. Like the Yakuza, the Triads have alliances with most other major transnational crime groups and are extensively involved in sex trafficking and prostitution of women and children globally. There are also vast sex crime groups in many other countries, notably including Thailand, Taiwan, Vietnam, South Korea, Albania, Italy, India, Nigeria and other West African and South African networks, as well as extensive Mexican, Central American and South American groups.[846] There are complex and extensive interrelations between all these major criminal groups making targeting them to shut them down, or to prosecute leaders or players within their organizations, exceptionally difficult.

In-Person Recruiting of Children

Children or young people are recruited into prostitution and the sex trade both directly and indirectly. Vulnerable girls are directly targeted for recruitment such as those in foster homes or youth shelters, as well as indirectly, on the internet.[847] The "in-person" process usually involves the recruiter establishing some sort of relationship with the child who then receives some form of reward (e.g. food, accommodation, drugs, alcohol, cigarettes, affection, gifts, money) in exchange for performing sexual activities with them or, thereafter, with others of their choice. Children are often picked up in a public location such as a park, cinema, outside their school, on the street, or at a friend's house. Some victims of "street grooming" may believe that the offender is in fact an older "boyfriend" as is so aptly presented in the film *Lilya4ever*.[848] As one recruiter said:

> If there's a few of them leaving school, I'll pick the one I want and say something like "Free at last, then?" using my friendliest voice. This is the golden moment. She will judge you in seconds, so you have to get everything right. Your personal appearance, manners and expression have to be just right. Some girls might hold your skin colour or age against you. You can't control this but you can make sure you scrub up well, and give the right kind of eye contact and facial expressions.
>
> You have to look confident and comfortable. If you don't look comfortable then no one will feel comfortable with you. Less than 10 percent of normal communication is verbal; everything else lies in body language and vocal tones. If I've done everything right then they will respond with a smile.[849]

Pimps have most success recruiting vulnerable children. Homeless youths, runaways, poor children, those who have already experienced sexual or physical abuse, children in foster care, or who are abusing substances, and children with LGBTQ2SIA+ identities are all more

199

vulnerable to recruitment.[850] The majority of girls who end up in sex work, at least in the UK, pass through the hands of social services who struggle to prevent them being recruited or re-recruited into the gangs. Two separate research studies estimate that, in the UK, more than 70% of adult street prostitutes were once in the care of social services.[851]

Social services are limited in what they can do to protect vulnerable children in their care homes. There are limited resources – such as psychologists – who can help children deal with the emotional, physical or sexual traumas that they have experienced, or to cope with lives linked to drugs, sex work, or inadequate parenting. In addition, at age eighteen they are expected to leave the home and be independent, without any adequate preparation for earning an income, having a job or better still, a career, or the education or means to develop one. Alone, without family or societal supports, they have few prospects. Society today expects and requires parental support for youth well into their twenties if they are to be able to find a meaningful job and become independent. In the UK, for example, those operating care homes cannot prevent the girls from leaving if they wish to. Nicki's story of one night out reflects a common pattern. Out of money, she recalled her mother telling her that "if you did it" often enough, eventually someone would fall in love with you. She could only think that that wouldn't happen, she wouldn't get to have sex with men in the hope one might fall in love with her, if she stayed in the care home. So she left to go out. The carers asked where she was going as she left the building, but could not stop her physically as this would then be regarded as assault. She walked until she found a hotel where a party was ongoing. There she met a "friend," Vinnie:

> He takes her into another room. Bed with mattress, metal frame, rough carpet, sink, toilet, filthy shower, high and small window with bars across. It smells so bad she wants to retch [...]
> Men come in, one at a time.
> She quickly loses count [...] She is sick over the bed while one of them is on her. Still they come [...]
> The men are cruel. They say awful things and hurt her on purpose.

When the last one comes in, Nikki is curled up in a corner of the room. Blood and vomit covers the bed. She tells him she can't. He doesn't listen. He is fat, old, sweaty. He pulls her up, throws her onto the bed and starts to beat her, over and over. She can hear someone screaming. It's her. Her ears fill with hissing, humming, feels the repeated shock of something pounding her, stops feeling any pain. The last thing she sees is the door opening.[852]

Some time after this incident, in 2003, Vicki died of a drug overdose:

Papers report that Victoria 'Vicky' Agoglia, fifteen, a white girl who absconded from her privately run Rochdale children's home twenty-one times in two months, died of a heroin overdose after being used for sex by older men who paid her in alcohol, coke and heroin.

Vicky, who had ambitions of becoming a model, had previously reported being raped. She was in the care of Manchester Social Services, who had placed her in a care home run by a company called "Green Corns."[853]

The challenges faced by social services, with limited financial or personnel resources, are huge if they are to prevent Vicky's story being retold a multitude of times.

The exploiters have power over children by virtue of their age, gender, intellect, physical strength and/or economic or other resources. Many use friendship to gain the trust of children while grooming them for closer – and eventual – sexual contact. After time spent encouraging children to talk about their worries, or their homes and families, and, perhaps, how they are not being understood, or treated as they would like, they are invited to meet in person. Coercion and intimidation follow, with threats to reveal their secrets, or their – possibly clandestine – meetings, to their parents. These then lead to sexual engagement with their new "friend" or, later, his friends – ostensibly to be paid by them and to earn money that could be exchanged for example, for nice clothes or travel prospects. Violence follows if these offers are not readily accepted and engaged in. With this, a life of prostitution, pimped out by the original "friend" commences.[854] Sarah's experiences regarding how she was drawn into a life of sexual exploitation are not unusual:

> I don't know how I ended up like this. I suppose I came from a bad home. Mum and Dad beat me, threw me out [...] I used to wake up every day in pain, hungry. I used to wake up with a hope that the answer would come. I used to think the answer was love. Then I thought it was money. Then I thought it was something else. Then I thought it was drugs. Every day I try not to remember what happened the night before.[855]

So-called friendships that turn out to be manipulative sexual slavery may be initiated using the internet. As Samantha (a pseudonym) reported:

> I was lured into human trafficking through the internet. I met someone online. He made me feel special. He listened to me. He was patient. Never pushy. I later learned that he had reached out to hundreds and hundreds of girls across Canada. This is a common practice among many traffickers. What started out as a fantasy turned into a nightmare. He slowly pushed me into having sex for money. I never saw a penny. I was abused and beaten, and many times I thought I would die. I wanted to believe the best of my trafficker. I wanted to leave but I felt compelled to stay for fear of what would happen if I didn't. I eventually escaped because my trafficker died in a knife fight. My best friend was not so lucky. She had tried to leave, and he strangled her to death with an extension cord.[856]

Consequences for Children

The lives of the few who are rescued or who manage to escape from their traffickers are badly scarred. In addition to their sexual abuse, they have lost their body autonomy, and self determination, being sexually, and likely, medically abused (with multiple abortions for example), without any ability to determine their actions at any time. They will have been labelled as criminals, prostitutes, and victims, and emotionally, physically and cognitively abused over extended periods of time. Re-establishing their identity, autonomy and their self worth is slow and difficult.

> Because of the men, I cannot have a child normally. To this day I have nightmares. Sometimes I sleep with the lights on. My trauma is deep, and I sometimes feel that I am frozen – or even worse, I feel damaged and not worthy.
> I was traded in legal establishments, street corners, and strip clubs. I even had a few trips across the Great Lakes servicing shipmen at the age of 13. The scariest thing that happened to me was being held captive for a period of 43 hours and raped and tortured repeatedly at 14 years of age by a sexual predator who preyed on exploited girls.[857]

Victims tell how difficult it is to escape from their traffickers. They develop strong bonds with their captors as a survival strategy, commonly referred to as Stockholm syndrome. If they are to live, they must develop a stronger bond with their tormentors that outweighs their hatred of him or her. It is preferable for them to live under false pretenses or hopes than die by facing the truth and opposing him/her. They force themselves to genuinely like their captors out of fear that if they fake such affection and it is noticed they would be punished, beaten or killed for their deception.[858]

For these girls, there is rarely any escape. One sixteen-year-old in New Brunswick, Canada, was lucky to escape: she called an emergency help line telling them she did not know where she was. She was traced to a hotel parking lot and rescued after experiencing a month of sexual assault. Two young men aged 30 and 28, were charged with sexual assault, unlawful confinement, administering a noxious substance and recruiting a young person for the purpose of exploiting sexual services.[859] Even if survivors of sexual assault escape, their climb back into personal, interpersonal and societal health is exceedingly difficult. They report being haunted by depression, long-term traumatic stress disorder, anxiety and fear, with feelings of inadequacy, worthlessness, guilt, humiliation, and insecurity dominating them for years to come.[860] It is difficult to re-integrate into their family settings, or to enter into society and find employment as they face personal emotional, cognitive and physical obstacles, as well as prejudicial or discriminatory legal, social, educational, and interpersonal challenges resulting from their experiences.

Consequences for Perpetrators

The legal consequences for traffickers who might be caught, often appear to be of minimal deterrence. Sentences for gang members who are occasionally brought to justice for child exploitation are sometimes inexplicable.

> Ahmed was convicted along with eight others. He was jailed for nineteen years for two counts of rape, aiding and abetting a rape, sexual assault, conspiracy and a count of trafficking within the UK for sexual exploitation. After his conviction, he was put on trial again. This time for a fourteen-year campaign of rape against a girl who was three years old when he first attacked her. The girl was Asian. Ahmed may have attacked her more than 700 times.[861]

He was sentenced to twenty-two years in prison to be served concurrently with his first sentence of nineteen years. The second offence, of fourteen years of abuse of a girl, starting at the age of three years old, added only three years to his sentence, illustrating the consequences of enforcing concurrent rather than sequential sentences even in the event of a horrific and long-term infant-child-adolescent sex abuse case. Ahmed's co-defendants – other gang members – brought glowing character references from local community leaders including from a former teacher, and another person who could recite huge parts of the Koran and was thus, ostensibly, a good, religious man. Ahmed and his friends did not believe they had done anything wrong. Ahmed's co-defendants argued that the girls knew what they were doing. They were outraged at finding themselves in court and at being found guilty.

What Can We Do?

World conferences representing all countries on the globe, and UN agencies including UNICEF, the International Organization for Migration and the International Labour Organization, have undertaken programs that try to end child trafficking and the sexploitation of children. Some Non-Government Organizations such as Captive Daughters specifically focus on ending the sex trafficking of children. Legal entities in multiple countries are working towards increasing the minimum age at which children can be married and to restrict internet-based child sex abuse and paedophile sex tourism through criminalizing these behaviours.[862] Yet these attempts are, to date, not able to overcome the significant obstacles that exist to ending the exploitation of children for prostitution and trafficking, due largely to the hidden and extensive nature of these crimes.

Despite there being almost daily news reports about children being sexually abused in one way or another, or rescued, or trafficked, people in society continue to virtually ignore the issue. We continue to expect families to provide sex education for their children in many countries – regardless of their ability and lack of preparation to do this – and even where such programs are introduced into schools, we still encounter objections to them from parents with many preferring ignorance rather than knowledge as the best protection for their children. Sex education is not just about interpersonal sexual interactions including gender diversity and the importance of consent, as well as intercourse, but about rape, prostitution, abuse, trafficking, abortion, predators, the misuse of the internet to facilitate such activities, and their consequences. Children need to be prepared for the world in which they live, including the world of predators and how to recognize and avoid them if at all possible. It should also explicitly target boys and men to educate them to respect women's bodies and to not abuse.

We also lack the will, and often the ability, to track child sex traffickers. Even in the modern world, with its access to technology that can track where any individual with a cell phone is at any one time, and where they move, we are still unable to, or unwilling to, target the multiple child sex offenders. Theoretically it is possible to identify the sex centres of the world – the pubs, clubs, nightclubs, brothels, known hotels used for sexual encounters, taxis that serve them, etc. – and to trace and identify users. We do not often focus on the people who abuse the children but sometimes regard the children, the victims, as somehow complicit in their demeaning activities, and therefore, to blame. We are occasionally able to crack internet groups that provide child sex pornography for millions of users, but we do not always trace the users aggressively. Taking down some of the people running these websites is about as much as we are able to do. Without political will, supported by society, innovative use of the internet, large scale data analysis, and the provision of alternate, safer, lifestyles for these abused children, we will continue to fail children caught up in the global pandemic of child sex abuse and will continue to enable their predators.

Adrian, a survivor of the sex trade in Canada, suggests that "John" school, or sex offender school, is most helpful in eliminating sexual slavery:

> "I believe john [sic] school should be mandatory," she said, referring to one-day seminars for men who are attempting to purchase sex. Johns are given the option of having their picture appear in the next day's paper or attending john school where survivors of human trafficking explain the reality victims face in being forced to service men.
> "I have taught in john schools across Ontario for many years [...] I can tell you this fight is about changing the mindset of men. Men truly believe that prostitution is a case of two consenting adults. They have no clue as to why or how a woman entered to begin with or if she is

even of age. They don't know the domino effect it has
on her life or even on his own life, of his wife's life or
his kids' lives. The men become oblivious to it. [...]
John schools should be key in educating the men who
buy sex. And we know they work. Eighty percent of
men who go through john school stop paying for
sex."[863]

Some countries have taken further steps towards ending sex
trafficking of children. Canadian laws, for example, following
Scandinavian countries' examples, have become increasingly severe in
their condemnation of sexual abuse of those who traffic or abuse
children or adults. Private Bill C-268, proposed by Jill Smith, a
Member of Parliament, and strong advocate on behalf of trafficked and
abused people, introduced a five-year minimum sentence for those
caught trafficking children under the age of eighteen.[864] This minimum
sentence allowed girls who were rescued (and whose pimps were
caught) to recover without fear of their trafficker being released from
prison and finding her to re-enslave her or kill her for testifying against
him. These girls then have a little longer to rebuild their lives than if
their tormentor were to be released only months after capture, as had
been the case prior to this bill being passed. Bill C-310, that followed,
resulted in Canadians who trafficked children or adults abroad being
tried in Canada as though they had committed this crime in Canada. A
minimum sentence of five years, however, remains ridiculously
inadequate for the crime of sexual abuse and trafficking of children
and reflects society's tolerance of, acceptance of, and enabling of, child
sex abuse.

Part 4: Preventing Abuse

We face a global climate that enables child sex abuse. A concerted effort to reduce or eliminate child sex abuse requires collaboration among global, national and regional organizations to change this conceptual model. Tackling child sex abuse in any society requires the co-ordination of multiple differing societal structures. Only the political organization and management of any region or society – such as the United Nations or many of the economic or regional subgroups such as the OECD, G7/8 or similar – could have the authority and responsibility to co-ordinate and implement programs that are designed to eliminate child sex abuse.

Preventive programs need to overcome the multiple ways in which we enable child sex abuse. These include not listening to and believing children's reports of abuse, i.e. respecting children's rights and agency; instituting or strengthening preparation for parenthood programs to incorporate these issues; closer monitoring of institutional care of children such as in schools or sports organizations; offering societal awareness programs that call for self identification of paedophilic tendencies; enhancing research into optimal treatment programs for both abusers and the survivors of their actions; providing societal supports for victims; facilitating education of government, educational, legal, and medical professionals regarding child sex abuse and abusers; supporting academic study of artificial intelligence methods of tracking and identifying internet sex abusers and sex traffickers; supporting ongoing efforts to eliminate sexual abuse in the military and in times of war; supporting media attention to these issues so that global awareness can be raised even further regarding the plight of these children; and overcoming our almost global aversion to discussion of sex in all its nuances that remains a primary obstacle to be overcome.

Strategic Goals

Our world has created a climate of abuse that ignores, or justifies, and even enables child sex abuse. The problem occurs on every level of our society: individual, institutional, societal, and global. It requires a multifaceted approach that targets all levels of society from global leaders, national politicians, religious leaders, educators, lawyers, police, psychologists and health care professionals, economic players, communities, parents, and the children themselves. Anything less will not be effective. The steps we need to take are many and varied. We need to:

Globally

- Create awareness of the extensiveness of child sexual abuse and particularly of how our world enables, facilitates, endorses and promotes child sex abuse.

- Recognize that children are not to blame and that perpetrators are. We need to reframe perpetrators and their facilitators, rather than primarily victims, as the targets of our interventions.

- Face and counter the corruption that lies beneath the economic incentives supporting the lucrative sex trade.

- Utilize substantial technical and intellectual intervention to address the misuse of the internet to exploit children sexually. This includes monitoring, identifying and prosecuting porn websites that include images of children in sexual activities and mobilize banking restrictions on perpetrators accessing child porn sites.

- Reform religious institutions to facilitate their prevention of child sex abuse among clergy, and their identification and treatment of offenders including referral to civil policing authorities.

Within the Family/Home Setting

- Create an environment in which children feel free to talk to their parents about sex and where they know they can report abuse and be believed and supported.

- Change our emphasis on teaching children, and particularly girls, how to avoid inciting abuse, or how to defend themselves against abuse, to instead, focus on teaching children of all genders to respect others and not to abuse. Teaching consent as an integral part of any sexual encounter, or indeed any interpersonal encounter, is central, and crucial.

- Overcome our reluctance to discuss sexuality, to prepare both parents and children for their sexual lives, as well as their teachers, professional caregivers and recreational leaders. We need to accept that sex is a part of life and is an evolutionary imperative. We need to learn how to enjoy it and how to prepare our children for a far healthier approach to sexuality and to their lives in a sexual world than they currently face. Developing an acceptance of the beauty and enjoyment that we can gain from healthy sexual interactions – in all their multiple variations – rather than shaming sex and hiding it under a guise of guilt is necessary.

At a Societal Level

- Increase children's rights and agency with regard to all aspects of their lives.

- Address some of the myths that serve to excuse child sex offenders, such as "men have needs they have to satisfy," "children or adolescents choose to engage in sex work as it helps them to earn money," "sex with children is a way of showing love for them."

- Condemn the commercialization of child sex abuse and establish effective means of countering offenders.

At a National Level

- Harness political will to address this issue and encourage strengthening of laws against child sex abusers.

- Educate, and implement monitoring of, policing, customs, and border control or other law enforcing authorities regarding child sex abuse.

- Monitor travel agency activity to identify, prevent and eliminate travel for child sex abuse.

- Revise laws to avoid victim blaming and protection for perpetrators.

- Modify legal proceedings to include greater sensitivity for victims and their families, and increase punishments for perpetrators.

At a Global Level

Action at the global level is essential if we are to counter the many aspects of child sex abuse that currently occur. Major United Nations Organizations have recently begun to address this issue within the context of all forms of violence against children and not only that of sexual abuse. In 2016, a global strategy named INSPIRE was initiated by ten agencies including the World Health Organization, the United States Centers for Disease Control and Prevention, the Global Partnership to End Violence Against Children, the Pan American Health Organization,

213

the President's Emergency Program for AIDS Relief, Together for Girls, the United Nations Children's Fund, the United Nations Office on Drugs and Crime, the United States Agency for International Development, and the World Bank.[865] INSPIRE includes seven strategies:

- I: Implementation and enforcement of laws.

- N: Norms and values.

- S: Safe environments.

- P: Parent and caregiver support.

- I: Income and economic strengthening.

- R: Response and support services.

- E: Education and life skills.

In addition, multi-sectorial action and coordination as well as monitoring and evaluation actions are advocated to help connect and strengthen the seven strategies. While a global strategy like the INSPIRE initiative will, no doubt, develop multiple helpful tools for implementation of each of the seven components of this program, and will also require national commitment to its global implementation, each country that signs on to the program will have to develop and undertake its own national implementation plan. A grand global initiative will only be as effective as each individual country's commitment to it. Child sex abuse is both a national problem and a global one, consequently, a truly intersectional development is needed.

Some of the steps advocated in this global outreach program, and detailed in this book, are summarized in this chapter, although these are only the first steps that we need to take. The problem is vast and resolving it is almost overwhelming. It is like fighting the Hydra: an enemy that is changeable, requiring us to remain vigilant regarding emerging systems of abuse. For example, as the residential schools closed in Canada, the abuse of Indigenous children transferred from residential schools to foster care. Further, as time and society changed, paedophiles became more likely to pick up children using social media rather than in parks or outside schools. We need to become far more assertive in demanding that our political, religious, professional, and business leaders, take up the challenge.

Preventing Child Sexual Abuse

Societal institutions that require change to reduce child sex exploitation include Education, the Family, Religion, Law and Policing, Cyberspace, Health and Welfare, and the Economy.

Unfortunately, only addressing one or a few of these levels of societal functioning, will be insufficient to reduce child sex abuse, as they are interdependent. Ideally all should be approached systematically so that the intrinsic links between them can be broken. At the root of the problem lies the failure of our world to accept that perpetrators still commit child sex abuse and that preventing perpetrators from taking abusive actions remains a primary need.

Until such time as this emphasis is widespread and pervasive, we need to improve education about child sex abuse among teachers, parents and children. It is not enough to alert teachers to the signs of abuse in families unless parents are also aware of this and are enabled to establish healthy, open relationships with their children so that the latter trust them to share activities that cause them discomfort before these become egregious events. Given that parents, step parents, siblings or close family friends may be the primary abuser/s the responsibility for providing an emotionally safe, and respectful place where children can share their experiences of abuse and be listened to, and believed, remains a shared responsibility among parents, teachers, and all those who have contact with them. Children's voices need to be heard, respected, and trusted. Parents need to be alerted to internet facilitated child sex abuse and how to assist if this is identified or suspected. A ripple effect occurs if a child is sexually abused in school or in the family. Such vulnerable children are increasingly prone to grooming and recruitment by predators outside the home, within child-oriented organizations such as sporting bodies, or religious institutions, or on the internet. These predatory individuals or groups may be linked to child sex abuse rings both locally and through global trafficking enterprises. These may in turn be facilitated by policing services and international travel authorities that turn a blind eye. Laws need to be severe enough to deter potential abusers and to punish them severely when caught. At present our punitive laws against perpetrators are sadly lacking in many parts of the world. Economic vulnerability also predisposes children to seek friends, occupations, and assistance outside the family including in potentially abusive situations. The entire cascade of failures across each and all these societal structures needs to be targeted to effectively prevent the sexual abuse of children.

Education

Sex education for children typically focuses on teaching potential victims – mostly girls – to avoid attracting sexual predators. A victim blaming philosophy underlies this. In contrast, teaching children to respect others at all times should be the central value. All interactions and especially intimate or sexual encounters must be based on respect and mutual consent. All children need to recognize and to say no to unwanted touching although such touching should never occur and should be targeted as the first step to condemn in eradicating child sex abuse. Education of children, their parents, teachers and child organization group leaders is a fundamental link in the chain of child sex abuse. While a start has been made towards including sex education of children in schools, these programs need to address not only the physiological basis of sexual organs and their functions but the psychological issues involved in negotiating sexual relationships with their peers or with adults. Such education should, ideally, go far beyond the immediate question of avoiding unwanted sexual harassment but extend to strengthening the self confidence and self assertiveness of the children. Children, and particularly the girl child who is so often taught to take a more submissive role, need to be encouraged to stand up for themselves, not only in a sexual context but in life. If we teach girls to be accommodating and compliant in everyday life, we cannot expect them to be assertive in their sexual encounters.

While it is hoped that such education will prevent unwanted sexual contact, it is still likely to occur, making teaching children how to react to or resist such touching becomes important. We have to teach children to say "no" to unwanted contact, to shout if necessary, while still acknowledging the unfortunate truth that this is not sufficient. We need to teach them the next step after that. Do we simply advise them to tell their parents or teachers? Do we encourage them to report unacceptable behavior they may observe with regard to either themselves or their friends to authority figures or can they stay silent out of fear, embarrassment or reluctance to "tell on" their friends or family? Will they be heard – really listened to – if they report abuse? Better still do we teach them to shout out if molested, to create a disturbance, to insist they will tell others? Even more importantly do we facilitate their learning methods of self defence, such as karate, that teaches defensive movements in addition to encouraging assertiveness?

We need to educate, not only children, but teachers, parents, doctors, camp counsellors, adolescent baby sitters, and any others who care for children, about how to respond if a child reports abuse. They need to know how to recognize signs of abuse and how to respond appropriately if a child shares this experience with them. They need to know that children's trust must be respected and their stories given credence. Their stories must also be acted on with further investigation and those responsible held to account. Not acting on these accounts, when you have the power to do so, makes the listener an accomplice to the abuse.

Such sex abuse education needs to address the threat of predators who use internet platforms. Teachers, parents and children need to be familiar with cybersex abuse. They need to become media and internet literate: i.e. understanding how the internet or media messages can be, or are, manipulative, persuasive, deceptive, and distorting of truth. The early signs of grooming, recruitment, temptation to participate or meet in person, leading to (misplaced) trust, emotional relationships, promises of benefits, provision of friendship until eventual abduction, kidnapping or forced sexual encounters and forced sexual activities with strangers. Simply teaching children not to talk to strangers, or to get into cars with strangers, is not sufficient. Predatory actions have progressed far beyond this in today's world and teachers, parents and children need to be warned about them. Remaining alert to such signs, keeping a close eye on all children but especially vulnerable children who might be more easily responsive to offers of "friendship" from outside the family, is essential for teachers and other child caregivers. Teacher education must encompass such concerns.

Advocating sex education in school presumes that those who teach such programs are comfortable with this subject matter as well as knowledgeable and skilled in discussing sexual issues with prepubescent and adolescent children of all genders. Recognition of the varying needs of children of all sexualities and genders (LGBTQ2SIA+) with regard to sexuality and sex abuse is a prerequisite. Do we meet this need in a respectful and sensitive manner? Training the teachers is also a necessary undertaking to facilitate education to prevent child sex abuse. Teachers need to be well trained and well reimbursed for undertaking these responsibilities. They also need to not be offenders themselves, unlike Ryan Jarvis, a former London, Canada, high school teacher, who was recently sentenced to six months in prison for secretly filming a fourteen-year-old female student's upper body and breasts during class, with a camera hidden in a pen.[866] Teachers also need to be given both the authority to manage sexual abuse situations as well as the responsibility to do so. At present, can they chastise a student for inappropriate predatory behaviour? Can they intervene to stop child bullying? Can they punish child-on-child abusers in the classroom? What action can they take if sexual abuse or bullying is suspected? Or reported to them? Is this currently well managed at its earliest manifestations in children's interactions?

Before such educational programs are instituted it is likely that education of government leaders will also be needed to obtain their endorsement and financial backing for such programs. We should develop child sex abuse education sessions for Politicians, Ministers of Education, Law and Order, Health and Welfare, Religion and others who determine child care within any global, regional or national government organizations. We need to recognize that some of these politicians and ministerial level authorities may also be perpetrators themselves.[867] We need to emphasize that having one or two sex education sessions in, for example, tenth grade and twelfth grade, is simply not enough to prevent a culture of sexual abuse in a school. As Rena Kosowsky reported regarding her high school's approach, an atmosphere of sexism pervaded her school life that requires far more than an hour or two of discussion to dispel.

> There were jokes about girls being less intelligent, jokes about women belonging in the kitchen, and constant objectification of female students' bodies. [...] Many boys did not understand the parameters of consent. For example, many were unaware that someone drunk cannot consent.[868]

It is time to take a more proactive stance and to teach children not to be abusers. We need to teach all children respectful attitudes and manners towards all others at all times, and particularly in sexual relationships We also need to teach them about their own bodies and how to manage them. We should teach children how to manage the internet and its perverted aspects, rather than to hide children from abusers or from the digital world around them. Teaching all children how to prepare for and achieve a positive and happy sexual life may be a more innovative and potentially positive approach.[869] Educating all children about their right to negotiate a respectful and positive sexual relationship with consenting parties being able to express, and have their partners respect their likes and dislikes, preferences and limits, may be a far more valuable approach to preventing abuse.

The Family

Much child sex abuse occurs within the family perpetrated by family members and friends of the family and is often ignored, or hidden from others, to avoid scandal or shame thereby enabling the perpetrator. Some parents and relatives abuse children in their families. How well prepared are parents for family life? Raising children? And addressing child sexual abuse issues that arise in the family? What cultural issues facilitate child sex abuse and how do we counter them? These include beliefs or societal customs that endorse paedophilic activities, or the use of rape as a means of retaliation for other rapes, or pubertal rites that involve sexual initiation? Virtually globally, we provide lengthy education for almost every career that we engage in as adults except that of parenting. When will we develop educational programs that provide preparation for parenthood, not only during pregnancy and in preparation for birth, but for child care, child rearing, child sex abuse recognition and prevention, discipline, parent-child relationships, conflict resolution, psychological sensitivity, and respect for each other and for children, adolescents and youth? Violence against women and children is a global phenomenon currently heightened due to the Covid-19 pandemic with its associated stay home admonitions. How well do we offer help, shelter, and safety for both women and children (the most common targets of familial sexual abuse) in our societies? Do we facilitate mothers' ability to report their partner's abusive behaviour, both towards themselves and/or to their children? Such mothers are often both victims in an abusive relationship and perpetrators if they do not report child abuse. And, even after saying this, we do not know if such educational programs or resources for assistance would prevent the abuse of children in family settings, although it is worthy of consideration.

In particular, we need to give particular consideration to the avoidance of sexual abuse of vulnerable children. The horrific experiences of the Duplessis orphans who were housed in psychiatric institutes in order to gain higher financial compensation for their carers, but with inadequate physical and psychological care, and children removed from their families through such actions as the Residential school system in Canada should never be allowed to reoccur. We need to recall that such abuse was imposed by the care authorities themselves, both religious and governmental, and justified by them for decades as being desirable means to dubious ends. These authorities avoided responsibility and accountability for their actions for decades – and still do. Recent discoveries of long-known about deaths of hundreds, if not thousands, of Residential school children's graves at Canadian Residential school sites, have again raised awareness of these injustices. And yet, even as I write this, Indigenous children in Canada continue to be removed from their families, often without cause, by social services, indicating that we are far from resolving this problem. Where poverty is used as a justification to remove Indigenous children from their families, it is not sufficient grounds for the same actions against non-Indigenous families. Social services that implement such colonial and racist policies need to be eliminated and replaced with equitable, supportive systems.

We also need to address child sex abuse in everyday society, such as when joining sports teams, or organizations such as the Boy Scouts, or even something as apparently innocuous as a ballet company[870] or a University School of the Arts.[871] We need to develop appropriate procedures to be followed for the prevention of child sex abuse in these child care settings, as well as adequate reporting, monitoring, and evaluation of such care settings and procedures. Families need to be made aware of the possibility that such settings are used by predators and to remain alert and respectful of accounts reported to them by their children. Any signs of reluctance to return to, or engage in, such activities by their children may well indicate fear of, or concern about, potential harm and should be investigated carefully and acted on/ reported if reflecting abusive experiences.

Sexual abuse of vulnerable children is a problem compounded by economic as well as physical vulnerability. Nowhere is this more obvious than in the institution of Child Marriage, where young girls are married, or sold, to much older men, and forced into sexual relationships even as prepubescent children, usually for the financial benefit of their parents. Government intervention to reduce poverty, reward parents for not involving their children in such schemes and for monitoring the incidence of child marriage is urgently needed in many countries.

221

Religion

Ideologies and religions have enabled child sex perpetrators for centuries. The Catholic Church has come under significant scrutiny globally for its horrendous child sex abuse actions, but even more so for its continued and sometimes continuing efforts to protect and enable perpetrators. But it is not alone in this charge. It is just the one that has received the most significant media coverage in recent decades and has been the one where the majority of known child sex abuse has occurred. Members of almost all major religions have been charged with child sex abuse at times. In addition, child sex abuse occurs in a-religious societies as well as in those swayed by cults that carry their followers along on the wave of an ideological, if not religious, passion. It is not religion itself that is the inspiration for child sex abuse but the protection that religious institutions or ideologically inspired cults offer that provides opportunities for child sex abuse and enables this cruelty. Countering child sex abuse must address the pernicious sexual abuse that has occurred and has been protected by such institutions.

The extensive negative publicity that the Catholic Church and schools have received in recent decades regarding the abuse and, particularly, sexual abuse of children has made the Church's position untenable in technologically advanced settings, at least, if not globally. Strong adherents to traditional values within the Church, however, make movement from their autocratic positions difficult. Issues such as the autonomy of the Church and its independence from secular society and judicial process, celibacy, the sanctity of the confessional, the role of women in the Church, controversies surrounding divorce, abortion, contraception and homophobia, as well as the importance of "saving souls" make significant changes in current approaches difficult to foresee. Until such time as these values shift towards a more liberal approach, the current decline in support for the institution of the Church – if not the Catholic faith itself – is likely to continue. Orders such as the notorious Christian Brothers – major culprits in the stories told here – are in steep decline and are likely to disappear, largely through a paucity of novitiate callings.[872]

222

Despite the extensive and dramatic global exposure of child sex abuse within the Catholic Church, particularly in recent decades, it is inappropriate to discount all other instances of child sex abuse as of lesser extent or importance, simply because they have not received as much media attention. Numerically speaking, child sex abuse is far more extensive within a global context due to sex trafficking, child marriage, and internet-based abuse. Currently these instances are exposed in global newspaper reports a few times a month but the reports are sparsely distributed geographically and lack focused media attention. Sex trafficking, child marriage, and internet-based abuse provide enormous challenges to combatting child sex abuse, far greater, numerically at least, than that occurring within religiously or ideologically inspired institutions.

Law

Child sex abusers have been shielded from law enforcement thus presenting little deterrence against child sex abuse. The legal system itself is often responsible for compounding the abuse. For example, a predictable and relatively common effect of child sex abuse is pregnancy, even in children younger than nine years old. In regions where abortion is banned or inaccessible due to legal and political impediments, those children are forced, by law, to survive a pregnancy and birth of their rapist's child. Some countries do not allow abortion even after rape or incest, the latter often requiring the child to remain in the same household as her abuser.

Only a tiny percentage of abusers are ever prosecuted and even fewer of these are ever convicted. Until recently, most countries have had statutes of limitations preventing any cases of child sex abuse from being brought against offenders when the abuse happened many years ago. In the USA, these statutes of limitations are currently being lifted or extended to at least fifty years after the offence is committed allowing many more charges to be brought against abusers.

Even more egregiously, the Church has prevented cases going to court by filing for bankruptcy. At least six dioceses have followed this path although none have actually gone bankrupt. In each case where a bankruptcy declaration was filed it was done on the day of, or the eve of, a trial that would have exposed secrets about how much the church officials knew or covered up for the sexual misconduct of Priests. As a bankruptcy filing halts all other forms of litigation against the debtor, those involved in the child abuse cases have been spared public exposure.[873] Settlements reached by the Catholic Church are estimated to be in the region of $3 billion, and with many more cases likely to be charged as the statute of limitations is extended or lifted, this figure could increase significantly in future.

The current and ongoing exposure of extensive child sex abuse within the Boy Scouts of America will likely also result in multiple settlements for abused children. The Organization has also declared bankruptcy, ostensibly to facilitate the legal settlements for the 100,000 children who have registered claims against the group.[874] Further reports regarding this will likely be forthcoming in future years.

Laws against child sex abuse in many countries are lax, or if stringent, are often not implemented. Such laws need to enforce the requirement that sex must always be consensual, and must take into account the severity of the crime for the victim. Recovery from rape or sexual assault can take decades or even a lifetime for most survivors, yet punishments for perpetrators may be short, often months or in many cases only a year or two, especially when sentences are reduced or commuted for "good behaviour."

Implementing new laws, or changing existing laws is often difficult and sometimes opposed by society. For example, following the rape and murder of a seven-year-old girl, Zainab Ansari, in 2018, Pakistan introduced a new law – the Alert, Response and Recovery Bill – to institute rapid police searches for missing children and commitment to finding the abusers within three months. Zainab's killer Imran Ali was found three weeks after her body was discovered but it was Zainab's relatives who had obtained the CCTV footage of the murderer rather than the criminal authorities. Ali had previously been found guilty of similar crimes against six other girls.[875] Public outcries against rape have led to measures to create a national sex offenders register, protect the identity of victims and allow the chemical castration of some offenders. Special fast-track courts will hear rape cases and will be expected to reach a verdict within four months.[876] At least, in Pakistan, virginity tests on survivors of sexual assault have recently been outlawed, in addition to a ban on such tests for all other reasons.[877] These tests, involving examination of the hymen and/or the insertion of two fingers into the vagina were customarily used to assess women who reported rape to determine whether or not sexual assault had occurred thereby assaulting the girl/woman again. Similarly, in Myanmar, the rape of a three-year-old girl, popularly named as "Victoria," allegedly assaulted at her nursery school, rocked the country. Although a staff member was charged with the crime, DNA evidence was inconclusive and staff denied his involvement in the assault, allowing him to escape punishment. Myanmar, however, is a largely rural country and elders in local communities often manage offences. Rape by men is not a crime in the country, and girls are often encouraged to marry their abuser.[878]

In Tanzania, legal punishments imposed for child sex abuse may not be implemented fully. Two men jailed for life for raping ten primary school girls were pardoned by the Tanzanian president after serving thirteen years of their sentence, indicative of the lack of concern evidenced in many places by crimes of sexual abuse, even, of multiple children.[879] In Sierra Leone, more than 8,500 cases – more than double the previous year's figures – of sexual abuse were reported in 2018 resulting in a new law imposing life imprisonment for sexual penetration of a minor. However, this law may not always be implemented with cases not often being prosecuted and punishments being minimal. For example, a fifty-six-year-old man who raped a six-year-old girl was recently sentenced to only one year in prison.[880]

Definitions of sexual abuse and sexual assault sometimes allow for vicious crimes and rape to be dealt with lightly. In Mexico, a judge was suspended after a public outcry regarding his lenient sentencing of a man accused of sexually abusing a ten-year-old girl. The judge refused to pursue a charge of "corrupting a minor" which carries a maximum sentence of eight years, instead accusing the perpetrator of sexual abuse which carries a lesser punishment of six years at most. The Judge's argument was based on his belief that the abuser's actions were not "corruption of a minor" unless they caused pleasure. The defendant, Luis Alonso, was head of human resources for the local police until his arrest. He has been suspended without pay and is now under investigation. Anger over numerous cases of violence against women has been building in the community.[881]

Under Spanish law evidence of violence or intimidation is required for a conviction of rape or sexual assault. In 2019, a Barcelona court convicted five men, who had taken turns raping a drugged and unconscious fourteen-year-old, of sexual abuse rather than sexual assault. They were sentenced to ten to twelve years instead of fifteen to twenty years, in consequence. Public reaction was strong and calls are being made for the country to change its law.[882] Recently, multiple reforms to child abuse laws in Spain have been driven by Spanish resident and pianist James Rhodes, himself abused as a child. These changes are making it easier for children to report abuse and they are now required to only testify once, before a specialized judge, in contrast to having to testify in court and even to face their rapist. The statute of limitations for reporting abuse has also been extended to fifteen years after the age of thirty compared to eighteen years after the event as existed previously. Sadly, sexual abuse of children is increasing in Spain, with a 40% increase in 2018 compared to the previous year.

Laws in many European countries such as in Denmark, as well as globally, put the onus on the victim to stop themselves being raped rather than on the perpetrator to not commit the act – which arises from, and reinforces, a pervasive victim blaming attitude. Such definitions do not acknowledge that in rape situations, women or girls may freeze, or they may be asleep, drunk, drugged or sedated. For example, in Canada in 2021, the Supreme Court upheld a conviction of a fifteen-year-old boy of sexual assault of a fourteen-year-old girl. They had both been drinking at a beach party and had intercourse a short distance from the bonfire. The girl did not, however, have any memory of the sexual activity. She was found to be unable to give consent and that the boy was clearly aware of this.[883] Only eight out of thirty-one European countries have a consent-based definition of rape indicating that in law, one's body is accessible until you say no or fight back. It should rather be that your body is not accessible until you say yes.[884] The right of rapists to have sex – or to control another's body with regard to sex – is inherent in these lax laws and their application.

The major world powers of China, Russia and the United States, have differing positions regarding laws against child sex abuse. While there are fewer reports of child sex abuse emerging from China, there is no reason to believe that this occurs there less often. One incident that did find its way into western media reports revealed that Chinese police were investigating claims of sexual molestation and "needlemarks" on children at a Beijing kindergarten: Children, some as young as three, relayed accounts of a naked adult male conducting so-called "medical check ups" on students, who were also unclothed.[885] In 2019, a thirteen-year-old Chinese minor sexually assaulted a ten-year-old girl, stabbed her to death, and then dumped her body in a ditch. Because the age of criminal responsibility in China is fourteen, the teenager was given three years of "rehabilitation," and will not spend any time in jail. Public protest has been significant calling for the law protecting thirteen-year-olds to be changed. It appears that, in recent years, there have been reports of Chinese gangs recruiting minors to implement sexual crimes, and who would not be severely prosecuted if caught, to exploit this Chinese law.[886] In Russia too, reports indicate that sexual "freedoms" since the collapse of the Soviet Union have exploded leading to increasing sexual abuse of children as well as adults. While a signatory to the UN Rights of Child, there are few laws in the country that comprehensively address child sex crimes as well as inadequate implementation of these. Record keeping and reporting is inconsistent, resulting in confusing accounts of child sexual abuse across this vast country.[887] The USA has also noted record levels of child sex abuse, particularly in the form of online photos and videos of children being sexually abused leading to an executive order issued by the President in 2020 to combat these and related events like human trafficking.[888]

Clearly, global standards of appropriate laws have yet to be achieved. Definitions of child sexual abuse vary regarding who is a child and when the age of responsibility is attained, for example in countries where child marriage is still common. How child sex abuse is defined varies widely ranging from a perpetrator-favouring approach in which the victim is blamed to one which condemns the abusers. Progressive laws are moving towards punishing the perpetrator rather than the victims: For example, targeting the users of sex workers rather than persecuting prostitutes in Canada, even though these still require more nuanced thought to be viewed as fair or safe laws for the women and girls involved. Finally, Bill C-36 made the purchase of sexual services in Canada illegal. Canadian laws now decriminalize the girls and women being prostituted and make the purchase of sex a crime as well as making it illegal to benefit from the work of sex workers. Instead of targeting the girls, they criminalize the men who pay for sex both in Canada and internationally.[889]

The child's ability or inability to refuse sexual contact or penetration is often disregarded in law such as when drugged: Date rape for example, is an acknowledged concern for many young girls. The severity of the punishment metered out bears little relation to the extent of injury to the sexually abused child or the lengthy recovery from the crime that is often required – both physically and psychologically. Nor do legal systems always acknowledge the immense difficulties faced by victims, especially child victims, regarding reporting their abuse and – often – repeatedly having to relive their experiences in front of police, carers, judges, juries, and even their abuser/s. Legal systems need to acknowledge and accommodate the psychological support that is required for both victims and their families when going through the legal confrontation system. As Allie reported, when she revealed that her mother's boyfriend had sexually abused her, the Canadian police response was humiliating. She was told that such sex abuse claims never result in convictions, and with chuckles, was encouraged not to pursue the case. Her mother persisted in approaching the police, with charges being ultimately laid against the perpetrator.[890]

Clearly legal systems globally have not reached any consensus of opinion on just what constitutes sexual abuse, particularly of children, and how this should be processed in law, or punished. Nor does the law recognize that most cases of sexual abuse never reach the courts.

Clearly, the obstacles to reporting abuse and pursuing legal action against perpetrators are significant enough to prevent most survivors from pursuing this line of action. Global legal systems currently enable child sex abuse by being lenient on perpetrators and making it difficult and disillusioning for children to report their abuse. A recent case in the USA clearly illustrates this problem: A young man pleaded guilty to the rape and sexual assault of four teenage girls when he was eighteen. While raping one sixteen-year-old who was crying throughout the attack, he told her to "stop being a baby."[891] He violated the terms of his probation while awaiting trial. Despite this, he was sentenced to only eight years of probation and registration as a sex offender, but was told by the judge, who admitted praying for guidance, that jail time was, to his mind, inappropriate.

Policing

Effective policing may or may not be present in many countries sometimes ignoring, facilitating or enabling child sex abuse. In some countries where child sex abuse is rampant, or economically advantageous to policing authorities, there may be little if any effective policing. In global trafficking networks, police are recruited by traffickers to protect them – and to return children or girls who run away from their forced sex captivity back to their captors. The global scourge of corruption extends into the various *mafiosi* involved in child sex abuse as well. Border police are also part of this international child sex trafficking network. So too are customs officials who turn a blind eye to transnational sex abuse and travel for sexual exploitation of children by tourists.

Children or girls who report sex abuse crimes often report being viewed as participants in the crime. Victim blaming is entrenched in rape myths with common perceptions that girls "ask for it." There are major global policing organizations that are undertaking ground-breaking efforts to monitor and arrest child sex abusers, such as Interpol and Europol. They are responsible for arresting most of the perpetrators of cybersex who provide images of children from babies to adolescents being abused on websites and who facilitate the viewing of such child photographs and videos across the globe.

Although not directly involved in daily police work within countries, the Military provides global or international policing services. This sector of society has also come under fire for its use of sexual services of women and, sometimes, some underage girls. In times of war or genocide, rape is used as a weapon of war, with targets ranging from toddlers to the elderly. Given the vast size of international forces, particularly in war, but also as peacekeepers, such services lead to the development of a prostitution work force in neighbouring areas. In some countries this has developed into a career choice for thousands of girls who have few other options open to them. Even in times of peace, soldiers, peacekeepers and aid organization have been reported for sexually abusing the people they have come to protect. Alternative approaches need to be developed: If sexual "R and R" is regarded as important by Military forces then they need to provide for this in legal and respectful ways.

Cyberspace

The enormous influence of global information sharing through the internet is a force for both good and evil. While most today cannot imagine how we ever lived before the digital age and are surprised on an almost daily basis at the stunning advances in information technology that are occurring today, mostly for our benefit, we can also acknowledge the deleterious impact that this is having as a result of increasing child sexual abuse. The internet fuels the sale of child sexual abuse images and consequently facilitates the need for, and abuse of children, to meet this increased demand for such images. It eases access to child sexual abuse while preserving privacy and concealment for both the perpetrator and the viewer. It also exposes viewers to violence in sex. Sex as rape, gang-rape, child sex, rough sex, abusive sex, and sex that depicts the satisfaction of men with little or any concern for the women's needs and preferences regarding sexual pleasure, is readily available. While violence in sex – both as fantasy or in reality – can be pleasurable if conducted with respect for each other's consensual agreement, it can also be potentially misleading if young people are not guided in its safe and appropriate use. Without substantial education regarding healthy, consensual, and respectful sex, in schools and in families, and as erotica on the internet, to counter the ready availability of abusive pornographic presentations of sexual encounters, there will be little to oppose the growing child's acceptance of violent and disrespectful sexual encounters that are readily available on the internet, as being the norm, and desired by both men and women. At the same time, we need to acknowledge the value and assistance that porn sites provide for adults and not condemn them in order to prevent child exposure to abusive sexual imagery.

The issue is complex. Exposing younger children to violent sexual pornography – before they are developmentally able to understand and comprehend this – appears to have negative consequences including an acceptance that this is what sex is about. Some have suggested requiring age verification before allowing young people access to online pornography sites, although how to facilitate this without restricting adult access to such sites, or how to identify falsified identities of users, is challenging and remains controversial.[892] On the other hand, consenting adults may well appreciate and enjoy such actions or fantasies, if they are produced safely, meaning that demonizing all violent sexual acts is not appropriate as they may be beneficial and enjoyed by many without leading to harm to sexual partners. More important is to provide a balanced and respectful means of educating youth about sexuality and its multiple variations to facilitate an understanding and ability to respectfully engage in consensual acts that are pleasurable to both or all partners, no matter what sexual variation is tried. Learning how to use the internet sexually and safely is urgently needed.

We need to use the digital technology we have towards preventing perpetrators from abusing children as well as to save victims. For instance, using the internet to find missing children – those abducted for service as beggars, in the sex trade, for organ trade, ransom, or sale – can be facilitated using "missing children" pages on such forums as

231

Facebook. These can help to locate and reunite children with their families as is happening in Egypt and Romania where missing children are particularly frequent.[893] Websites that include child sex images – or thinly disguised child sex abuse – are readily available. Those on the dark web are more difficult to access but can be identified by skilled personnel. It is now virtually impossible to hide our identities on the internet. Surely, we can use this knowledge to trace and apprehend child sex abusers and facilitators? Most importantly, using big data analysis should allow us to "follow the money" globally to identify and trace corrupt transactions when perpetrators are identified. No doubt many are already working on such solutions but there needs to be major political, financial, technological and material support directed towards strengthening such approaches.

Creating a database of violence against children to monitor child sex abuse is needed. Both prevalence studies and qualitative studies that explain the settings in which abuse occurs are required. At present, much of the available information on child sex abuse is based on limited local or country analyses, Interpol and/or Europol reports, personal accounts of experiences of child sexual abuse, newspaper reports of specific instances of crime, and some International Aid agency reports of programs and initiatives undertaken to try to combat this problem. It is not surprising that efforts to counter the tragedy of child sex abuse are insufficient, given that the crime is global, vast, takes many different forms, is largely hidden on the internet, by corrupt authorities, by inadequate monitoring tools, or within families, and is virtually taboo to address. In Canada, for example, neither the Criminal Code nor the Immigration and Refugee Protection Act differentiate between sexual, labour, and other forms of exploitation, making it extremely challenging to specifically identify sex trafficking.[894] The rapid development of big data analysis coupled with global internet access, may facilitate monitoring, or more precise monitoring, of global child sexual abuse, as well as the potential implementation of curbs to such behaviours. Identifying global criminal groups, or local perpetrators, monitoring them and assessing their activities is a necessary start. We need to explore how to utilize artificial intelligence to track child sex abusers, identify and follow child sex trafficking routes, find centres where abuse takes place and monitor the abusers who frequent them – both for sale of children or for their sexual abuse.

Health and Welfare

Caring for both those who are abused, and those who abuse, falls within the remit of the health care services of any country. Victims need physical care whether it be children examined within a family practice, or hospital, or survivors who are rescued from forced sexual exploitation or transnational sex trafficking. All require psychological assistance and support, sometimes for years, to recover. Their parents will also need assistance to welcome their previously abducted child back into the family if at all possible. Social support services are needed, likely for years, to provide safe and sheltered accommodation and care for as long as it takes to recuperate from the self-denigration that results from extended forced sexual abuse. Educational needs may have also been interrupted and support is needed to return to education to prepare for a life ahead.

We have, to date, been woefully unsuccessful in treating paedophiles, with most being unable to refrain from re-abusing children. Chemical castration has harsh side effects and behaviour therapy has limited success. Social programs that call for those who identify as "liking children more than they should" are at least encouraging potential abusers to self identify and seek assistance. Exposing perpetrators to education programs given by girls who have been rescued from or escaped from forced child sex abuse appears to create some understanding among perpetrators of what their actions do to their victims. Especially for casual users of such child sex workers, such training may well provide sufficient insight to overcome erroneous beliefs that their payment for the sexual services of a child or young girl is really something of benefit for the child, such as a way to earn money to survive. We still need to develop adequate assistance for perpetrators to facilitate them managing their inclinations.

233

Commercialization of Children

Child sex abuse through trafficking for sexual exploitation is unbelievably lucrative. The number of children involved in this trade is staggering. It is one of the most financially rewarding trades in existence for perpetrators, on a par or nearly so with the global drugs and arms trades and trafficking of people for labour.

The massive multi-billion-dollar incomes reported by sex websites reveals another source of financial gain emerging from the abuse of women, and sometimes children, of all ages. Political will to combat sexual abuse of children is called for, together with appropriate legislation, policies and programs that prevent as well as respond to, violence against children and that enforce accountability on perpetrators for these acts. Politicians, educators, internet providers, criminal gangsters and abusing families need to be held accountable for these crimes, or at least, for inaction to counter them. Sentences need to reflect the severity, immorality, and criminality of these acts. The vast millions that are spent on utilizing sex websites or sex services by people across the globe, and earned by sex websites, would be a welcome resource if directed towards eliminating the criminal activities related to inappropriate and illegal sexual exploitation of children. Internet sites that include child sex images should be targeted, financially and legally, and their revenue for the period that the children's images were on their site, redirected towards combatting child sex abuse.

Creating Awareness: The Media

Child sex abuse has only reached some public awareness in very recent decades. There is a dearth of information available about child sex abuse virtually everywhere in the world, with few exceptions. Even the United Nations Declaration of the Rights of the Child, while incorporating child sexual abuse as one of many forms of child maltreatment, has not yet resulted in a globally effective method of its elimination. The relevant clauses from the Declaration of the Rights of the Child follow:

Article 34

States Parties undertake to protect the child from all forms of sexual exploitation and sexual abuse. For these purposes, States Parties shall in particular take all appropriate national, bilateral and multilateral measures to prevent:

(a) The inducement or coercion of a child to engage in any unlawful sexual activity;

(b) The exploitative use of children in prostitution or other unlawful sexual practices;

(c) The exploitative use of children in pornographic performances and materials.

Article 35

States Parties shall take all appropriate national, bilateral and multilateral measures to prevent the abduction of, the sale of or traffic in children for any purpose or in any form.

Article 39

States Parties shall take all appropriate measures to promote physical and psychological recovery and social reintegration of a child victim of: any form of neglect, exploitation, or abuse; torture or any other form of cruel, inhuman or degrading treatment or punishment; or armed conflicts. Such recovery and reintegration shall take place in an environment which fosters the health, self-respect and dignity of the child.[895]

Despite this responsible and worthy declaration, we do not have a globally accurate estimate of child sex abuse in all its various guises. Estimates of frequency of various crimes are scattered throughout the academic, government, and popular media and use different terminology and definitions of crimes making comparison or integration of data unmanageable. At best we can estimate that at least 250 million children worldwide are abused before the age of eighteen, although how accurate or comprehensive this estimate is, is open to question given the hidden nature of much child sex abuse.

The hundred or so news reports referred to throughout this book reflect the role that the media are playing in bringing child sex abuse incidents to public awareness. Emerging on average about once every two weeks over the past five years, at least on the BBC (UK), Reuters (Global), CNN (USA), and CBC (Canada), these reports are valuable but too isolated to have a significant impact on creating global or even local community awareness or to creating sufficient political will to rectify the problem. The movie industry has fared better in exposing these horrific crimes. In Canada, tragedies such as that made public in Newfoundland, Canada, through the film *The Boys of St Vincent's*[896] and Michael Harris's book on the same subject, *Unholy Orders*[897] expose the cover-up of abuse and particularly sexual abuse of young boys that characterized the Church's approach to these children. The horrors of unmarried mothers' homes and the forced adoption of their offspring was exposed in the book[898] and multiple award-winning film[899] *Philomena*. The forced labour of girls in Irish laundries was aptly portrayed in the film *The Magdalen Sisters,*[900] and in such books as *Whispering Hope*.[901] Similarly, the abuse of children by Priests in the USA and the cover up of their ignominious activities as highlighted by the multiple award winning, including an Oscar for Best Picture, film *Spotlight*[902] has opened the floodgates of public attention towards these hitherto concealed crimes of the religious. The film *Tell No One*[903] created in Poland, that went viral within days of being uploaded onto the web, as well as *By the Grace of God*[904] in France and *Prey*[905] in Canada, reflect increasing national awareness and intolerance of child sex abuse.

Social media have also facilitated the sexual abuse of children. Children are most likely in more danger of sexual abuse because of the widespread abuse of the world wide web and its dark side. In many places around the world, child sex abuse is sanctioned as a societally approved practice. In a number it is condemned but there are few societal sanctions imposed to implement restrictions on its practice. In most countries the use of "disguised websites"[906] that are accessible on the open web but hidden behind adverts and popups – is virtually occurring "in the open." Much of child sexual exploitation, however, is still ignored or concealed: This time hiding on the "dark web."

Social media is also used to combat sexual abuse of women and teenagers. The internet based viral spread of the "#MeToo" hashtag has led the exposure and global condemnation of sexual abuse of women and teenagers, by those in prominent social positions – leading most often to their resignation or expulsion from public office by the pressure brought to bear on them through social condemnation. The #MeToo twitter hashtag, initiated in 2006 by Tarana Burke, an American social activist, was made famous when used by actress Alyssa Milano in 2017 resulting in it rapidly going viral. It was copied more than 55,000 times within two days after Milano asked victims of sexual assault to come forward in a show of solidarity.[907] Popular media sources suggest retweet estimates as above 200,000 times within forty-eight hours.[908] Within a short period of months, millions of women contributed to the conversation or used the #MeToo hashtag. A subsequent movement, started in Britain, referring to sexual abuse of teenagers at schools and colleges is being called a "#MeToo movement" for schools. It was created by twenty-two-year-old Soma Sara to oppose the rape culture within teenage social circles where sexual abuse is being normalized. Called "Everyone's Invited"[909] the stories recounted refer to behaviours that are not normal being normalized, such as groping at a Christmas party, non-consensual sharing of intimate photos, forced sexual acts, or derogatory sexist remarks. Over 11,000 young people, in exclusive private schools as well as in state schools, uploaded teenage experiences of sexual harassment or abuse to the site within a few weeks of its creation.[910] The government has set up a helpline and review into sexual abuse at schools in response.[911]

Future Actions

Our multiple societal institutions including the Family, Education, Law, Policing, Cyberspace, Health and Welfare, as well as Religious belief or Ideology, are all involved in various ways in justifying, covering-up, ignoring, enabling or promoting child sex abuse. We need to think about child sexual abuse from within a far larger perspective than is currently adopted. We need to mobilize major societal change agents such as the media; digital technologies; educational institutions; any and all child-directed authorities; social organizations for children, and for the protection of children; the economic sector that currently benefits from child sex abuse, trafficking, tourism, and forced sex work; societal systems that promote child marriage or condone child sex use or abuse; the legal profession with its often inadequate laws or unwillingness to implement severe punishments, its insensitivity to the experiences of minors, as well as its related segments of law and order authorities; and most importantly the political leadership of countries, regions or the globe. Without the political will to implement change across all these dimensions, and to target perpetrators rather than to primarily assist victims, child sex abuse will continue unabated and will likely flourish.

Clearly, it is long past time to stop justifying, concealing, ignoring, enabling and facilitating child sex abuse at all levels of society. As in Dante's Inferno, the world of child sex abuse is akin to Dante's multi-layered levels of Hell populated by individuals displaying lust, gluttony, avarice, wrath, heresy, violence, fraud and, most devastating of all, and at the deepest level of Hell, betrayal. Bystanders, whether these are family members, politicians, law enforcement agencies, business leaders and technology developers, religious authorities, educational directors, or just ordinary people who fail to speak out or take action, are guilty of such betrayal, and of facilitating child sex abuse. It is time to focus on what can be done to eradicate this climate of sexual abuse; this scourge against our children, our societies and our world.

Notes

1 UNICEF, "Sexual Violence against Children," UNICEF.
2 Berhard Gallagher, "The Extent and Nature of Known Cases of Institutional Child Sexual Abuse," *British Journal of Social Work* 30 (2003).
3 Dana Solomon, Personal Communication, 2021.
4 Adele D Jones and Ena Trotman Jemmott, "Status, Privilege and Gender Inequality: Cultures of Male Impunity and Entitlement in the Sexual Abuse of Children: Perspectives from a Caribbean Study," *International Social Work* 59, no. 6 (2016).
5 Justice Ryan, "The Commission to Enquire into Child Abuse Report," (Ireland 2009).
6 Scott Ronis and Laura Kabbash, "Sexual Assault and Harassment," in *Human Sexuality: A Contemporary Introduction*, ed. Caroline Pukall (Canada: Oxford University Press, 2020), 397.
7 Reuters, "France Outlaws Sex with Children Aged under 15," Reuters, https://www.cnn.com/2021/04/16/europe/france-consent-age-intl/index.html.
8 Interpol, "Appropriate Terminology," UN, https://www.interpol.int/en/Crimes/Crimes-against-children/Appropriate-terminology.
9 Felecia Marie Knaul, Flavia Bustreo, and Richard Horton, "Countering the Pandemic of Gender-Based Violence and Maltreatment of Young People: The Lancet Commission," *The Lancet* (2019).
10 Mannat Mohanjeet Singh, Shradha S. Parsekar, and Sreekumaran N. Nair, "An Epidemiological Overview of Child Sexual Abuse," *Journal of Family Medicine and Primary Care.* 3, no. 4 (2014).
11 Ibid.
12 Kris Hollington, *Unthinkable: The Shocking Scandal of the UK Sex Traffickers* (London: Simon and Schuster, 2013), 245.
13 Marije Stoltenborgh et al., "A Global Perspective on Child Sexual Abuse: Meta-Analysis of Prevalence around the World," *Child Maltreatment* 16, no. 2 (2011).

14 Singh, Parsekar, and Nair, "An Epidemiological Overview of Child Sexual Abuse."; Caroline Pukall, ed. *Human Sexuality: A Contemporary Introduction*, 2nd ed. (Don Mills, Ontario: Oxford University Press, 2017); Ben Mathews and Delphine Collin-Vezine, "Child Sexual Abuse: Raising Awareness and Empathy Is Essential to Promote New Public Health Responses," *Journal of Public Health Policy* 37, no. 3 (2016).

15 EG Krug et al., *The World Report on Violence and Health* (Geneva: World Health Organization, 2002).

16 Singh, Parsekar, and Nair, "An Epidemiological Overview of Child Sexual Abuse."

17 Diane Russell, *The Secret Trauma: Incest in the Lives of Girls and Women* (New York: Basic Books Inc, 1986), 12.

18 Singh, Parsekar, and Nair, "An Epidemiological Overview of Child Sexual Abuse."

19 Russell, *The Secret Trauma: Incest in the Lives of Girls and Women*, 12.

20 A Barett, Y Kamiya, and V O'Sullivan, "Childhood Sexual Abuse and Later Life Economic Consequences," *Journal of Behavioural and Experimental Economics* 53 (2014).

21 SS Stroebel et al., "Brother-Sister Incest: Data from Anonymous Computer Assisted Self Interviews.," *Journal of Child Sexual Abuse* 22 (2013).

22 Knaul, Bustreo, and Horton, "Countering the Pandemic of Gender-Based Violence and Maltreatment of Young People: The Lancet Commission."

23 Mathews and Collin-Vezine, "Child Sexual Abuse: Raising Awareness and Empathy Is Essential to Promote New Public Health Responses."

24 Florence Rush, *The Best-Kept Secret: Sexual Abuse of Children* (USA: McGraw Hill, 1980).

25 Ellen Bass and Louise Thornton, *I Never Told Anyone: Writings by Women Survivors of Child Sexual Abuse* (New York: Harper and Row 1983).

26 Jeremy Black, *Slavery* (London: Running Press, 2011).

27 Paul Boge, *The True Story of Canadian Human Trafficking* (Canada: Castle Quay Books, 2018); Lydia Cacho, *Slavery Inc.: The Untold Story of International Sex Trafficking* (London: Portobello Books, 2012).

28 Steven O'Riordan and Sue Leonard, *Whispering Hope: The True Story of the Magdalene Women* (London: Orion, 2015); Colm O'Gorman, *Beyond Belief* (UK: Hodder and Stoughton, 2009).

29 Amy Neustein, *Tempest in the Temple: Jewish Communities and Child Sex Scandals* (Lebanon, New Haven, USA: University Press of New England, 2009); Michael Lesher, *Sexual Abuse, Shonda and Concealment in Orthodox Jewish Communities.* (Jefferson, North Carolina: McFarland and Company, 2014); Richard Breitman Walter Laqueur, *Breaking the*

Silence (Hanover: Brandeis University Press, 1986).as well as that of Bass and Thornton

30   Beverley Chalmers, *Betrayed: Child Sex Abuse in the Holocaust* (UK: Grosvenor House Publishers, 2020).

31   Mike Milotte, *Banished Babies: The Secret History of Ireland's Baby Export Business* (Dublin: New Island, 2012); O'Gorman, *Beyond Belief*; Martin Sixsmith, *Philomena: A Mother, Her Son and a Fifty-Year Search* (London: Pan Books, 2010); O'Riordan and Leonard, *Whispering Hope: The True Story of the Magdalene Women*

32   Theodore Fontaine, *Broken Cicle: The Dark Legacy of Indian Residential Schools. A Memoir* (Canada: Heritage House Publishing Company, 2010); Suzanne Fournier and Ernie Grey, *Stolen from Our Embrace: The Abduction of First Nations Children and the Restoration of Aboriginal Communities* (Vancouver: Douglas & McIntyre, 1997); Bev Sellars, *They Called Me Number One* (Vancouver: Talon Books, 2013); Elizabeth Furniss, *Victims of Benevolence: The Dark Legacy of the Williams Lake Residential School* (Vancouver: Arsenal Pulp Press, 1992).

33   Kate Skylark and Lucy Gilbert, *Daddy's Wicked Parties* (Bolton Ontario: Createspace, 2015); Nujood Ali and Delphine Minoui, *I Am Nujood: Age 10 and Divorced* (New York: Broadway Paperbacks, 2010); Cathy Glass, *Innocent* (London: Harper, 2019); Celeste Jones, Kristina Jones, and Juliana Buhring, *Not without My Sister* (London: Harper Element, 2007); Anna Ruston, *Secret Slave* (London: Blink Publishing, 2016); Hollington, *Unthinkable: The Shocking Scandal of the UK Sex Traffickers*.

34   Mathews and Collin-Vezine, "Child Sexual Abuse: Raising Awareness and Empathy Is Essential to Promote New Public Health Responses."

35   BBC, "Turpin: Shackled Siblings Found in Perris, California Home," BBC www.bbc.com/news/world-us-canada-42698562; "Argentina Father Jailed for Keeping Daughter as 'Sex Slave'," BBC, www.bbc.com/news/world-latin-america-42517711.

36   Frances Mao, "Jeni Haynes: The Woman Who Created 2,500 Personalities to Survive," BBC, www.bbc.com/news/world-australia-49589160.

37   Jones and Jemmott, "Status, Privilege and Gender Inequality: Cultures of Male Impunity and Entitlement in the Sexual Abuse of Children: Perspectives from a Caribbean Study."

38   Katherine Sutton, ed. *Variations in Sexual Behaviour*, third ed., Human Sexuality: A Contemporary Introduction (Canada: Oxford University Press, 2020), 351.

39   Jones and Jemmott, "Status, Privilege and Gender Inequality: Cultures of Male Impunity and Entitlement in the Sexual Abuse of Children: Perspectives from a Caribbean Study."

40 BBC, "Police: California Man Admits to Molesting 50 Children," BBC www.bbc.com/news/world-us-canada-42226750.
41 "France: Former Surgeon Goes on Trial on Child Rape and Assault Charges.," BBC, www.bbc.com/news/world-europe-51883495
42 Lucy Williamson, "Olivier Duhamel: French Incest Allegations Prompt Victims to Speak Out.," BBC, https://www.bbc.com/news/world-europe-55707613.
43 Reuters, "Macron Says France Will Tighten Legislation on Incest," Reuters, https://www.reuters.com/article/us-france-incest/macron-says-france-will-tighten-legislation-on-incest-idUSKBN29S0KY.
44 World Health Organization, "Global Status Report on Preventing Violence against Children," World Health Organization.
45 Skylark and Gilbert, *Daddy's Wicked Parties*.
46 Ibid., 110.
47 Bass and Thornton, *I Never Told Anyone: Writings by Women Survivors of Child Sexual Abuse*.
48 Bobby Histrova, "Families of Paul Bernardo's Victims File for Access to Records of Parole Hearing.," CBC, https://www.cbc.ca/news/canada/hamilton/paul-bernardo-parole-files-1.5538586.
49 BBC, "Coronavirus: Domestic Abuse Victims 'Still Allowed to Leave Home'," BBC, www.bbc.com/news/uk-52081280.
50 Kate Razzall, "Coronavirus: 'Worryingly Low Number' of at-Risk Children in School," BBC, https://www.bbc.com/news/uk-52228772.
51 BBC, "UK Lockdown: Calls to Domestic Abuse Hotline Jump by Half," BBC, https://www.bbc.com/news/uk-52433520.
52 Meagan Fitzpatrick, "Online Sexual Predators Eager to Take Advantage of Greater Access to Kids During Covid-19, Police Warn," CBC, https://www.cbc.ca/news/canada/sexual-predators-children-online-pandemic-1.5542166.
53 Elisabeth Thompson, "Child Sex Exploitation Is on the Rise in Canada During the Pandemic," CBC, https://www.cbc.ca/news/politics/pandemic-child-sexual-abuse-1.5645315.
54 Ibid.
55 BBC, "India Coronavirus: 14-Year-Old Sexually Assaulted at Delhi Covid Centre," BBC, https://www.bbc.com/news/world-asia-india-53522998.
56 Fitzpatrick, "Online Sexual Predators Eager to Take Advantage of Greater Access to Kids During Covid-19, Police Warn".
57 BBC, "India's Covid Crisis Sees Rise in Child Marriage and Trafficking," BBC, https://www.bbc.com/news/world-asia-india-54186709.
58 "Coronavirus Risks "Greatest Surge in Child Marriages in 25 Years"." BBC, https://www.bbc.com/news/world-54370316; Sophie Cousins, "2.5

Million More Child Marriages Due to Covid-19 Pandemic," *The Lancet* Oct 10 (2020).

59 BBC, "Man Charged with Child Sex Offences in Hampshire and Berkshire," BBC, www.bbc.com/news/uk-england-hampshire-39337878.

60 "Singapore Anger at 'Too Lenient' Child Sex Sentence," BBC www. BBC.com/news/world-asia-39202215.

61 "Australian Police Charge Seven with Abusing Boys," BBC, www.bbc. com/news/world-australia-42954474; Tom Westbrook, "Australian Police File Hundreds of Sex Abuse Charges against Seven People," Reuters, www.reuters.com/article/us-australia-sexabuse/australian-police-file-hundreds-of-sex-abuse-charges-against-seven-people-idUSKBN1FS17L.

62 BBC, "Australian Toddler's Alleged Rape Was a 'Foreseeable Risk'," BBC, www.bbc.com/news/world-australia-44063602.

63 Judith Burns, "MPs Seek Better Plan to Fight School Sexual Harassment," BBC News, http://www.bbc.com/news/education-37338712.

64 Linda Pressly, "The Community of 2000 People with 151 Cases of Sex Crimes," BBC, www.bbc.com/news/stories-43478396.

65 A Sethi, " Domestic Sex Trafficking of Aboriginal Girls in Canada: Issues and Implications," *First Peoples Child & Family Review* 3, no. 3 (2007): 57.

66 Sutton, *Variations in Sexual Behaviour*, 350.

67 Hollington, *Unthinkable: The Shocking Scandal of the UK Sex Traffickers*, 270.

68 Sutton, *Variations in Sexual Behaviour*, 352.

69 Ibid., 351.

70 Dick Wolf, *Angels, Law and Order Special Victims Unit 4th Year* (USA: Universal Studios, 2007).

71 *Pandora, Law and Order Special Victims Unit 3rd Year* (USA: Universal Studios, 2007).

72 Sutton, *Variations in Sexual Behaviour*.

73 Caroline Pukall, *Human Sexuality: A Contemporary Introduction*, Third ed. (Canada: Oxford University Press, 2020), 381.

74 Ibid.

75 *Human Sexuality: A Contemporary Introduction*, 379.

76 Nazim Baksh, "Order of Canada Recipient Peter Dalglish Found Guilty of Child Sex Assault in Nepal," CBC, www.cbc.ca/news/world/peter-dalglish-conviction-nepal-1.5170122.

77 Thomas Rogers, "A Major German Political Party Used to Support Pedophilia - and It's Coming Back to Haunt Them," https://newrepublic.com/article/120379/german-green-party-pedophilia-scandal.

78 Ibid.

79 Russell, *The Secret Trauma: Incest in the Lives of Girls and Women*, 5.

80 Ibid., 7-8.
81 Ibid., 8.
82 Lucian Valsan, "Simone De Baeuvoir: A Nazi, a Pedophile, and a Misogynist," http://www.avoiceformen/feminism/simone-de-beauvoir-a-nazi-a-pedophile-and-a-misogynist.
83 Ibid.; Carole Seymour-Jones, *A Dangerous Liaison: A Revelatory New Biography of Simone De Beauvoir and Jean-Paul Sartre* (USA: Harry Abrams, 2009).
84 Hannah L. Merdian et al., "Transnational Child Sexual Abuse: Outcomes from a Roundtable Discussion," *Environmental Research and Public Health* 16 (2019).
85 Ibid.
86 Rogers, "A Major German Political Party Used to Support Pedophilia - and It's Coming Back to Haunt Them".
87 Sutton, *Variations in Sexual Behaviour*, 352.
88 Calcasa, "Pedophiles and Child Molesters: The Differences," www.calcasa.org/wp-content/uploads/2007/11/pedophiles-and-child-molesters.doc.
89 Ibid.
90 BBC, "Chemical Castration: Alabama Enacts New Paedophile Law.," BBC, www.bbc.com/news/world-us-canada-48593699.
91 J Raboch, H Cerna, and P Zemek, "Sexual Aggressivity and Androgens," *British Journal of Psychiatry* 151 (1987).
92 BBC, "Nigeria's Kaduna Passes Law to Castrate Child Rapists," BBC, https://www.bbc.com/news/world-africa-54117462.
93 A Ananthalakshmi, "How Malaysia Allows Child Abuse to Go Unpunished," Reuters, www.reuters.com/article/us-malaysia-sexcrimes-insight-idUSKBN1390AT.
94 BBC, "Pakistan Anti-Rape Ordinance Signed into Law by President," BBC, https://www.bbc.com/news/world-asia-55314493.
95 "Dutch Police Give 'Stop Paedophile Hunts' Warning after Arnhem Death," BBC, https://www.bbc.com/news/world-europe-54930488.
96 Priyanka Pathak, "India Catholic Cardinal Oswald Gracias 'Failed Abuse Victims'," BBC, www.bbc.com/news/world-asia-india-47302447.
97 Denise Hruby, "Where Survivors of Sexual Abuse Are Sued by the Perpetrators," CNN, www.cnn.com/2019/01/23/europe/austria-skiers-sexual-assault-int/index.html.
98 Kara Fox and Antoine Crouin, "Men Are Suing Women Who Accuse Them of Harassment. Will It Stop Others from Speaking Out?," CNN, www.cnn.com/2019/06/05/europe/metoo-defamation-trials-sandra-muller-france-intl/index.html.
99 Ibid.
100 Jones, Jones, and Buhring, *Not without My Sister*, ix.

101 Ibid., xiii.

102 Ibid., vii.

103 BBC, "NXIVM 'Sex Cult' Case: Co-Founder Pleads Guilty to Racketeering," BBC, www.bbc.com/news/world-us-canada-47563045.

104 "NXIVM Sex Cult Case: Seagram Heiress among Four Women Arrested," BBC, https://www.bbc.com/news/world-us-canada-44946059.

105 Sonia Moghe, "NXIVM Founder Sentenced to the Remainder of His Life in Prison," CNN, https://www.cnn.com/2020/10/27/us/nxivm-keith-raniere-sentencing-supporters/index.html.

106 BBC, "Spanish Father Accused of 'Evil Spirits' Rape," BBC, www.bbc.com/news/world-europe-44107300.

107 "La Luz Del Mundo Church Leader Charged with Child Rape in US," BBC, www.bbc.com/news/world-us-canada-48524878.

108 "La Luz Del Mundo Sex Crimes Case Dropped by US Court," BBC, https://www.bbc.com/news/world-us-canada-52217977.

109 Norma Galeana, "Mexico-Based Church Leader Charged with Sex Crimes Ordered Held on $90 Million Bail," Reuters, https://www.reuters.com/article/us-usa-mexico-church-court/mexico-based-church-leader-charged-with-sex-crimes-ordered-held-on-90-million-bail-idUSKCN2523FS.

110 Aaron Akinyemi, "'No Sex without Fighting' - Tackling Toxic Masculinity in DR Congo," BBC Africa Eye, www.bbc.com/news/world/africa/48094438.

111 Ibid.

112 BBC, "Bosco Ntaganda Sentenced to 30 Years for Crimes in DR Congo," BBC, www.bbc.com/news/world-africa-50329503

113 Akinyemi, "'No Sex without Fighting' - Tackling Toxic Masculinity in DR Congo".

114 BBC, "'Tortured' and Shackled Pupils Freed from Nigerian Islamic School," BBC, www.bbc.com/news/world-africa-50053725.

115 Oren Gruenbaum, "Malawi: The Human Hyenas," *The Round Table: The Commonwealth Journal of International Affairs* September (2016); Ed Butler, "The Man Hired to Have Sex with Children," BBC News Malawi, www.bbc.com/news/magazine-36843769.

116 "The Man Hired to Have Sex with Children".

117 Gruenbaum, "Malawi: The Human Hyenas."

118 Ibid.

119 Ibid.

120 Ibid.

121 Jones and Jemmott, "Status, Privilege and Gender Inequality: Cultures of Male Impunity and Entitlement in the Sexual Abuse of Children: Perspectives from a Caribbean Study."

122 Eileen Meier, "Child Rape in South Africa," *Paediatric Nursing* 28, no. 5 (2002).

123 Douglas Bowley and Graeme Pitcher, "Motivation Behind Infant Rape in South Africa," *The Lancet* 359, no. 9314 (2002).

124 Ibid.

125 Meier, "Child Rape in South Africa."

126 Africa Check, "Factsheet: South Africa's Crime Statistics for 2019/20," Africa Check, https://africacheck.org/fact-checks/factsheets/factsheet-south-africas-crime-statistics-201920.

127 Ernest Mabuza, "Children Victims in 42% of All Rape Cases Recorded.," Times Alive, www.timeslive.co.za/news/south-africa/2018-05-16-children-victims-in-42-of-all-rape-cases-recorded/.

128 BBC, "South Africa Anger after Girl 'Raped' in Restaurant," BBC News, www.bbc.com/new/world-africa-45652729.

129 Bowley and Pitcher, "Motivation Behind Infant Rape in South Africa."

130 Mabuza, "Children Victims in 42% of All Rape Cases Recorded.".

131 BBC, "South Africa Anger after Girl 'Raped' in Restaurant".

132 "Somali Outrage at Rape of Girls Aged Three and Four," BBC, www.bbc.com/news/world-africa-52172609.

133 "Militiamen Jailed in DR Congo's Kavumu for Raping 40 Children," BBC www.bbc.com/news/world-africa-42345705.

134 "Pakistan Village Council Orders 'Revenge Rape' of Girl," BBC www/bbc.com/news/world-asia-india-40731035.

135 "India Stepmother Arrested for 'Ordering' Gang Rape of Girl, 9," BBC, www.bbc.co.uk/news/world-asia-india-45417725.

136 Julie Anne Laser, "Prevalence and Correlates of Enjo Kousai, School Girl and Boy Prostituion, in Japan," *Journal of Asian Research* 2, no. 1 (2018).

137 Ibid.

138 Kento Sahara, "Japan Exhibition Puts Child Prostitution in the Limelight," Reuters, http://www.reuters.com/article/us-japan=prostitution-idUSKCN1180IT.

139 Laser, "Prevalence and Correlates of Enjo Kousai, School Girl and Boy Prostituion, in Japan."

140 Ibid.

141 Ibid.

142 Ibid.

143 Ibid.

144 Sahara, "Japan Exhibition Puts Child Prostitution in the Limelight".

145 The Economist, "The Sexualization of Children: Innocents and Experience," *The Economist*, July 21 2018.

146 BBC, "Japan Child Abuse at Record High, Police Data Shows," BBC, www.bbc.com/news/world-asia-pacific-10979109.

147   Geeta Pandey, "Abuse of Indian Children 'Common'," BBC, http://
       news.bbc.co.uk/2/hi/south_asia/6539027.stm.
148   Divya Arya, "Child Sex Crime: Does India Have a Growing Problem?,"
       BBC, www.bbc.com/news/wsorld-asia-india-44497312.
149   BBC, "Indian Man Allegedly Rapes Girl, Five, on Embassy Grounds "
       BBC, www.bbc.com/news/world-aasia-india-51398295.(94%)
150   Geeta Pandey, "Why an MP Wants India to Talk About Child Sex
       Abuse," BBC, www.bbc.com/news/world-asia-india-34971791.
151   Esha Mitra et al., "Girl, 16, Says She Was Raped by Hundreds of Men in
       Western India," CNN, https://www.cnn.com/2021/11/16/india/india-
       girl-rape-hundreds-men-intl-hnk/index.html.
152   BBC, "India Outrage over Brutal Rape and Murder of Six-Year-Old,"
       BBC www.bbc.com/news/world-asia-india-42305395.
153   "India Rape: Two Men Arrested from 13-Year-Old's Rape and Murder,"
       BBC, https://www.bbc.com/news/world-asia-india-53799036.
154   "India Uncles Convicted of Raping and Impregnating Child Aged 10,"
       BBC www.bbc.com/news/world-asia-india-41817519.
155   Soutik Biswas, "Why India's Rape Crisis Shows No Sign of Abating,"
       BBC, www.bbc.com/news/world-asia-india-43782471.
156   BBC, "Indian Man Allegedly Rapes Girl, Five, on Embassy Grounds ".
157   "India Rape: 17 Men Accused of Multiple Attacks on 11-Year-Old Girl
       in Chennai," BBC, www.bbc.com/news/world-asia-india-44877729.
158   Malini Menon, "Two Teenagers Gang Raped in India, One Commits
       Suicide,"   Reuters,   www.reuters/com/article/us-india-rape/two-
       teenagers-gang-raped-in-india-one-commits-suicide-idUSKBN1I412J.
159   Biswas, "Why India's Rape Crisis Shows No Sign of Abating".
160   BBC, "India Rape: Two Men Arrested from 13-Year-Old's Rape and
       Murder".
161   Esha Mitra et al., "Four Men Charged with Rape and Murder of 9-Year-
       Old Girl in India," CNN, https://www.cnn.com/2021/08/30/india/dalit-
       rape-men-charged-india-intl-hnk/index.html.
162   Swati Gupta and Jessie Yeung, "Dozens of Men Arrested in India Are
       Accused of Gang Raping a 15-Year-Old Girl Repeatedly," CNN, https://
       www.cnn.com/2021/09/24/india/india-gang-rape-mumbai-girl-intl-hnk/
       index.html.
163   BBC, "India Outcry after Eight-Month-Old Raped," BBC www.bbc.
       com/news-world-asia-india-42869010.
164   "India Arrests after Women's Heads Shaved for Resisting Rape," BBC,
       www.bbc,com/news/world-asia-india-48783253.
165   Biswas, "Why India's Rape Crisis Shows No Sign of Abating".
166   Swati Gupta, "Kathua Child Rape and Murder: Indian Court Finds Sex
       Guilty in Case That Outraged Nation.," CNN, www.cnn.com/2019/06/10/
       asia/india-jammu-rape-trial-verdict=intl-hnk/index.html.

167 M Ybarra et al., "X-Rated Material and Perpetration of Sexually Aggressive Behaviour among Children and Adolescents: Is There a Link?," *Aggressive Behaviour* 37, no. 1 (2011).

168 Divya Arya, "Why Smartphones Are Skewing Young Indian's Ideas of Sex," BBC, ww.bbc.com/news/world-asia-india-46602885.

169 Jeremy Black, *A Brief History of Slavery: A New Global History* (London: Constable and Robinson, 2011), 242-3.

170 Biswas, "Why India's Rape Crisis Shows No Sign of Abating".

171 UN Ministry of Statistics and Programme implementation, "Sex Ratio of India," UN, http://statisticstimes.com/demographics/sex-ratio-of-india.php.

172 UNICEF, "Together for Girls: Sexual Violence Fact Sheet," UNICEF, www.unicef.org/protection/files/Together-for-Girls-Sexual-Violence-Fact-Sheet-July2012.pdf.

173 UNDATA, "Legal Age for Marriage," UN, https://data.un.org/DocumentData.aspx?id=336.

174 UNICEF, "Child Marriage: Latest Trends and Future Perspectives," UNICEF, www.data.unicef.org/wp-content/uploads/2018/06/Child-marriage-data-brief.pdf.

175 Emily Chow, "Malaysians Outraged over Reports of Child Marriage," Reuters,www.reuters.com/article/us-malaysia-child-marriage/malaysians-outraged-over-reports-of-child-marriage-idUSKBN1JQ0R6.

176 Ibid.

177 UNICEF, "Together for Girls: Sexual Violence Fact Sheet"; Plan International Canada, "Child Marriage," https://plancanada.ca/child-marriage.

178 UNICEF, "Together for Girls: Sexual Violence Fact Sheet"; Plan International Canada, "Child Marriage".

179 Government of Canada, "Child, Early and Forced Marriage," Government of Canada, https://www.international.gc.ca/world-monde/issues_development-enjeux_developpement/human_rights-droits_homme/child_marriage-mariages_enfants.aspx?lang=eng.

180 Plan International Canada, "Child Marriage".

181 Ibid.

182 Ali and Minoui, *I Am Nujood: Age 10 and Divorced*, 74.

183 Ibid., 92-3.

184 Ibid., 183.

185 Ibid., 173.

186 Real Life News Life, "It's Hard to Believe That Bride Kidnapping Exists in 2017," Real Life News Life, /www.news.com.au/lifestyle/real-life/news-life/its-hard-to-believe-that-bride-kidnapping-exists-in-2017/news-story/9e7a445078231d94da67be33e3bb9157.

187 United Nations Commission on Human Rights, "Culture of Abduction, Rape and Forced Marriage Violates Women's Rights in Kyrgyzstan, UN

Experts Find," United Nations Commission on Human Rights, www.ohchr.org/EN/NewsEvents/Pages/DisplayNews.aspx?NewsID=23583&LangID-E.

188   Courtney Brooks and Amina Umarova, "Despite Official Measures, Bride Kidnapping Endemic in Chechnya," Radio Free Europe/Radio Liberty, www.rferl.org/a/Despite_Official_Measures_Bride_Kidnapping_Endemic_In_Chechnya/2197575.html.

189   Diane Cole, *Kidnapped and Raped at Age 13, She's Finally Found Justice* (NPR News: USA, 2016); Real Life News Life, "It's Hard to Believe That Bride Kidnapping Exists in 2017".

190   Cole, *Kidnapped and Raped at Age 13, She's Finally Found Justice*; Real Life News Life, "It's Hard to Believe That Bride Kidnapping Exists in 2017".

191   "It's Hard to Believe That Bride Kidnapping Exists in 2017".

192   Nawal al-Maghafi, "The Teenager Married Too Many Times to Count," BBC, www.bbc.co.uk/news/extra/iuKTEGjKgS/teenage_iraq_brides; Katherine Sutton and Karen Blair, "Perspectives on Sexuality," in *Human Sexuality: A Contemporary Inroduction*, ed. Caroline Pukall (Canada: Oxford University Press, 2020), 14.

193   Shakito Murata, "Muta' Temporary Marriage in Islamic Law," Al Islam.org, https://www.al-islam.org/muta-temporary-marriage-islamic-law-sachiko-murata/permanent-marriage#iii-divorce-talaq.

194   al-Maghafi, "The Teenager Married Too Many Times to Count".

195   Ibid.

196   UNICEF, "Child Marriage: Latest Trends and Future Perspectives".

197   "Together for Girls: Sexual Violence Fact Sheet".

198   UNICEF-UNFPA, "Global Programme to End Child Marriage," UNICEF-UNFPA, https://www.unicef.org/protection/unfpa-unicef-global-programme-end-child-marriage.

199   Canada's Human Rights History, "Duplessis Orphans," https://historyofrights.ca/encyclopaedia/main-events/duplessis-orphans/.

200   R Vienneau, *Collusion: The Dark History of the Duplessis Orphans* (Canada: Kindle, 2010).

201   Quebec Ombudsman, "The "Children of Duplessis" a Time for Solidarity," in *Assemblee Nationale Quebec* (QuebecJanuary 22, 1997), 15.

202   Ibid., 10.

203   Ibid., 15.

204   Canada's Human Rights History, "Duplessis Orphans".

205   Quebec Ombudsman, "The "Children of Duplessis" a Time for Solidarity," 15.

206   Ibid., 17.

207 Ibid., 33.
208 Ibid.
209 Canada's Human Rights History, "Duplessis Orphans".
210 Mary Raftery and Eoin O'Sullivan, *Suffer the Little Children: The inside Story of Ireland's Industrial Schools* (Dublin, Ireland: New Island Books, 1999), 16.
211 Ryan, "The Commission to Enquire into Child Abuse Report," 13.
212 Solomon.
213 O'Gorman, *Beyond Belief*, 36.
214 Raftery and O'Sullivan, *Suffer the Little Children: The inside Story of Ireland's Industrial Schools*, 267.
215 The Economist, "Hearts, Minds and Souls," *The Economist*, July 30th 2016.
216 BBC, "Pope Francis Makes It Mandatory for Clergy to Report Sex Abuse," BBC, www.bbc.com/news/world-europe-48213135.
217 The Economist, "Bully Pulpit," *The Economist*, June 25th 2016.
218 Bass and Thornton, *I Never Told Anyone: Writings by Women Survivors of Child Sexual Abuse*, 36.
219 Ibid., 34-5.
220 Ibid.
221 Rush, *The Best-Kept Secret: Sexual Abuse of Children*, 17.
222 Bass and Thornton, *I Never Told Anyone: Writings by Women Survivors of Child Sexual Abuse*, 34-5.
223 Ibid.
224 Ibid.
225 Ibid.
226 O'Gorman, *Beyond Belief*, 255.
227 Ibid.
228 Ibid.
229 Ibid.
230 Bass and Thornton, *I Never Told Anyone: Writings by Women Survivors of Child Sexual Abuse*.
231 Ibid.
232 Paul Isely, "Child Sexual Abuse and the Catholic Church: An Historical and Contemporary Review," *Pastoral Psychology* 45, no. 4 (1997): 280-2.
233 O'Gorman, *Beyond Belief*, 289; Tomasz Sekielski, *Tell No One* (Poland: YouTube, 2019); Thomas Doyle, *The 1962 Vatican Instruction: Crimen Sollicitationis: Promulgated on March 16, 1962* (April 1 2008).
234 Sekielski, *Tell No One*; Doyle, *The 1962 Vatican Instruction: Crimen Sollicitationis: Promulgated on March 16, 1962*.
235 Mavis Arnold and Heather Lasky, *Children of the Poor Clares: The Story of an Irish Orphanage* (Belfast: Appletree Press, 1985), 11.

236 Ibid.; Raftery and O'Sullivan, *Suffer the Little Children: The inside Story of Ireland's Industrial Schools*, 18-20.

237 Arnold and Lasky, *Children of the Poor Clares: The Story of an Irish Orphanage*, 11; Raftery and O'Sullivan, *Suffer the Little Children: The inside Story of Ireland's Industrial Schools*, 18-20.

238 *Suffer the Little Children: The inside Story of Ireland's Industrial Schools*, 69-71.

239 Ryan, "The Commission to Enquire into Child Abuse Report."

240 Raftery and O'Sullivan, *Suffer the Little Children: The inside Story of Ireland's Industrial Schools*, 280-1.

241 BBC, "Magdalene Laundries Victim Mary Cavner to Get Compensation," BBC, www.bbec.com/news/uk-england-hampshire-49393418.

242 Ryan, "The Commission to Enquire into Child Abuse Report."

243 Raftery and O'Sullivan, *Suffer the Little Children: The inside Story of Ireland's Industrial Schools*, 53.

244 Ryan, "The Commission to Enquire into Child Abuse Report."

245 Raftery and O'Sullivan, *Suffer the Little Children: The inside Story of Ireland's Industrial Schools*, 227.

246 Ibid., 271.

247 Ryan, "The Commission to Enquire into Child Abuse Report."

248 Ben Robinson and Michael Buchanan, "Bodies of 'Hundreds' of Children Buried in Mass Grave," BBC News, www.bbc.com/news/uk-41200949.

249 Arnold and Lasky, *Children of the Poor Clares: The Story of an Irish Orphanage*, 78-9.

250 O'Riordan and Leonard, *Whispering Hope: The True Story of the Magdalene Women* 67-8.

251 Raftery and O'Sullivan, *Suffer the Little Children: The inside Story of Ireland's Industrial Schools*, 155.

252 Ryan, "The Commission to Enquire into Child Abuse Report," 12-13.

253 Irene Kelly, *Sins of the Mother* (London: Pan Books, 2015), 82-3.

254 Raftery and O'Sullivan, *Suffer the Little Children: The inside Story of Ireland's Industrial Schools*, 114.

255 Tom Mackenzie, *The Last Foundling* (London: Pan Books, 2014), 5.

256 Arnold and Lasky, *Children of the Poor Clares: The Story of an Irish Orphanage*, 76.

257 Raftery and O'Sullivan, *Suffer the Little Children: The inside Story of Ireland's Industrial Schools*, 110.

258 Ann Thompson, *Say Sorry: A Harrowing Childhood in Catholic Orphanages* (Kindle, 2009), Chapter 2.

259 Ibid., Chapter 7.

260 Ryan, "The Commission to Enquire into Child Abuse Report," 12.

261 Arnold and Lasky, *Children of the Poor Clares: The Story of an Irish Orphanage*, 76.
262 Ibid., 76-7.
263 Ibid., 53-4.
264 Kelly, *Sins of the Mother*, 80-1.
265 Raftery and O'Sullivan, *Suffer the Little Children: The inside Story of Ireland's Industrial Schools*, 249.
266 Arnold and Lasky, *Children of the Poor Clares: The Story of an Irish Orphanage*, 69.
267 Raftery and O'Sullivan, *Suffer the Little Children: The inside Story of Ireland's Industrial Schools*, 176-8.
268 Arnold and Lasky, *Children of the Poor Clares: The Story of an Irish Orphanage*, 97.
269 Ibid., 108.
270 Raftery and O'Sullivan, *Suffer the Little Children: The inside Story of Ireland's Industrial Schools*, 327-8.
271 Ibid., 50-1.
272 Ibid., 176-8.
273 Thompson, *Say Sorry: A Harrowing Childhood in Catholic Orphanages*, Chapter 8.
274 Ryan, "The Commission to Enquire into Child Abuse Report," 12.
275 Arnold and Lasky, *Children of the Poor Clares: The Story of an Irish Orphanage*, 52.
276 Ibid., 53.
277 Raftery and O'Sullivan, *Suffer the Little Children: The inside Story of Ireland's Industrial Schools*, 240.
278 Ibid., 206-7.
279 Ibid., 173.
280 Ibid., 165.
281 Ibid., 320.
282 Ibid.
283 Kelly, *Sins of the Mother*, 111-2.
284 Arnold and Lasky, *Children of the Poor Clares: The Story of an Irish Orphanage*, 107.
285 Raftery and O'Sullivan, *Suffer the Little Children: The inside Story of Ireland's Industrial Schools*, 204.
286 Scotland, "Systematic Child Abuse Claims Published," www.bbc.news/uk-scotland-38566857.
287 BBC, "Scottish Child Abuse Inquiry Hears Apologies over 'Deplorable' Attacks," BBC, www.bbc.com/news/uk-scotland-40093270.
288 O'Gorman, *Beyond Belief*, 210.
289 The Stationary Office, "Lost in Care: Report of the Tribunal of Inquiry into the Abuse of Children in Care in the Former County Council Aras

of Gwynedd and Clwyd since 1974.," (Department of Health, Wales 1999).

290 Mackenzie, *The Last Foundling*, 212.

291 BBC, "US Elite School Choate Rosemary Hall 'Sorry' over Sexual Abuse," BBC news, www.bbc.com/news/world-us-canada-39604353.

292 Michael Harris, *Unholy Orders: Tragedy at Mount Cashel* (Toronto: Penguin Books, 1990).

293 Raftery and O'Sullivan, *Suffer the Little Children: The inside Story of Ireland's Industrial Schools*, 262.

294 Ibid.

295 Ibid., 265-6.

296 Ibid.

297 Thompson, *Say Sorry: A Harrowing Childhood in Catholic Orphanages*, Chapter 1.

298 Ibid., Chapter 4.

299 Ibid.

300 Raftery and O'Sullivan, *Suffer the Little Children: The inside Story of Ireland's Industrial Schools*, 266-7.

301 Ryan, "The Commission to Enquire into Child Abuse Report," 12.

302 Kelly, *Sins of the Mother*, 94-7.

303 Ibid., 102.

304 Thompson, *Say Sorry: A Harrowing Childhood in Catholic Orphanages*, Chapter 2.

305 Raftery and O'Sullivan, *Suffer the Little Children: The inside Story of Ireland's Industrial Schools*, 268.

306 Kelly, *Sins of the Mother*, 105-6.

307 Raftery and O'Sullivan, *Suffer the Little Children: The inside Story of Ireland's Industrial Schools*, 326.

308 Arnold and Lasky, *Children of the Poor Clares: The Story of an Irish Orphanage*, 130-1,43; Raftery and O'Sullivan, *Suffer the Little Children: The inside Story of Ireland's Industrial Schools*, 43-4, 120.43, 278-9.

309 *Suffer the Little Children: The inside Story of Ireland's Industrial Schools*, 273.

310 Ibid., 272-3.

311 Ibid., 273.

312 Harris, *Unholy Orders: Tragedy at Mount Cashel*, 34.

313 Ibid., 36.

314 Raftery and O'Sullivan, *Suffer the Little Children: The inside Story of Ireland's Industrial Schools*, 278-9.

315 Harris, *Unholy Orders: Tragedy at Mount Cashel*, 41.

316 Ibid.

317 Ibid., 189.

318 Ibid., 43.

319 Ibid., 90.

320 Raftery and O'Sullivan, *Suffer the Little Children: The inside Story of Ireland's Industrial Schools*, 264; A Gill, *Children of the Empire: The Shocking Story of Child Migration to Australia* (UK: Random House, 1998), 350.

321 Raftery and O'Sullivan, *Suffer the Little Children: The inside Story of Ireland's Industrial Schools*, 263-4.

322 Arnold and Lasky, *Children of the Poor Clares: The Story of an Irish Orphanage*, 129.

323 Ibid.

324 Raftery and O'Sullivan, *Suffer the Little Children: The inside Story of Ireland's Industrial Schools*, 300-1.

325 Ibid., 382.

326 Ibid., 385.

327 Arnold and Lasky, *Children of the Poor Clares: The Story of an Irish Orphanage*, 105.

328 Ibid., 125.

329 Raftery and O'Sullivan, *Suffer the Little Children: The inside Story of Ireland's Industrial Schools*, 35.

330 Ibid., 327-8.

331 Thompson, *Say Sorry: A Harrowing Childhood in Catholic Orphanages*, Chapter 9.

332 Ibid., Chapter 12.

333 Ibid., Chapter 11.

334 Raftery and O'Sullivan, *Suffer the Little Children: The inside Story of Ireland's Industrial Schools*, 268.

335 Tom Wesbrook, "Australian Report into Child Sex Abuse Wants to Break Confessional Seal," Reuters, www.reuters.com/article/us-australia-abuse-idUSKCN1AU0R7.

336 Ibid.

337 Arnold and Lasky, *Children of the Poor Clares: The Story of an Irish Orphanage*, 131.

338 O'Gorman, *Beyond Belief*, 149.

339 Harris, *Unholy Orders: Tragedy at Mount Cashel*, 19.

340 Ibid., 384.

341 Raftery and O'Sullivan, *Suffer the Little Children: The inside Story of Ireland's Industrial Schools*, 278-9.

342 Arnold and Lasky, *Children of the Poor Clares: The Story of an Irish Orphanage*, 130.

343 Rush, *The Best-Kept Secret: Sexual Abuse of Children*, 45.

344 Martin Bashir, "How Will Pope Francis Deal with Abuse in the Catholic Church?," BBC, www.bbc.com/news/world-47201647.

345 Ibid.

346 Raftery and O'Sullivan, *Suffer the Little Children: The inside Story of Ireland's Industrial Schools*, 240.

347 Ibid., 395.

348 BBC, "Church of England Failures 'Allowed Child Sex Abusers to Hide'," BBC, https://www.bbc.com/news/uk-54433295; Alexis Jay et al., *Interim Report: A Summary: Independent Inquiry into Child Sexual Abuse* (UK: Crown, 2018).

349 Timothy Sawa, "Ontario Christian School Tells Court It Was Unaware Abuse Would Cause Emotional Damage," CBC News, https://www.cbc.ca/news/canada/toronto/grenville-christian-college-lawsuit-appeal-1.6014135.

350 CBC, "Catholic Archdiocese of Vancouver Aware of 36 Cases of Clergy Sex Abuse since 1950s, CBC Learns," CBC News, www.cbc.ca/news/canada/fifth-estate-sexual-abuse-vancouver-catholic-diocese-1.5360493.

351 SNAP, "Snap SW Ontario Releases List of Credibly Accused Priests of the Roman Catholic Diocese of London (Ont)," SNAP Network, www.snapnetwork.org/list_of_credibly_accused_priests_diocese_of_london_ont_dec19.

352 Aislinn Laing, "Chile's National Prosecutor Requesting Vatican Sex Abuse Files," Reuters, www.reuters.com/article/us-chile-abuse-church/chiles-national-prosecutor-requesting-vatican-sex-abuse-files-idUSK-BN1KM6BT.

353 BBC, "German Catholic Priests 'Abused Thousands of Children'," www.bbc.co.uk/news/world-europe-45500072; Independent Inquiry, "The Independent Inquiry into Child Sexual Abuse in Germany," (Berlin, Germany: Aufarbeitungskommission, 2020).

354 Delia Gallagher, Nadine Schmidt, and Kara Fox, "Top German Church Official Offers Resignation over 'Catastrophe of Sexual Abuse'," CNN, https://www.cnn.com/2021/06/04/europe/cardinal-marx-germany-resignation-pope-intl/index.html.

355 BBC, "Clerical Abuse: Film Gets Go-Ahead after Legal Challenge," BBC, www.bbc.com/news/world-europe-47280764.

356 Saskya Vandoorne, Simon Bouvier, and Sam Bradpiece, "More Than 200,000 Children Sexually Abused by French Catholic Clergy, Damning Report Finds," CNN, https://www.cnn.com/2021/10/05/europe/france-catholic-church-abuse-report-intl/index.html.

357 Ibid.

358 James Babcock, "Spain Child Abuse: Victims Fight Back and Appeal for Change," BBC, www.bbc.com/news/world-europe-46064017.

359 Tomasz Sekielski, *Tylko Nie Mów Nikomu (2019) (Tell No One)* (Poland: IMDb, 2019).

360 Praveen Menon, "New Zealand Child Abuse Inquiry Finds Quarter of a Million Harmed in State and Faith-Based Care," Reuters, https://www.

reuters.com/article/newzealand-abuse/new-zealand-inquiry-finds-quarter-of-a-million-abused-in-state-and-faith-based-care-idUSKBN-28Q0C6.

361 Peter McClelland et al., "Royal Commission into Institutional Responses to Child Sexual Abuse," ed. Australian Government (UK2017).

362 Wesbrook, "Australian Report into Child Sex Abuse Wants to Break Confessional Seal".

363 Peter McClelland et al., "Royal Commission into Institutional Responses to Child Sexual Abuse," (Australia2017).

364 BBC, "Cardinal Bernard Law: Disgraced US Cardinal Dies in Rome," BBC, www.bbc.com/news/world-us-canada-42421423.

365 Philip Pullella and Scott Malone, "Vatican Voices: 'Shame and Sorrow' over Damning Sex Abuse Report," Boston, www.rreuters.com/article/us-pennsylvania-religion-mccarrick/vatican-voices-shame-and-sorrow-over-damning-sex-abuse-report-idUSKBN1L11W5.

366 BBC, "Pope Francis on Side of Victims of 'Predator' Priests," BBC, www.bbc.co.uk/news/world-us-canada-45211942.

367 "Theodore McCarrick: Defrocked US Cardinal Charged with Assault and Battery," BBC, https://www.bbc.com/news/world-us-canada-58019652.

368 CBC Radio, "How a Sexual Assault Victim's Lawsuit Set a Precendent That Alarmed the Catholic Church," CBC Radio, www.cbc.ca/radio/thesundayedition/the-sunday-edition-for-april-14-2019-1.509537/.

369 Harris, *Unholy Orders: Tragedy at Mount Cashel*, 12.

370 Ibid., 15.

371 Ibid.

372 Ibid., 385.

373 Ibid., 386.

374 Ibid., 373.

375 Ibid., 370.

376 Ibid.

377 Ibid., 375.

378 Ryan Cooke, "Damning Decisions," CBC News, https://newsinterac-tives.cbc.ca/longform/mount-cashel.

379 CBC, "Supreme Court of Canada Rejects Catholic Archdiocese Appeal over Mount Cashel," CBC, https://www.cbc.ca/news/canada/newfound-land-labrador/mount-cashel-supreme-court-thursday-1.5871478.

380 "Former Priest Pleads Guilty to 17 Sex Charges," CBC News, www.cbc.ca/news/canada/windsor/former-priest-pleads-guilty-to-17-sex-charges-1.999662.

381 Linda Clementson and Gillian Findlay, "'It's Overwhelming': Survivors Create Public List of Catholic Clerics Accused of Sexual Abuse," CBC News, www.cbc.ca/news/canada/catholic-sexual-abuse-london-diocese-1.5384217.

382 CBC Radio, "How a Sexual Assault Victim's Lawsuit Set a Precendent That Alarmed the Catholic Church".

383 BBC, "Church Sexual Abuse: French Priest Preyant Admits 'Caressing' Boys," BBC, www.bbc.com/news/world-europe-51090077.

384 "Clerical Abuse: Film Gets Go-Ahead after Legal Challenge".

385 "Phillipe Barbarin: French Cardinal Guilty of Abuse Cover-Up," BBC, www.bbc.com/news/world-europe-47481618.

386 "Cardinal Barbarin: France's Top Cleric Cleared of Abuse Cover-Up," BBC, www.bbc.com/news/world-europe-51308751.

387 Tom Symonds, "The Child Abuse Scandal of the British Children Sent Abroad," BBC News, www,bbc.com/news/u7k-39078652.

388 Ibid.

389 BBC, "Archbishop of Brisbane: Catholic Church's Credibility 'Shot to Pieces'," BBC, www.bbc.com/news/ay/world-47348171/archbishop-of-brisbane-catholic-church-s-credibility-shot-to-pieces.

390 Ryan, "The Commission to Enquire into Child Abuse Report."

391 Philip Pullella and Caroline Stauffer, "Key Cardinal Rebukes Pope over Abuse Comment in Rare Move," Reuters, www.reuters/com/article/us-pope-latum-abuse/key-cardinal-rebukes-pope-over-abuse-comment-in-rare-move-idUSKBN1F90ZH.

392 BBC, "Vatican Abuse Summit: Cardinal Says Files Were Destroyed," BBC, www.bbc.com/news/world-europe-47343458.

393 Ryan, "The Commission to Enquire into Child Abuse Report," 13-4.

394 Arnold and Lasky, *Children of the Poor Clares: The Story of an Irish Orphanage*, 82.

395 Kelly, *Sins of the Mother*, 174-5.

396 Ibid., 182.

397 Arnold and Lasky, *Children of the Poor Clares: The Story of an Irish Orphanage*, 10.

398 BBC, "Chile Church Scandal: 'How I Escaped the Priest Who Abused Me for Decades.'," BBC, www.bbc.co.uk/news/stories-45486176.

399 "Child Abuse Priest Fernando Karadima Removed by Vatican," BBC, www.bbc.com/news/world-middle-east-45677534.

400 Nicholas Harrison, June 16, 2019.

401 Dr Nicholas J Harrison to Starwarssavedmylife, August 17, 2019, https://starwarssavedmylife.wordpress.com/2018/08/17/the-art-of-precious-scars/.

402 Coping International, "Welcome to Coping International," Coping: Children of Priests International, www.copinginternational.com/.

403 Sarah McDermott, "My Father, the Catholic Priest Who Doesn't Want to Know Me," BBC, www.bbc.com/news/stories-42085065.

404 BBC, "Silenced Children of Priests to Share Stories with French Bishops," BBC, www.bbc.com/news/world-europe-48620284.

405 Elizabeth Auvillain, "Break the Silence: French Bishops Start Dialogue with Children of Priests.," National Catholic Reporter, www.ncronline. org/news/accountability/break-the-silence-french-bishops-start-dialogue-children-priests.

406 Truth and Reconciliation Commission, *Honouring the Truth, Reconciling for the Future* (Canada: Government of Canada, 2015), v.

407 John S Milloy, *A National Crime: The Canadian Government and the Residential School System 1879-1986* (Manitoba: University of Manitoba Press, 1999), xv.

408 Truth and Reconciliation Commission, *Honouring the Truth, Reconciling for the Future*, v.

409 Fontaine, *Broken Cicle: The Dark Legacy of Indian Residential Schools. A Memoir*, 171-2.

410 Travis Hay, Cindy Blackstock, and Michael Kirlew, "Dr Peter Bryce (1853-1932): Whistleblower on Residential Schools," *CMAJ* 192, no. 9 (2020).

411 Truth and Reconciliation Commission, *Honouring the Truth, Reconciling for the Future*, 54.

412 Ibid., 9.

413 Ibid., v-vi.

414 Milloy, *A National Crime: The Canadian Government and the Residential School System 1879-1986*, 91.

415 Truth and Reconciliation Commission, *Honouring the Truth, Reconciling for the Future*, 3.

416 Milloy, *A National Crime: The Canadian Government and the Residential School System 1879-1986*, 52.

417 Truth and Reconciliation Commission, *Honouring the Truth, Reconciling for the Future*, 3,71.

418 Ibid., 105-7.

419 Milloy, *A National Crime: The Canadian Government and the Residential School System 1879-1986*, 154-5.

420 Truth and Reconciliation Commission, *Honouring the Truth, Reconciling for the Future*, 39.

421 Ibid., 38.

422 Ibid., 40.

423 Ibid., 82.

424 Fournier and Grey, *Stolen from Our Embrace: The Abduction of First Nations Children and the Restoration of Aboriginal Communities*, 34.

425 Milloy, *A National Crime: The Canadian Government and the Residential School System 1879-1986*, 12.

426 Ibid., 142-3.

427 Furniss, *Victims of Benevolence: The Dark Legacy of the Williams Lake Residential School*, 67.

428   Ibid.
429   Truth and Reconciliation Commission, *Honouring the Truth, Reconciling for the Future*, 86.
430   Milloy, *A National Crime: The Canadian Government and the Residential School System 1879-1986*, 284.
431   Ibid.
432   Truth and Reconciliation Commission, *Honouring the Truth, Reconciling for the Future*, 89.
433   Ibid.
434   Milloy, *A National Crime: The Canadian Government and the Residential School System 1879-1986*, 140.
435   Ibid., 139.
436   Ibid., 142-3.
437   Ibid.
438   Ibid.
439   Ibid.
440   Ibid., 150.
441   Ibid., 150-1.
442   Fontaine, *Broken Cicle: The Dark Legacy of Indian Residential Schools. A Memoir*, 111.
443   Milloy, *A National Crime: The Canadian Government and the Residential School System 1879-1986*, 284.
444   Ibid., 296-7.
445   Ibid.
446   Fournier and Grey, *Stolen from Our Embrace: The Abduction of First Nations Children and the Restoration of Aboriginal Communities*, 121.
447   Ibid.
448   Milloy, *A National Crime: The Canadian Government and the Residential School System 1879-1986*, 298.
449   Truth and Reconciliation Commission, *Honouring the Truth, Reconciling for the Future*, 107-8.
450   Ibid., 107.
451   Ibid., 107-8.
452   Fontaine, *Broken Cicle: The Dark Legacy of Indian Residential Schools. A Memoir*, 13-8.
453   Ibid., 19.
454   Truth and Reconciliation Commission, *Honouring the Truth, Reconciling for the Future*, 107-8.
455   Ibid.
456   Fournier and Grey, *Stolen from Our Embrace: The Abduction of First Nations Children and the Restoration of Aboriginal Communities*, 31-2.
457   Ibid., 47.
458   Ibid., 48.

459 Ibid.

460 Ibid.

461 Ibid., 140.

462 Ibid., 64-9.

463 Ibid., 71-2.

464 Alanna Mitchell, "From the Survivors' Circle," *Canadian Geographic* 2017, 66.

465 Ibid., 68.

466 Ibid., 71.

467 Fournier and Grey, *Stolen from Our Embrace: The Abduction of First Nations Children and the Restoration of Aboriginal Communities*, 120.

468 Ibid.

469 Jessica Doria-Brown, "Hidden History: Survivor Stories Fom the Indian Day School on Lennox Island, Located Just Off PEI's North Shore," CBC, https://newsinteractives.cbc.ca/longform/hidden-history.

470 Fournier and Grey, *Stolen from Our Embrace: The Abduction of First Nations Children and the Restoration of Aboriginal Communities*, 81.

471 Ibid., 82.

472 Tanya Talaga, *Seven Fallen Feathers: Racism, Death and Hard Truths in a Northern City* (Canada: Anansi Press, 2017), 203.

473 Ibid.

474 Fournier and Grey, *Stolen from Our Embrace: The Abduction of First Nations Children and the Restoration of Aboriginal Communities*, 88-9.

475 Ibid., 91.

476 Truth and Reconciliation Commission, *Honouring the Truth, Reconciling for the Future*, 140-1.

477 Ibid.

478 Ibid.

479 APTN News, "Indigenous Newborn 'Baby H' Returned to Parents on Brink of Court Hearing," APTN News, https://aptnnews.ca/2019/06/27 indigenous-newborn-baby-h-returned-to-parents-on-the-brink-of-court-hearing.

480 CBC Radio, "Indigenous Women Kept from Seeing Their Newborn Babies until Agreeing to Sterilization," www.cbc.ca/radio/thecurrent/the-current-for-november-13-2018-1.4902670/indigenous-women-kept-from-seeing-their-newborn-babies-until-agreeing-to-sterilization; Yvonne Boyer and Judith Bartlett, "External Review: Tubal Ligation in the Saskatoon Health Region: The Lived Experience of Aboriginal Women," (Canada: Health Region Saskatoon, 2017).

481 Sylvie Fournier, "Black, Indigenous Mothers Say They Were Sterilized without Full Consent at Quebec Hospitals," CBC, https://www.cbc.ca/news/canada/montreal/quebec-hospital-sterilization-1.6188269; Susan

Bell, "Quebec Indigenous Groups Collecting Stories of Forced Sterilization," CBC, https://www.cbc.ca/news/canada/north/indigenous-forced-sterilization-quebec-study-cree-1.6186212.

482   Truth and Reconciliation Commission, *Honouring the Truth, Reconciling for the Future*, 140-1.

483   K E Macleans, "When You Have to Give Birth in Secret," Today's Parent, www.todaysparent.com/family/parenting/when-you-have-to-give-birth-in-secret.

484   André Picard, "Cindy Blackstock: Advocate for First Nations Children," *The Lancet* (2018).

485   Solomon.

486   Fournier and Grey, *Stolen from Our Embrace: The Abduction of First Nations Children and the Restoration of Aboriginal Communities*, 37-8.

487   Ibid., 52.

488   Ibid., 43.

489   Ibid., 121.

490   Ibid., 139.

491   Truth and Reconciliation Commission, *Honouring the Truth, Reconciling for the Future*, 105-7.

492   Milloy, *A National Crime: The Canadian Government and the Residential School System 1879-1986*, 145.

493   Truth and Reconciliation Commission, *Honouring the Truth, Reconciling for the Future*, 105-7.

494   Ibid.

495   Milloy, *A National Crime: The Canadian Government and the Residential School System 1879-1986*, 145.

496   Truth and Reconciliation Commission, *Honouring the Truth, Reconciling for the Future*, 119.

497   Ibid.

498   Furniss, *Victims of Benevolence: The Dark Legacy of the Williams Lake Residential School*, 14.

499   Ibid., 67.

500   Ibid., 93.

501   Truth and Reconciliation Commission, *Honouring the Truth, Reconciling for the Future*, 117-8.

502   Ibid.

503   Hay, Blackstock, and Kirlew, "Dr Peter Bryce (1853-1932): Whistleblower on Residential Schools."

504   Simon Solomon, 13 December 2017.

505   Hay, Blackstock, and Kirlew, "Dr Peter Bryce (1853-1932): Whistleblower on Residential Schools."

506   Fontaine, *Broken Cicle: The Dark Legacy of Indian Residential Schools. A Memoir*, 175.

507 Fournier and Grey, *Stolen from Our Embrace: The Abduction of First Nations Children and the Restoration of Aboriginal Communities*, 115.

508 Ibid., 211.

509 Ibid., 210.

510 Talaga, *Seven Fallen Feathers: Racism, Death and Hard Truths in a Northern City.*

511 Fournier and Grey, *Stolen from Our Embrace: The Abduction of First Nations Children and the Restoration of Aboriginal Communities*, 118.

512 Ibid., 117.

513 Ibid.

514 Hay, Blackstock, and Kirlew, "Dr Peter Bryce (1853-1932): Whistleblower on Residential Schools."

515 Ibid.

516 Olivia Stefanovich, "NDP MP Calls on Lemetti to Preserve St Anne's Residential School Abuse Documents," CBC News, https://www.cbc.ca/news/politics/st-anne-documents-angus-lametti-letter-1.5839805.

517 Simon Nakonechny, "As Catholic Church Balked at Paying Residential School Settlement, Quebec Nuns Sold Nearly $25m in Real Estate," CBC, https://www.cbc.ca/news/canada/montreal/residential-school-financial-settlements-quebec-catholic-church-1.6092215.

518 Jason Warick, "Critics Blast Catholic Church for Spending after Commitment to Residential School Survivors Went Unmet," CBC News, https://www.cbc.ca/news/canada/saskatoon/critics-blast-catholic-church-1.6086030.

519 Nakonechny, "As Catholic Church Balked at Paying Residential School Settlement, Quebec Nuns Sold Nearly $25m in Real Estate".

520 Julie Ireton, "'Far from Bankrupt': Catholic Order That Ran 48 Residential Schools Faces Criticism," CBC, https://www.cbc.ca/news/canada/ottawa/oblates-complex-corporate-structure-protect-money-from-liabilities-residential-school-1.6259013.

521 Warick, "Critics Blast Catholic Church for Spending after Commitment to Residential School Survivors Went Unmet".

522 Jason Warick and Justin Li, "Catholic Bishops Pledge $30m for Residential School Survivors, AFN Expresses Skepticism," CBC, https://www.cbc.ca/news/canada/catholic-bishops-30-million-1.6191677.

523 Truth and Reconciliation Commission, *Honouring the Truth, Reconciling for the Future*, 8.

524 Lesher, *Sexual Abuse, Shonda and Concealment in Orthodox Jewish Communities.*, 7-8.

525 Ibid.

526 Neustein, *Tempest in the Temple: Jewish Communities and Child Sex Scandals*, 1.

527   Ibid.
528   Ibid.
529   Ibid., 2,127.
530   Ibid., 130.
531   BBC, "Malka Leifer: Israel Court Approves Extradition of Sex Abuse Suspect to Australia," BBC, https://www.bbc.com/news/world-australia-55302667.
532   R Yehuda et al., "History of Past Sexual Abuse in Married Observant Jewish Women," *American Journal of Psychiatry* 164 (2007).
533   Neustein, *Tempest in the Temple: Jewish Communities and Child Sex Scandals*, 77.
534   Ibid., 6.
535   Ibid., 96-7.
536   Ibid., 3.
537   Ibid., 7.
538   Ibid., 91.
539   MC Spiegel, "Survival and Recovery: Jewish Women Confront Abuse," in *Shine the Light: Sexual Abuse and Healing in the Jewish Community*, ed. R Lev (Boston: Northwestern University Press, 2003), 147.
540   Neustein, *Tempest in the Temple: Jewish Communities and Child Sex Scandals*, 94.
541   Ibid., 116.
542   Lesher, *Sexual Abuse, Shonda and Concealment in Orthodox Jewish Communities.*, 70-1.
543   Ibid., 73.
544   Neustein, *Tempest in the Temple: Jewish Communities and Child Sex Scandals*, 114.
545   Steven H Resnicoff, "Jewish Law and the Tragedy of Sexual Abuse of Children: The Dilemma within the Orthodox Jewish Community" *Rutgers Journal of Law and Religion* 13, no. 2 (2012): 4-6; Lesher, *Sexual Abuse, Shonda and Concealment in Orthodox Jewish Communities.*, 112.
546   Torah Academy of Bergen County, "The Mesirah Dilemma by Rabbi Chaim Jachter," Torah Academy of Bergen County, https://www.kolto-rah.org/halachah/the-mesirah-dilemma-by-rabbi-chaim-jachter; Herschel Schachter, "Regarding Mesirah," The Torahweb Foundation, https://www.torahweb.org/torah/special/2007/rsch_mesirah.html.
547   Lesher, *Sexual Abuse, Shonda and Concealment in Orthodox Jewish Communities.*, 113.
548   Neustein, *Tempest in the Temple: Jewish Communities and Child Sex Scandals*, 88-90.
549   Resnicoff, "Jewish Law and the Tragedy of Sexual Abuse of Children: The Dilemma within the Orthodox Jewish Community ".

550 David Mandel and David Pelcovitz, *Breaking the Silence: Sexual Abuse in the Jewish Community* (Jersey City, NJ, USA: Ktav Publishing House, Inc., 2011), xii-xiii.

551 Ibid.

552 Ibid.

553 Ibid.

554 Lesher, *Sexual Abuse, Shonda and Concealment in Orthodox Jewish Communities.*, 213.

555 Mandel and Pelcovitz, *Breaking the Silence: Sexual Abuse in the Jewish Community*, 3.

556 Lesher, *Sexual Abuse, Shonda and Concealment in Orthodox Jewish Communities.*, 90.

557 Resnicoff, "Jewish Law and the Tragedy of Sexual Abuse of Children: The Dilemma within the Orthodox Jewish Community " 10-1.

558 Leonard Shengold, *Soul Murder Revisited* (New Haven Conn: Yale University Press, 1999); Neustein, *Tempest in the Temple: Jewish Communities and Child Sex Scandals*, 78.

559 Nicole Brockbank, "Dark Days at Camp," CBC News, https://newsinteractives.cbc.ca/longform/camp-wahanowin-abuse.

560 BBC Sport, "Simone Biles: Larry Nassar Abused Me, Says Four-Time Olympic Champion," BBC, www.bbc.com/sport/gymnastics/42697952; BBC, "Larry Nassar Case: The 156 Women Who Confronted a Predator," BBC News, www.bbc,com/news/world-us-canada-42725339; "Larry Nassar Jailed for Another 40-125 Years.," BBC, www.bbc.com/news/world-us-canada-42950478.

561 Reuters, "Gymnastics: U.S Governing Body Shocked over Death of Former Coach," Reuters, https://www.usnews.com/news/top-news/articles/2021-02-26/gymnastics-us-governing-body-shocked-over-death-of-former-coach.

562 BBC, "George Tyndall: Ex-USC Doctor Arrested over Sex Abuse " BBC, www.bbc.com/news/world-us-canada-48794597.

563 "Ohio State University Doctor 'Abused 177 Male Students'," BBC, www.bbc.com/news/world-us-canada-48319878.

564 Jim Reed and Louis Lee Ray, *Lawn Tennis Association 'Missed Chances' to Stop Abuse* (UK: BBC, 2019).

565 BBC, "Tennis Child Abuse Apology after Wrexham Coach Case," BBC www.bbc.com/news/uk-wales-north-east-wales-42102382.

566 "Barry Bennell: A Mother's Horror at Her Son's Sexual Abuse," BBC News, www.bbc.com/news/uk-wales-43106572.

567 "Neil Harris: How Abusive Dance Teacher Went Unchecked for Decades," BBC, https://www.bbc.com/news/uk-england-birmingham-53388634.

568 "Peter Seisenbacher: Austrian Judo Champion Jailed for Child Sex Abuse," BBC, bbc.com/news/world-europe-50631219.

569 "Sarah Abitbol: French Ice Skating Boss Quits Amid Sex Abuse Scandal," BBC, www.bbc.com/news/world-europe-51425860.

570 Ibid.

571 CBC, "Maple Leafs Gardens Sex Offender Gordon Stuckless Dead, Lawyer Says," The Canadian Press, https://www.cbc.ca/news/canada/toronto/maple-leaf-garden-s-sex-offender-gordon-stuckless--lawyer-1.5528992.

572 Paola Loriggio, "Sexual Abuse Victims Tell of Lifelong Suffering from Gordon Stuckless," Macleans, https://www.macleans.ca/news/canada/sexual-abuse-victims-tell-of-lifelong-suffering-from-gordon-stuckless/.

573 Ibid.

574 Ibid.

575 Ministry of the Attorney General, "Handouts: Child Sex Abuse," Ministry of the Attorney General, https://www.attorneygeneral.jus.gov.on.ca/inquiries/cornwall/en/hearings/exhibits/Peter_Jaffe/pdf/Sports.pdf.

576 Ibid.

577 Ibid.

578 Chalmers, *Betrayed: Child Sex Abuse in the Holocaust*, 170.

579 Robin Levinson-King, "The Brutal Secret of School Sport Initiations," BBC News, www.bbc.com/news/world-us-canada-46282988.

580 Ibid.

581 Sarah Rieger, "Calgary Minor Hockey Club Probes 'Disturbing' Video That Shows Boy Passing out, Convulsing," CBC, https://www.cbc.ca/news/canada/calgary/calgary-hockey-seizure-video-1.5775894.

582 University of Alberta, "University of Alberta: Hazing Information," University of Alberta, https://www.ualberta.ca/current-students/student-groups/hazing/index.html.

583 BBC, "Boy Scouts of America: Almost 100,000 Make Sexual Abuse Compensation Claims," BBC, https://www.bbc.com/news/world-us-canada-54971579.

584 "Boy Scouts of America Files for Bankruptcy over Sex Abuse Lawsuits," BBC, www.bbc.com/news/world-us-canada-51542401.

585 CNN, "Boy Scouts Plan Fund with at Least $300 Million for Sex Abuse Victims, Court Documents Show," CNN, https://www.cnn.com/2021/03/02/us/boy-scouts-sexual-abuse-bankruptcy/index.html.

586 BBC, "Boy Scouts of America: Almost 100,000 Make Sexual Abuse Compensation Claims".

587 "Boy Scouts: A Wholesome US Institution Poisoned by Predators," BBC, https://www.bbc.com/news/world-us-canada-51552576.

588 Ibid.
589 "Boy Scouts of America: Almost 100,000 Make Sexual Abuse Compensation Claims".
590 "Thousands of US Child Migrants Sexually Abused," CNN, www.bbc.com/news/world-us-canada-47377889.
591 Ibid.
592 UNICEF, "Together for Girls: Sexual Violence Fact Sheet".
593 Susan Anderson, *High Glitz: The Extravagent World of Child Beauty Pageants* (USA: Powerhouse, 2009).
594 Ibid.
595 The Economist, "The Sexualization of Children: Innocents and Experience."
596 EL Zurbriggen et al., "Report of the APA Task Force on the Sexualization of Girls," (Washington DC: American Psychological Association, 2007); Elke Reissing and Heather Armstrong, "Sexuality over the Lifespan," in *Human Sexuality: A Contemporary Introduction*, ed. Caroline Pukall (Canada: Oxford University Press, 2020), 207.
597 Zurbriggen et al., "Report of the APA Task Force on the Sexualization of Girls."
598 S Grabe, JS Hyde, and SM Lindberg, "Body Objectification and Depression in Adolescents: The Role of Gender, Shame and Rumination," *Psychology of Women Quarterly* 31, no. 2 (2007).
599 Zurbriggen et al., "Report of the APA Task Force on the Sexualization of Girls."
600 Rush, *The Best-Kept Secret: Sexual Abuse of Children*, 16-40.
601 Ibid.
602 Amber Haque, "Breast Ironing Awareness 'Needed in School'," BBC, www.bbc.com/news/education-47695169.
603 B Chalmers and K Omer-Hashi, *Female Genital Mutilation and Obstetric Care* (Vancouver, BC, Canada: Trafford Publishers, 2003), 10.
604 Francesco Rubino et al., "Joint International Consensus Statement for Ending Stigma of Obesity," *Nature Medicine* (2020).
605 BBC, "Tennis Child Abuse Apology after Wrexham Coach Case".
606 The Lancet Editorial, "The Erosion of Women's Sexual and Reproductive Rights," *The Lancet* 393, no. 10183 (2019).
607 Hollington, *Unthinkable: The Shocking Scandal of the UK Sex Traffickers*, 221.
608 Ibid.
609 Solomon.
610 Hollington, *Unthinkable: The Shocking Scandal of the UK Sex Traffickers*, 161.
611 Ibid., 220.
612 Boge, *The True Story of Canadian Human Trafficking*, 243.

613 Ibid., 237.
614 Hollington, *Unthinkable: The Shocking Scandal of the UK Sex Traffickers*, 254.
615 Cacho, *Slavery Inc.: The Untold Story of International Sex Trafficking*, 24.
616 Ibid., 240.
617 Ronis and Kabbash, "Sexual Assault and Harassment," 403-4.
618 Ibid., 403.
619 J O'Conner et al., "Students' Articulation of Subtle Rape Myths Surrounding Campus Sexual Assault.," *Journal of College Student Development* 59 (2018).
620 KM Budd and DM Bierie, "Victims of Sexual Assault Perpetrated by Female Youth: An Exploratory Study of Gender Differences," *Journal of Sexual Aggression* 24, no. 3 (2018).
621 LA Greenfield, "Sex Offences and Offenders: An Analysis of Data on Rape and Sexual Assault.," (Washington DC: U S Department of Justice, 1997).
622 Ronis and Kabbash, "Sexual Assault and Harassment," 403-4.
623 Ibid.
624 C Rotenberg and A Cotter, "Police Reported Sexual Assaults in Canada before and after #Metoo, 2016 and 2017," in *Juristat: Candian Centre for Justice Statistics* (Statistics Canada Catalogue no.85-002-x, 2018).
625 Ronis and Kabbash, "Sexual Assault and Harassment," 403-4.
626 Ibid.
627 Ibid.
628 Ibid.
629 Ibid.
630 Ibid., 405.
631 The Economist, "The Sexualization of Children: Innocents and Experience."
632 BBC, "Egypt Sex Attacks Fuel 'Feminist' Revolution," BBC, https://www.bbc.com/news/world-middle-east-54643463.
633 Mayuri Mei Lin, "Malaysia Revised 'Victim-Shaming' School Text Book," BBC News, www.bbc.com/news/world-asia-46888332.
634 Bradlyn Oakes and John Last, "Women on Arctic Mission Told Not to Wear Tight-Fitting Clothing," CBC, https://www.cbc.ca/news/canada/north/mosaic-dress-code-sexism-arctic-research-1.5739547.
635 The Economist, "The Sexualization of Children: Innocents and Experience."
636 Chalmers and Omer-Hashi, *Female Genital Mutilation and Obstetric Care*, 10.
637 The Economist, "The Sexualization of Children: Innocents and Experience."

638 Kathrin F. Stanger-Hall and David W. Hall, "Abstinence-Only Education and Teen Pregnancy Rates: Why We Need Comprehensive Sex Education in the U.S," *PLOS-ONE* 6, no. 10 (2011).

639 Sutton, *Variations in Sexual Behaviour*, 430.

640 Ibid.

641 Ibid.

642 Ibid., 431.

643 M Ybarra and K Mitchell, "Exposure to Internet Pornography among Children and Adolescents: A National Survey," *CyberPsychology and Behaviour* 8, no. 5 (2005).

644 M Flood, "The Harms of Pornography Exposure among Children and Young People," *Child Abuse Review* 18, no. 6 (2009).

645 Ibid.

646 Ybarra et al., "X-Rated Material and Perpetration of Sexually Aggressive Behaviour among Children and Adolescents: Is There a Link?."

647 J Peter and PM Valkenburg, "Adolescents and Pornography: A Review of 20 Years of Research," *Journal of Sex Research* 53 (2016).

648 S Kraus and B Russell, "Early Sexual Experiences: The Role of Internet Access and Sexually Explicit Material," *CyberPsychology and Behavior* 11, no. 2 (2008).

649 R Collins et al., "Sexual Media and Childhood Well-Being and Health," *Pediatrics* 140, no. 5, Supp 2 (2017).

650 J Peter and P Valkenburg, "Adolescents' Exposure to Sexually Explicit Internet Material and Sexual Satisfaction: A Longitudinal Study," *Human Communication Research* 35, no. 2 (2009).

651 JM Allbright, "Sex in America Online: An Exploration of Sex, Marital Status and Sexual identity in Internet Sex Seeking and Its Impacts," *Journal of Sex Research* 45, no. 2 (2008).

652 Dana Solomon, Personal Communication, 2020.

653 E L James, *Fifty Shades of Grey* (UK: Doubleday, 2013).

654 Solomon.

655 Pukall, *Human Sexuality: A Contemporary Introduction*, 349.

656 Interpol, "International Child Sexual Exploitation Database," UN, https://www.interpol.int/en/Crimes/Crimes-against-children/International-Child-Sexual-Exploitation-database.

657 BBC, "Eric Eoin Marques: Irish Man Jailed in US for Child Abuse Images," https://www.bbc.com/news/world-europe-58582817.

658 "Dark Web Paedophile Mathew Falder's Sentence Reduced," BBC, www.bbc.com/news/uk-england-45875275.

659 Ibid.

660 Mathew Falder, "Dark Web Paedophile Mathew Falder Jailed for 32 Years," BBC, www.bbc.com/news/uk-england-43114471.

661 BBC, "Dark Web Paedophile Mathew Falder's Sentence Reduced".

662 Jessica Damiana, Kanupriya Kapoor, and Clarence Fernandez, "Indonesian Police Probe Foreign 'Orders' for Child Pornography," Reuters, www.reuters.com/article/us-indonesia-pornography/indonesian-police-probe-foreign-orders-for-child-pornography-idUSKBN1EY10O.

663 BBC, "Paedophile Richard Huckle Stabbed to Death at Full Sutton Prison," BBC, www.bbc.com/news/uk-50042406.

664 Lucy Adams, "Online Child Sex Abuse Investigation Identifies 523 Potential Victims," BBC, www.bbc.com/ness/uk-scotland-36922820.

665 BBC, "Rotherham Warning over Child Sex Exploitation in Scotland," BBC http://bbc.com/uk-scotland-29175287.

666 Morris Steven, "Revealed: Child Sex Abuse Gang 'with Tentacles That Go around the World'," The Guardian, www.theguardian.com/uk-news/2015/apr/22/child-sex-paedophile-abuse-gang-revealed--two-convictions.

667 Michael Nienaber, "German Police Make Arrests over Massive Child Pornography Website," Reuters, http://www.reuters.com/article/us-germany-sexcrimes-idUSKBN19R0VD; Riham Alkousaa, "German Prosecutors Charge Child-Porn Website Operators," Reuters, www.reuters.com/article/us-germany-sexcrimes/german-prosecutors-charge-child-porn-website-operators-idSKCN1IG1NT.

668 James Frate and Claudia Otto, "German Police Bust Child Sex Abuse Imagery Network with 400,000 Users," CNN, https://www.cnn.com/2021/05/03/europe/germany-child-sex-abuse-imagery-ring-intl/index.html.

669 BBC, "Major Child Sexual Abuse Trial Begins in Germany," BBC, https://www.bbc.com/news/world-europe-53813249.

670 "Paedophile Ring Sentenced in Germany," BBC, https://www.bbc.com/news/world-europe-57735317.

671 Atika Shubert, Nadine Schmidt, and Claudia Otto, "Children and Parents Reported Sex Abuse for Years in Central Germany. Why Did No One Believe Them?," CNN, www.cnn.com/2019/04/05/europe/german-sex-abuse-michaela-andreas-v-intl/index.html.

672 Nadine Schmidt and Sheena McKenzie, *Two Men Convicted in One of Germany's Worst Child Sex Abuse Scandals* (USA: CNN, 2019).

673 Reuters, "Australian Police Arrests 14 Men on Child Abuse Charges," Reuters, https://www.reuters.com/article/australia-crime-int/australian-police-arrests-14-men-on-child-abuse-charges-idUSKBN-27R05C.

674 BBC, "Fifty Children Saved as International Paedophile Ring Busted.," BBC, www.bbc.com/news/world-48379983.

675 Ananthalakshmi, "How Malaysia Allows Child Abuse to Go Unpunished".

676 Stacey Dooley, "Stacy Dooley Investigates: 'My Daughter Was Tormented by Spycam Sex Crime'," BBC, https://www.bbc.co.uk/bbc-three/article/63de169c-dfbb-4b22-9da3-b5f3a55628a2.

677 Ibid.

678 BBC, "Brazil Police Arrests 108 in Major Anti-Paedophile Operation," BBC, www.bbc.com/news/world-latin-america-41704429.

679 Malone Mullin, "Sending Nudes Can Have Dire Consequences. So Why Are N.L. Teens Still Doing It?," CBC News, https://www.cbc.ca/news/canada/newfoundland-labrador/teen-sexting-nl-1.5483672; Alexandra S. Marcotte et al., "Women's and Men's Reactions to Receiving Unsolicited Genital Images from Men," *The Journal of Sex Research* 58, no. 4 (2020).

680 The Economist, "The Sexualization of Children: Innocents and Experience."

681 Jason Proctor, "Instagram Evidence Convinces B.C. Judge Teen Was 'Set up' on Sexual Assault Charges," CBC News, https://www.cbc.ca/news/canada/british-columbia/sexual-assault-instagram-teenager-1.5995282.

682 National Crime Agency, "Man Sentenced over Some of the Worst Child Abuse Content NCA Investigators Have Ever Seen," National Crime Agency, https://www.nationalcrimeagency.gov.uk/news/man-sentenced-over-some-of-the-worst-child-abuse-content-nca-investigators-have-ever-seen.

683 Ibid.

684 National Center for Education Statistics, "Student Access to Digital Learning Resources Outside of the Classroom," U.S. Department of Education, https://nces.ed.gov/fastfacts/display.asp?id=46.

685 Hollington, *Unthinkable: The Shocking Scandal of the UK Sex Traffickers*, 52.

686 Nicholas Kristoff, "The Children of Pornhub: Why Does Canada Allow This Company to Profit Off Videos of Exploitation and Assault?," New York Times, https://www.nytimes.com/2020/12/04/opinion/sunday/pornhub-rape-trafficking.html?smid=em-share.

687 John Paul Tasker, "Senator Aims to Curb 'Violent' Porn, Pitches Mandatory Age Verification for Online Sites," CBC, https://www.cbc.ca/news/politics/senator-violent-porn-mandatory-age-pornhub-1.5810603.

688 Kristoff, "The Children of Pornhub: Why Does Canada Allow This Company to Profit Off Videos of Exploitation and Assault?".

689 Ibid.

690 Ibid.

691 BBC, "Sajid Javid Threatens Tech Giants over Online Child Sex Abuse," BBC www.bbc.co.uk/news/uk-45389937.

692 "Facebook Removes 11.6 Million Child Abuse Posts," BBC, www.bbc. com/news/technology-50404812.

693 Kristoff, "The Children of Pornhub: Why Does Canada Allow This Company to Profit Off Videos of Exploitation and Assault?".

694 Ibid.; BBC, "Pornhub Bans User Uploads after Abuse Allegations," BBC, https://www.bbc.com/news/technology-55231181.

695 Kristoff, "The Children of Pornhub: Why Does Canada Allow This Company to Profit Off Videos of Exploitation and Assault?"; BBC, "Pornhub Bans User Uploads after Abuse Allegations".

696 Jazmin Goodwin, "Mastercard, Visa and Discover Cut Ties with Pornhub Following Allegations of Child Abuse," CNN, https://www. cnn.com/2020/12/14/business/mastercard-visa-discover-pornhub/index. html; BBC, "Pornhub: Mastercard Severs Links with Pornography Site," https://www.bbc.com/news/technology-55267311.

697 CBC, "40 Women in California Launch Lawsuit against Montreal-Based Parent Company of Pornhub," CBC, https://www.cbc.ca/news/ canada/montreal/women-california-lawsuit-pornhub-1.5844705.

698 Karen Pauls, "New Rules on Removal of Illegal Online Content Could Help in Battle against Child Pornography," CBC, https://www.cbc.ca/ news/canada/manitoba/canada-illegal-online-content-child-porn-1.5847695.

699 BBC, "Facebook Child Abuse Detection Hit by New EU Rules," BBC, https://www.bbc.com/news/technology-55399509.

700 "Child Abuse Images Being Traded Via Secure Apps," BBC, www.bbc. com/news/technology-47279256.

701 Megha Mohan, "I Was Raped at 14, and the Video Ends up on a Porn Site," BBC, www.bbc.com/news/stories-51391981.

702 Ybarra et al., "X-Rated Material and Perpetration of Sexually Aggressive Behaviour among Children and Adolescents: Is There a Link?."

703 Alys Harte, "A Man Tried to Choke Me During Sex without Warning," BBC Radio 5 Live Investigators Unit, www.bbc.com/news/ uk-50546184.

704 CNN, "Instagram Is Leading Social Media Platform for Child Grooming," CNN, www.cnn.com/2019/03/01/uk/nspcc-grooming-social-media-report-scli-gbr-intl/index.html.

705 Karen Pauls and Cameron MacIntosh, "Woman Who Spent Years Scrubbing Explicit Video from Internet Urges Tech Firms to Make It Easier to Remove," CBC, https://www.cbc.ca/news/canada/manitoba/ canada-internet-children-abuse-pornography-1.5822042.

706 BBC, "WhatsApp Child Sex Images Led to Arrests," BBC, www.bbc. uk/news/technology-39629184.

707 "Fears over Fake Bieber and Styles Accounts," BBC, www.bbc.com/ news/blogs-trending-39670673

708   Yoonjung Seo, "Dozens of Young Women in South Korea Were Allegedly Forced into Sexual Slavery on an Encrypted Messaging App," CNN, https://www.cnn.com/2020/03/27/asia/south-korea-telegram-sex-rooms-intl-hnk/index.html

709   Ibid.

710   BBC, "Choju-Bin: South Korea Chatroom Sex Abuse Suspect Named after Outcry.," BBC, www.bbc.com/news/world-asia-52030219.

711   Seo, "Dozens of Young Women in South Korea Were Allegedly Forced into Sexual Slavery on an Encrypted Messaging App".

712   BBC, "Choju-Bin: 40 Years Jail for South Korean Chatroom Sex Abuse Group Leader," BBC, https://www.bbc.com/news/world-asia-55082072.

713   "Netherlands 'Hosts Most Child Sex Abuse Images'," BBC, www.bbc.com/news/technology-48022950.

714   Tim Whewell, "Norway's Hidden Scandal," BBC, www.bbc.co.uk/news/resources/idt-sh/norways_hidden_scandal.

715   BBC, "Denmark Facebook Sex Video: More Than 1000 Young People Charged," BBC www.bbc,com/news/world-europe-42694218.

716   "Belgium Gang Rape: Five Arrested over Assault on Teenager," BBC, https://www.bbc.com/news/world-europe-57315750.

717   Ibid.

718   BBC Panorama, "Pimps Caught Exploiting Women on Popular Classified Ads Website," BBC, https://www.bbc.com/news/uk-59219411.

719   Noel Titheradge, "OnlyFans: How It Handles Illegal Sex Videos - BBC Investigation," BBC.

720   Noel Titheradge and Rianna Croxford, "The Children Selling Explicit Videos on OnlyFans," BBC, https://www.bbc.com/news/uk-57255983.

721   Ibid.

722   BBC, "German Couple Jailed for Selling Son to Paedophiles on Dark Net," BBC, www.bbc.co.uk/news/world-eu45096183.

723   Reuters, "German Police Detain Man after Posting Child Abuse Victim's Photo," Reuters, www.reuters.com/article/us-germany-crime/german-police-detain-man-after-posting-child-abuse-victims-photo-idUSKBN1CF1F3.

724   Damiana, Kapoor, and Fernandez, "Indonesian Police Probe Foreign 'Orders' for Child Pornography".

725   Mike Thomson, "Westeners 'Fuelling Phillipine Child Sex Video Rise'," BBC, www.bbc.com/news/world-asis-48517437.

726   Angus Crawford, "UK Paedophiles Pay to Watch Webcam Child Sex Abuse in Philippines," BBC, www.bbc.com/news/uk-25729140.

727   Thomson, "Westeners 'Fuelling Phillipine Child Sex Video Rise'".

728   BBC, "Steep Rise in Child Abuse Images Online, Charity Reports," BBC www.bbc.co.uk/news/technology-43796380.

729   Interpol, "Crimes against Children," UN, https://www.interpol.int/Crimes/Crimes-against-children.

730   Kathryn Farr, *Sex Trafficking: The Global Market in Women and Children* (New York: Worth Publishers, 2005), 163.

731   Ibid., 164-7.

732   Ibid., 191-2.

733   Cacho, *Slavery Inc.: The Untold Story of International Sex Trafficking*, 159.

734   Ibid., 158.

735   Farr, *Sex Trafficking: The Global Market in Women and Children*, 167.

736   Ibid.

737   Ibid., 164.

738   Ibid., 170.

739   Ibid., 199.

740   Ibid.

741   Black, *Slavery*, 238.

742   Charles River Editors, *The Rape of Nanking* (San Bernadino, California: Charles River Editors, 2016).

743   Ibid.

744   Ibid.

745   Farr, *Sex Trafficking: The Global Market in Women and Children*, 163.

746   Ibid.

747   Ibid., 173.

748   UNICEF, "Children under Attack: Six Grave Violations against Children in Times of War," UNICEF, https://www.unicef.org/stories/children-under-attack-six-grave-violations-against-children-times-war.

749   Ibid.

750   Bethlehem Feleke et al., "Practically This Has Been a Genocide," CNN, https://www.cnn.com/2021/03/19/africa/ethiopia-tigray-rape-investigation-cmd-intl/index.html.

751   UNICEF, "Children under Attack: Six Grave Violations against Children in Times of War".

752   Ibid.

753   Anna Coren, Jessie Yeung, and Abdul Basir Bina, "She Was Sold to a Stranger So Her Family Could Eat as Afghanistan Crumbles," CNN, https://www.cnn.com/2021/11/01/asia/afghanistan-child-marriage-crisis-taliban-intl-hnk-dst/index.html.

754   Chalmers, *Betrayed: Child Sex Abuse in the Holocaust*.

755   Ibid.

756   Emmanuel Sehene Ruvugiro, "Rwanda: The Gruesome Plight of Children During the Tutsi Genocide.," Justiceinfo.net, www.justiceinfo.

net/en/tribunals/ictr/34925-online-exhibition-pays-gruesome-tribute-to-child-suffering-in-rwandan-genocide.html.

757 Musa Wakhungu Olaka, "Living a Genocide: Rape," USF Tampa Library, http://exhibits.lib.usf.edu/exhibits/show/darfur-genocide/modeofdestruction/rape.

758 V Dadrian, "Armenian Children Victims of Genocide," http://www.genocide-museum.am/eng/online_exhibition_3.php.

759 Ruvugiro, "Rwanda: The Gruesome Plight of Children During the Tutsi Genocide.".

760 United to End Genocide, "The Cambodian Genocide," United to End Genocide, http://endgenocide.org/learn/past-genocides/the-cambodian-genocide/.

761 The History Place, "Stalin's Forced Famine: 1932-9133: 7,000,000 Deaths," The History Place, http://www.historyplace.com/worldhistory/genocide/stalin.htm.

762 Lisa Alfredson, "Sexual Exploitation of Child Soldiers: An Exploration and Analysis of Global Dimensions and Trends," *Minerva* 23, no. May (2002): 3.

763 Ibid., 3-4.

764 Ibid., 7.

765 Ibid., 6-7.

766 Ibid., 13.

767 Rosemary Grey, "Sexual Violence against Child Soldiers: The Limits and Potential of International Criminal Law," *International Feminist Journal of Politics* 16, no. 4 (2014): 602.

768 E Benjamin Skinner, *A Crime So Monstrous: A Shocking Expose of Modern-Day Sex Slavery, Human Trafficking and Urban Child Markets* (Edinburgh: Mainstream Publishing, 2008), 207; Farr, *Sex Trafficking: The Global Market in Women and Children*, 208.

769 Skinner, *A Crime So Monstrous: A Shocking Expose of Modern-Day Sex Slavery, Human Trafficking and Urban Child Markets*, 207; Farr, *Sex Trafficking: The Global Market in Women and Children*, 208.

770 WHO, "WHO Horrified over Sexual Exploitation by Aid Workers in DR Congo," BBC, https://www.bbc.com/news/world-africa-58710200.

771 Skinner, *A Crime So Monstrous: A Shocking Expose of Modern-Day Sex Slavery, Human Trafficking and Urban Child Markets*, 207; Farr, *Sex Trafficking: The Global Market in Women and Children*, 208.

772 Cacho, *Slavery Inc.: The Untold Story of International Sex Trafficking*, 164.

773 BBC, "United States Dilutes UN Rape-in-War Resolution," BBC, www.bbc.com/news/world-us-canada-48028773.

774 Ibid.

775 Farr, *Sex Trafficking: The Global Market in Women and Children*, 5.

776 Cacho, *Slavery Inc.: The Untold Story of International Sex Trafficking*, 4; John W Whitehead, "The Essence of Evil: Sex with Children Has Become Big Business in America," *Global Research* April 24 (2019).

777 Cacho, *Slavery Inc.: The Untold Story of International Sex Trafficking*, 223.

778 Ibid.

779 Ibid., 3.

780 Interpol, "Interpol Annual Report," UN, INTERPOL_Annual Report 2019_EN (1).pdf.

781 Farr, *Sex Trafficking: The Global Market in Women and Children*, xv11, 3; Black, *A Brief History of Slavery: A New Global History*, 242-3; Cacho, *Slavery Inc.: The Untold Story of International Sex Trafficking*, 3; Boge, *The True Story of Canadian Human Trafficking*, 7.

782 UN Gift, "Sex Trafficking of Minors in America," Global Initiative to fight Human Trafficking, www.ungift.org/2017/09/17/sex-trafficking-of-minors-in-america.

783 StatsCan, "Trafficking in Persons in Canada, 2018," Statistics Canada, https://www150.statcan.gc.ca/n1/pub/85-002-x/2020001/article/00006-eng.htm; Global News, "25% of Human Trafficking Victims in Canada AreChildren:StatsCan,"GlobalNews,https://globalnews.ca/news/4314916/25-of-human-trafficking-vistims-in-canada-are-children-statscan/.

784 Farr, *Sex Trafficking: The Global Market in Women and Children*, 25.

785 Ibid.

786 Cacho, *Slavery Inc.: The Untold Story of International Sex Trafficking*, 225-6.

787 Ibid., 226.

788 UN Gift, "Sex Trafficking of Minors in America".

789 Kevin Alderson, "Selling and Buying Sex," in *Human Sexuality: A Contemporary Introduction*, ed. Caroline Pukall (Canada: Oxford University Press, 2020).

790 Ibid.

791 M Farley, J Lynne, and AL Cotton, "Prostitution in Vancouver: Violence and the Colonization of First Nations Women," *Transcultural Psychiatry* 42, no. 2 (2005).

792 Jones and Jemmott, "Status, Privilege and Gender Inequality: Cultures of Male Impunity and Entitlement in the Sexual Abuse of Children: Perspectives from a Caribbean Study."

793 Ibid.

794 Merdian et al., "Transnational Child Sexual Abuse: Outcomes from a Roundtable Discussion."

795 Sutton, *Variations in Sexual Behaviour*, 355.

796 Merdian et al., "Transnational Child Sexual Abuse: Outcomes from a Roundtable Discussion."

797   Ibid.

798   Farr, *Sex Trafficking: The Global Market in Women and Children*, 204.

799   Cacho, *Slavery Inc.: The Untold Story of International Sex Trafficking*, 171.

800   BBC, "North Korean Women 'Forced into Sex Slavery' in China-Report," BBC, www.bbc.com/news/world-asia-48340210; Julie Zaugg, "These North Korean Defectors Were Sold into China as Cybersex Slaves. Then They Escaped.," CNN, www.cnn.com/2019/06/09/asia/north-korea-defectors-intl-hnk/index.html.

801   Farr, *Sex Trafficking: The Global Market in Women and Children*, 232-3; Cacho, *Slavery Inc.: The Untold Story of International Sex Trafficking*, 243.

802   Hollington, *Unthinkable: The Shocking Scandal of the UK Sex Traffickers*, 54.

803   CNN, "157 Children Rescued from West Africa Trafficking Ring," CNN, www.cnn.com/2019/04/25/africa/dozens-of-human-trafficking-rescued-africa-intl/index.html.

804   Farr, *Sex Trafficking: The Global Market in Women and Children*, 117-9.

805   Rahul Kalvapalle, "An Indian Train Passenger's Tweet Helped Save 25 Girls from Child Traffickers," Global News, www.globalnews.ca/news/4319117/india-girls-rescued-from-human-traffickers-tweet.

806   Farr, *Sex Trafficking: The Global Market in Women and Children*, 132.

807   Ibid., 133-4.

808   Boge, *The True Story of Canadian Human Trafficking*, 9.

809   Ronis and Kabbash, "Sexual Assault and Harassment," 399.

810   Boge, *The True Story of Canadian Human Trafficking*, 236.

811   Ronis and Kabbash, "Sexual Assault and Harassment," 399.

812   Talaga, *Seven Fallen Feathers: Racism, Death and Hard Truths in a Northern City*; Solomon.

813   BBC, "India Women: Anti-Trafficking Activists Raped after Staging Street Play," BBC, www.bbc.com/news/world-asia-india-44572276.

814   Cacho, *Slavery Inc.: The Untold Story of International Sex Trafficking*, 212.

815   Whitehead, "The Essence of Evil: Sex with Children Has Become Big Business in America."

816   Ibid.

817   Farr, *Sex Trafficking: The Global Market in Women and Children*, 232-3; Cacho, *Slavery Inc.: The Untold Story of International Sex Trafficking*, 243.

818   Farr, *Sex Trafficking: The Global Market in Women and Children*, 231.

819   Whitehead, "The Essence of Evil: Sex with Children Has Become Big Business in America."

820 Farr, *Sex Trafficking: The Global Market in Women and Children*, 20.
821 Whitehead, "The Essence of Evil: Sex with Children Has Become Big Business in America."
822 Ibid.; Boge, *The True Story of Canadian Human Trafficking*, 13.
823 Whitehead, "The Essence of Evil: Sex with Children Has Become Big Business in America."
824 Ibid.
825 Cacho, *Slavery Inc.: The Untold Story of International Sex Trafficking*, 234.
826 Ibid., 25.
827 Farr, *Sex Trafficking: The Global Market in Women and Children*, 21-2.
828 Ibid., 22.
829 Department of Justice Canada, "Criminal Code: Human Trafficking," Department of Justice Canada, https://www.justice.gc.ca/eng/cj-jp/tp/legis-loi.html.
830 Cacho, *Slavery Inc.: The Untold Story of International Sex Trafficking*, 217.
831 Farr, *Sex Trafficking: The Global Market in Women and Children*, 232-3.
832 Cacho, *Slavery Inc.: The Untold Story of International Sex Trafficking*, 243.
833 Solomon.
834 Cacho, *Slavery Inc.: The Untold Story of International Sex Trafficking*, 2.
835 Ibid.
836 Ibid., 3.
837 Ibid., 123-34.
838 Ibid., 127.
839 Ibid., 128.
840 Farr, *Sex Trafficking: The Global Market in Women and Children*, 99.
841 Ibid., 100-1.
842 Ibid., 101.
843 Ibid., 103.
844 Ibid., 104.
845 Ibid.
846 Ibid., 99-119.
847 Whitehead, "The Essence of Evil: Sex with Children Has Become Big Business in America."
848 Lukas Moodysson, *Lilya 4-Ever* (Metrodome Distribution and BBC Four, 2002).
849 Hollington, *Unthinkable: The Shocking Scandal of the UK Sex Traffickers*, 256-7.
850 UN Gift, "Sex Trafficking of Minors in America".

851 Hollington, *Unthinkable: The Shocking Scandal of the UK Sex Traffickers*, 161.
852 Ibid., 120-21.
853 Ibid., 156.
854 Ibid., xiii.
855 Ibid., 154.
856 Boge, *The True Story of Canadian Human Trafficking*, 237.
857 Ibid.
858 Ibid., 240-1.
859 Blair Rhodes, "Human Trafficking Charges Laid after N.B. Girl Rescued in N.S. Hotel Parking Lot," CBC, https://www.cbc.ca/news/canada/nova-scotia/human-trafficking-charges-laid-teen-found-hotel-1.6247021.
860 Ronis and Kabbash, "Sexual Assault and Harassment," 400.
861 Hollington, *Unthinkable: The Shocking Scandal of the UK Sex Traffickers*, 198-9.
862 Farr, *Sex Trafficking: The Global Market in Women and Children*, 234.
863 Boge, *The True Story of Canadian Human Trafficking*, 237.
864 Ibid., 325-6.
865 World Health Organization, "Global Status Report on Preventing Violence against Children".
866 Colin Butler, "Ex-Teacher Who Filmed Students with Spy Pen, Ontario School Board Named in $200k Civil Suit," CBC, https://www.cbc.ca/news/canada/london/ryan-jarvis-beal-voyeurism-civil-lawsuit-1.5996802.
867 Boge, *The True Story of Canadian Human Trafficking*, 135-9.
868 Rena Kosovsky, "It's Time Schools Took Sexual Assault Seriously," Jewish Women's Archive, https://jwa.org/blog/its-time-schools-took-sexual-assault-seriously.
869 The Economist, "The Sexualization of Children: Innocents and Experience."
870 Melissa Alonso, "A Former Boston Ballerina and Her Husband Have Been Accused of Sexually Abusing Young Dancers, According to a Federal Lawsuit," CNN, https://www.cnn.com/2021/09/29/us/ballerina-dusty-button-husband-lawsuit/index.html.
871 Madeline Holcombe and Lauren del Valle, "Lawsuit Alleges Past Culture of Sexual Abuse at University of North Carolina School of the Arts," CNN, https://www.cnn.com/2021/10/05/us/sexual-abuse-lawsuit-north-carolina-school-of-the-arts/index.html.
872 Rodney Stark and Roger Finke, "Catholic Religious Vocations: Decline and Revival," *Review of Religious Research* 42, no. 2 (2000).
873 Neustein, *Tempest in the Temple: Jewish Communities and Child Sex Scandals*, 185.

874 BBC, "Boy Scouts of America: Almost 100,000 Make Sexual Abuse Compensation Claims".

875 M Ilyas Khan, "Pakistan Zeinab Murder: New Law Aims to Catch Child Abusers," BBC, www.bbc.com/news/world-asia-51852381.

876 BBC, "Pakistan Anti-Rape Ordinance Signed into Law by President".

877 Helen Regan and Sophia Saifi, "Pakistan's Most Populous Province Bans Virginity Tests for Rape Survivors in Landmark Ruling," CNN, https://www.cnn.com/2021/01/05/asia/pakistan-court-virginity-test-ban-intl-hnk/index.html.

878 BBC, "'Justice for Victoria': Toddler Testifies in Myanmar 'Nursery Rape' Case," BBC, www.bbc.com/news/world-asia-49660087.

879 "Tanzanian President Magufuli Pardons Child Rapists," BBC www.bbc.com/news/world-africa-42309501.

880 "Sierra Leone Declares Emergency over Rape and Sexual Assault," BBC, www.bbc.com/news/world-africa-47169729.

881 Reuters, "Mexican Judge Suspended after Outcry over Child Abuse Case," Reuters, https://www.reuters.com/article/us-mexico-crime/mexican-judge-suspended-after-outcry-over-child-abuse-case-idUSKCN25D067.

882 BBC, "Spanish Anger as Five Men Acquited of Gang-Raping Teenager," BBC, www.bbc.com/news/world-europe-50257922.

883 CBC, "Supreme Court Upholds Sexual Assault Conviction in Case Involving Teens, Alcohol," CBC https://www.cbc.ca/news/politics/scc-youth-sexual-assault-1.6017773.

884 Ashitha Nagesh, "Does Denmark Have a 'Pervasive' Rape Problem," BBC www.bbc,com/news/world-europe-47470353.

885 Philip Wen and Adam Jourdan, "China Kindergarten Sex Abuse and 'Needlemark' Claims Prompt Police Probe," Reuters, www.reuters.com/article/us-ryb-education-china/china-kindergarten-sex-abuse-and-needlemarks-claims-prompt-police-probe-idUSKBN1DO01D.

886 BBC, "Chinese Minor, 13, Receives Three Year Penalty for Murder," BBC, www.bbc.com/news/world-asia-china-50210961.

887 Svetlana Huntley, "Russian Legislation on the Protection of Children against Sexual Abuse and Sexual Exploitation: A Review," https://www.icmec.org/wp-content/uploads/2015/10/Russian_Legislation_on_Protection_of_Children_Against_Sexual_Abuse_and_Exploitation_FINAL.pdf.

888 Donald Trump, "Executive Order on Combating Human Trafficking and Online Child Exploitation in the United States," ed. Law and Justice (Washington, USA: The White House, January 2020).

889 Boge, *The True Story of Canadian Human Trafficking*, 325-6.

890 Meghan Grant, "Victim of Alleged Child Sex Assault Says Interview with Lethbridge Office 'Like a Slap in the Face'," CBC News, https://

www.cbc.ca/news/canada/calgary/lethbridge-police-historic-sexual-assault-complaint-1.6100895.

891   Eric Levenson, Sahar Akbarzai, and Taylor Romine, *No Prison Time for Man Who Pleaded Guilty to Rape and Sexual Assault of Four Teenage Girls* (USA: CNN, 2021).

892   Tasker, "Senator Aims to Curb 'Violent' Porn, Pitches Mandatory Age Verification for Online Sites".

893   Dina Aboughazala, "Egypt Facebook Page Raises Hopes for Missing Children," BBC, https://www.bbc.com/news/world-middle-east-53564935.

894   StatsCan, "Trafficking in Persons in Canada, 2018".

895   Office of the High Commissioner of Human Rights, "Convention on the Rights of the Child," (Geneva: United Nations, 1989), 8.

896   John Smith, *The Boys of St Vincent* (Frankfurt, Germany: Pro-Fun Media, 2011).

897   Harris, *Unholy Orders: Tragedy at Mount Cashel*.

898   Sixsmith, *Philomena: A Mother, Her Son and a Fifty-Year Search*.

899   Stephen Frears, *Philomena* (20th Century Fox 2013).

900   Peter Mullen, *The Magdalene Sisters* (Ireland: PEP Films, 2002).

901   O'Riordan and Leonard, *Whispering Hope: The True Story of the Magdalene Women*

902   Tom McCarthy, *Spotlight* (Open Road Films, 2015).

903   Sekielski, *Tell No One*.

904   BBC, "Clerical Abuse: Film Gets Go-Ahead after Legal Challenge".

905   CBC, ""Prey": A Documentary by Windsor Director Shines a Light on Sexual Abuse by Priests," CBC www.cbc.ca/news/canada/windsor/prey-documentary-windsor-director-sexual-abuse-1.5097909.

906   BBC, "Steep Rise in Child Abuse Images Online, Charity Reports".

907   Ronis and Kabbash, "Sexual Assault and Harassment," 393.

908   Rozina Sini, "How 'Metoo' Is Exposing the Scale of Sexual Abuse," BBC NEws, www.bbc.com/news/blogs-trending-41633857.

909   Estelle Shirbon, "'#Metoo Movement' in British Schools as Teens Recount Sexual Abuse," Reuters, https://www.reuters.com/article/uk-britain-schools-sexual-abuse/metoo-movement-in-british-schools-as-teens-recount-sexual-abuse-idUSKBN2BM20L.

910   Ibid.

911   BBC, "Tackling Sexual Abuse in Schools through the Arts," BBC, https://www.bbc.com/news/av/education-56597853.

Bibliography

Aboughazala, Dina. "Egypt Facebook Page Raises Hopes for Missing Children." BBC, https://www.bbc.com/news/world-middle-east-53564935.

Adams, Lucy. "Online Child Sex Abuse Investigation Identifies 523 Potential Victims." BBC, www.bbc.com/ness/uk-scotland-36922820.

Africa Check. "Factsheet: South Africa's Crime Statistics for 2019/20." Africa Check, https://africacheck.org/fact-checks/factsheets/factsheet-south-africas-crime-statistics-201920.

Akinyemi, Aaron. "'No Sex without Fighting' - Tackling Toxic Masculinity in DR Congo." BBC Africa Eye, www.bbc.com/news/world/africa/48094438.

al-Maghafi, Nawal. "The Teenager Married Too Many Times to Count." BBC, www.bbc.co.uk/news/extra/iuKTEGjKgS/teenage_iraq_brides.

Alderson, Kevin. "Selling and Buying Sex." In *Human Sexuality: A Contemporary Introduction*, edited by Caroline Pukall, 420-37. Canada: Oxford University Press, 2020.

Alfredson, Lisa. "Sexual Exploitation of Child Soldiers: An Exploration and Analysis of Global Dimensions and Trends." *Minerva* 23, no. May (2002): 70-78.

Ali, Nujood, and Delphine Minoui. *I Am Nujood: Age 10 and Divorced.* New York: Broadway Paperbacks, 2010.

Alkousaa, Riham. "German Prosecutors Charge Child-Porn Website Operators." Reuters, www.reuters.com/article/us-germany-sexcrimes/german-prosecutors-charge-child-porn-website-operators-idSKCN1IG1NT.

Allbright, JM. "Sex in America Online: An Exploration of Sex, Marital Status and Sexual Identiy in Internet Sex Seeking and Its Impacts." *Journal of Sex Research* 45, no. 2 (2008): 175-86.

Alonso, Melissa. "A Former Boston Ballerina and Her Husband Have Been Accused of Sexually Abusing Young Dancers, According to a Federal Lawsuit." CNN, https://www.cnn.com/2021/09/29/us/ballerina-dusty-button-husband-lawsuit/index.html.

Ananthalakshmi, A. "How Malaysia Allows Child Abuse to Go Unpunished." Reuters, www.reuters.com/article/us-malaysia-sexcrimes-insight-idUSKBN1390AT.

Anderson, Susan. *High Glitz: The Extravagent World of Child Beauty Pageants.* USA: Powerhouse, 2009.

APTN News. "Indigenous Newborn 'Baby H' Returned to Parents on Brink of Court Hearing." APTN News, https://aptnnews.ca/2019/06/27indigenous-newborn-baby-h-returned-to-parents-on-the-brink-of-court-hearing.

Arnold, Mavis, and Heather Lasky. *Children of the Poor Clares: The Story of an Irish Orphanage.* Belfast: Appletree Press, 1985.

Arya, Divya. "Child Sex Crime: Does India Have a Growing Problem?" BBC, www.bbc.com/news/wsorld-asia-india-44497312.

———. "Why Smartphones Are Skewing Young Indian's Ideas of Sex." BBC, ww.bbc.com/news/world-asia-india-46602885.

Auvillain, Elizabeth. "Break the Silence: French Bishops Start Dialogue with Children of Priests." National Catholic Reporter, www.ncronline.org/news/accountability/break-the-silence-french-bishops-start-dialogue-children-priests.

Babcock, James. "Spain Child Abuse: Victims Fight Back and Appeal for Change." BBC, www.bbc.com/news/world-europe-46064017.

Baksh, Nazim. "Order of Canada Recipient Peter Dalglish Found Guilty of Child Sex Assault in Nepal." CBC, www.cbc.ca/news/world/peter-dalglish-conviction-nepal-1.5170122.

Barett, A, Y Kamiya, and V O'Sullivan. "Childhood Sexual Abuse and Later Life Economic Consequences." *Journal of Behavioural and Experimental Economics* 53 (2014): 10-16.

Bashir, Martin. "How Will Pope Francis Deal with Abuse in the Catholic Church?" BBC, www.bbc.com/news/world-47201647.

Bass, Ellen, and Louise Thornton. *I Never Told Anyone: Writings by Women Survivors of Child Sexual Abuse.* New York: Harper and Row 1983.

BBC. "Archbishop of Brisbane: Catholic Church's Credibility 'Shot to Pieces'."BBC,www.bbc.com/news/ay/world-47348171/archbishop-of-brisbane-catholic-church-s-credibility-shot-to-pieces.

———. "Argentina Father Jailed for Keeping Daughter as 'Sex Slave'." BBC, www.bbc.com/news/world-latin-america-42517711.

———. "Australian Police Charge Seven with Abusing Boys." BBC, www.bbc.com/news/world-australia-42954474.

———. "Australian Toddler's Alleged Rape Was a 'Foreseeable Risk'." BBC, www.bbc.com/news/world-australia-44063602.

———. "Barry Bennell: A Mother's Horror at Her Son's Sexual Abuse." BBC News, www.bbc.com/news/uk-wales-43106572.

———. "Belgium Gang Rape: Five Arrested over Assault on Teenager." BBC, https://www.bbc.com/news/world-europe-57315750.

———. "Bosco Ntaganda Sentenced to 30 Years for Crimes in DR Congo." BBC, www.bbc.com/news/world-africa-50329503

———. "Boy Scouts of America Files for Bankruptcy over Sex Abuse Lawsuits." BBC, www.bbc.com/news/world-us-canada-51542401.

———. "Boy Scouts of America: Almost 100,000 Make Sexual Abuse Compensation Claims." BBC, https://www.bbc.com/news/world-us-canada-54971579.

———. "Boy Scouts: A Wholesome US Institution Poisoned by Predators." BBC, https://www.bbc.com/news/world-us-canada-51552576.

———. "Brazil Police Arrests 108 in Major Anti-Paedophile Operation." BBC, www.bbc.com/news/world-latin-america-41704429.

———. "Cardinal Barbarin: France's Top Cleric Cleared of Abuse Cover-Up." BBC, www.bbc.com/news/world-europe-51308751.

———. "Cardinal Bernard Law: Disgraced US Cardinal Dies in Rome." BBC, www.bbc.com/news/world-us-canada-42421423.

———. "Chemical Castration: Alabama Enacts New Paedophile Law." BBC, www.bbc.com/news/world-us-canada-48593699.

———. "Child Abuse Images Being Traded Via Secure Apps." BBC, www.bbc.com/news/technology-47279256.

———. "Child Abuse Priest Fernando Karadima Removed by Vatican." BBC, www.bbc.com/news/world-middle-east-45677534.

———. "Chile Church Scandal: 'How I Escaped the Priest Who Abused Me for Decades.'." BBC, www.bbc.co.uk/news/stories-45486176.

———. "Chinese Minor, 13, Receives Three Year Penalty for Murder." BBC, www.bbc.com/news/world-asia-china-50210961.

———. "Choju-Bin: 40 Years Jail for South Korean Chatroom Sex Abuse Group Leader." BBC, https://www.bbc.com/news/world-asia-55082072.

———. "Choju-Bin: South Korea Chatroom Sex Abuse Suspect Named after Outcry." BBC, www.bbc.com/news/world-asia-52030219.

———. "Church of England Failures 'Allowed Child Sex Abusers to Hide'." BBC, https://www.bbc.com/news/uk-54433295.

———. "Church Sexual Abuse: French Priest Preyant Admits 'Caressing' Boys." BBC, www.bbc.com/news/world-europe-51090077.

———. "Clerical Abuse: Film Gets Go-Ahead after Legal Challenge." BBC, www.bbc.com/news/world-europe-47280764.

———. "Coronavirus Risks "Greatest Surge in Child Marriages in 25 Years"." BBC, https://www.bbc.com/news/world-54370316.

———. "Coronavirus: Domestic Abuse Victims 'Still Allowed to Leave Home'." BBC, www.bbc.com/news/uk-52081280.

———. "Dark Web Paedophile Mathew Falder's Sentence Reduced." BBC, www.bbc.com/news/uk-england-45875275.

———. "Denmark Facebook Sex Video: More Than 1000 Young People Charged." BBC www.bbc,com/news/world-europe-42694218.

———. "Dutch Police Give 'Stop Paedophile Hunts' Warning after Arnhem Death." BBC, https://www.bbc.com/news/world-europe-54930488.

———. "Egypt Sex Attacks Fuel 'Feminist' Revolution." BBC, https://www.bbc.com/news/world-middle-east-54643463.

———. "Eric Eoin Marques: Irish Man Jailed in US for Child Abuse Images." https://www.bbc.com/news/world-europe-58582817.

———. "Facebook Child Abuse Detection Hit by New EU Rules." BBC, https://www.bbc.com/news/technology-55399509.

———. "Facebook Removes 11.6 Million Child Abuse Posts." BBC, www.bbc.com/news/technology-50404812.

———. "Fears over Fake Bieber and Styles Accounts." BBC, www.bbc.com/news/blogs-trending-39670673

———. "Fifty Children Saved as International Paedophile Ring Busted." BBC, www.bbc.com/news/world-48379983.

———. "France: Former Surgeon Goes on Trial on Child Rape and Assault Charges." BBC, www.bbc.com/news/world-europe-51883495

———. "George Tyndall: Ex-USC Doctor Arrested over Sex Abuse " BBC, www.bbc.com/news/world-us-canada-48794597.

———. "German Catholic Priests 'Abused Thousands of Children'." www.bbc.co.uk/news/world-europe-45500072.

———. "German Couple Jailed for Selling Son to Paedophiles on Dark Net." BBC, www.bbc.co.uk/news/world-eu45096183.

———. "India's Covid Crisis Sees Rise in Child Marriage and Trafficking." BBC, https://www.bbc.com/news/world-asia-india-54186709.

———. "India Arrests after Women's Heads Shaved for Resisting Rape." BBC, www.bbc,com/news/world-asia-india-48783253.

———. "India Coronavirus: 14-Year-Old Sexually Assaulted at Delhi Covid Centre." BBC, https://www.bbc.com/news/world-asia-india-53522998.

———. "India Outcry after Eight-Month-Old Raped." BBC www.bbc.com/news-world-asia-india-42869010.

———. "India Outrage over Brutal Rape and Murder of Six-Year-Old." BBC www.bbc.com/news/world-asia-india-42305395.

———. "India Rape: 17 Men Accused of Multiple Attacks on 11-Year-Old Girl in Chennai." BBC, www.bbc.com/news/world-asia-india-44877729.

————. "India Rape: Two Men Arrested from 13-Year-Old's Rape and Murder." BBC, https://www.bbc.com/news/world-asia-india-53799036.

————. "India Stepmother Arrested for 'Ordering' Gang Rape of Girl, 9." BBC, www.bbc.co.uk/news/world-asia-india-45417725.

————. "India Uncles Convicted of Raping and Impregnating Child Aged 10." BBC www.bbc.com/news/world-asia-india-41817519.

————. "India Women: Anti-Trafficking Activists Raped after Staging Street Play." BBC, www.bbc.com/news/world-asia-india-44572276.

————. "Indian Man Allegedly Rapes Girl, Five, on Embassy Grounds" BBC, www.bbc.com/news/world-asia-india-51398295.

————. "Japan Child Abuse at Record High, Police Data Shows." BBC, www.bbc.com/news/world-asia-pacific-10979109.

————. "'Justice for Victoria': Toddler Testifies in Myanmar 'Nursery Rape' Case." BBC, www.bbc.com/news/world-asia-49660087.

————. "La Luz Del Mundo Church Leader Charged with Child Rape in US." BBC, www.bbc.com/news/world-us-canada-48524878.

————. "La Luz Del Mundo Sex Crimes Case Dropped by US Court." BBC, https://www.bbc.com/news/world-us-canada-52217977.

————. "Larry Nassar Case: The 156 Women Who Confronted a Predator." BBC News, www.bbc,com/news/world-us-canada-42725339.

————. "Larry Nassar Jailed for Another 40-125 Years." BBC, www.bbc.com/news/world-us-canada-42950478.

————. "Magdalene Laundries Victim Mary Cavner to Get Compensation."BBC,www.bbec.com/news/uk-england-hampshire-49393418.

————. "Major Child Sexual Abuse Trial Begins in Germany." BBC, https://www.bbc.com/news/world-europe-53813249.

————. "Malka Leifer: Israel Court Approves Extradition of Sex Abuse Suspect to Australia." BBC, https://www.bbc.com/news/world-australia-55302667.

————. "Man Charged with Child Sex Offences in Hampshire and Berkshire." BBC, www.bbc.com/news/uk-england-hampshire-39337878.

———. "Militiamen Jailed in DR Congo's Kavumu for Raping 40 Children." BBC www.bbc.com/news/world-africa-42345705.

———. "Neil Harris: How Abusive Dance Teacher Went Unchecked for Decades." BBC, https://www.bbc.com/news/uk-england-birmingham-53388634.

———. "Netherlands 'Hosts Most Child Sex Abuse Images'." BBC, www.bbc.com/news/technology-48022950.

———. "Nigeria's Kaduna Passes Law to Castrate Child Rapists." BBC, https://www.bbc.com/news/world-africa-54117462.

———. "North Korean Women 'Forced into Sex Slavery' in China-Report." BBC, www.bbc.com/news/world-asia-48340210.

———. "NXIVM 'Sex Cult' Case: Co-Founder Pleads Guilty to Racketeering." BBC, www.bbc.com/news/world-us-canada-47563045.

———. "NXIVM Sex Cult Case: Seagram Heiress among Four Women Arrested." BBC, https://www.bbc.com/news/world-us-canada-44946059.

———. "Ohio State University Doctor 'Abused 177 Male Students'." BBC, www.bbc.com/news/world-us-canada-48319878.

———. "Paedophile Richard Huckle Stabbed to Death at Full Sutton Prison." BBC, www.bbc.com/news/uk-50042406.

———. "Paedophile Ring Sentenced in Germany." BBC, https://www.bbc.com/news/world-europe-57735317.

———. "Pakistan Anti-Rape Ordinance Signed into Law by President." BBC, https://www.bbc.com/news/world-asia-55314493.

———. "Pakistan Village Council Orders 'Revenge Rape' of Girl." BBC www/bbc.com/news/world-asia-india-40731035.

———. "Peter Seisenbacher: Austrian Judo Champion Jailed for Child Sex Abuse." BBC, bbc.com/news/world-europe-50631219.

———. "Phillipe Barbarin: French Cardinal Guilty of Abuse Cover-Up." BBC, www.bbc.com/news/world-europe-47481618.

———. "Police: California Man Admits to Molesting 50 Children." BBC www.bbc.com/news/world-us-canada-42226750.

———. "Pope Francis Makes It Mandatory for Clergy to Report Sex Abuse." BBC, www.bbc.com/news/world-europe-48213135.

———. "Pope Francis on Side of Victims of 'Predator' Priests." BBC, www.bbc.co.uk/news/world-us-canada-45211942.

———. "Pornhub Bans User Uploads after Abuse Allegations." BBC, https://www.bbc.com/news/technology-55231181.

———. "Pornhub: Mastercard Severs Links with Pornography Site." https://www.bbc.com/news/technology-55267311.

———. "Rotherham Warning over Child Sex Exploitation in Scotland." BBC http://bbc.com/uk-scotland-29175287.

———. "Sajid Javid Threatens Tech Giants over Online Child Sex Abuse." BBC www.bbc.co.uk/news/uk-45389937.

———. "Sarah Abitbol: French Ice Skating Boss Quits Amid Sex Abuse Scandal." BBC, www.bbc.com/news/world-europe-51425860.

———. "Scottish Child Abuse Inquiry Hears Apologies over 'Deplorable' Attacks." BBC, www.bbc.com/news/uk-scotland-40093270.

———. "Sierra Leone Declares Emergency over Rape and Sexual Assault." BBC, www.bbc.com/news/world-africa-47169729.

———. "Silenced Children of Priests to Share Stories with French Bishops." BBC, www.bbc.com/news/world-europe-48620284.

———. "Singapore Anger at 'Too Lenient' Child Sex Sentence." BBC www.BBC.com/news/world-asia-39202215.

———. "Somali Outrage at Rape of Girls Aged Three and Four." BBC, www.bbc.com/news/world-africa-52172609.

———. "South Africa Anger after Girl 'Raped' in Restaurant." BBC News, www.bbc.com/new/world-africa-45652729.

———. "Spanish Anger as Five Men Acquited of Gang-Raping Teenager." BBC, www.bbc.com/news/world-europe-50257922.

———. "Spanish Father Accused of 'Evil Spirits' Rape." BBC, www.bbc.com/news/world-europe-44107300.

———. "Steep Rise in Child Abuse Images Online, Charity Reports." BBC www.bbc.co.uk/news/technology-43796380.

———. "Tackling Sexual Abuse in Schools through the Arts." BBC, https://www.bbc.com/news/av/education-56597853.

———. "Tanzanian President Magufuli Pardons Child Rapists." BBC www.bbc.com/news/world-africa-42309501.

———. "Tennis Child Abuse Apology after Wrexham Coach Case." BBC www.bbc.com/news/uk-wales-north-east-wales-42102382.

———. "Theodore McCarrick: Defrocked US Cardinal Charged with Assault and Battery." BBC, https://www.bbc.com/news/world-us-canada-58019652.

———. "Thousands of US Child Migrants Sexually Abused." CNN, www.bbc.com/news/world-us-canada-47377889.

———. "'Tortured' and Shackled Pupils Freed from Nigerian Islamic School." BBC, www.bbc.com/news/world-africa-50053725.

———. "Turpin: Shackled Siblings Found in Perris, California Home." BBC www.bbc.com/news/world-us-canada-42698562.

———. "UK Lockdown: Calls to Domestic Abuse Hotline Jump by Half." BBC, https://www.bbc.com/news/uk-52433520.

———. "United States Dilutes UN Rape-in-War Resolution." BBC, www.bbc,com/news/world-us-canada-48028773.

———. "US Elite School Choate Rosemary Hall 'Sorry' over Sexual Abuse." BBC news, www.bbc.com/news/world-us-canada-39604353.

———. "Vatican Abuse Summit: Cardinal Says Files Were Destroyed." BBC, www.bbc.com/news/world-europe-47343458.

———. "WhatsApp Child Sex Images Led to Arrests." BBC, www.bbc.uk/news/technology-39629184.

Bell, Susan. "Quebec Indigenous Groups Collecting Stories of Forced Sterilization." CBC, https://www.cbc.ca/news/canada/north/indigenous-forced-sterilization-quebec-study-cree-1.6186212.

Biswas, Soutik. "Why India's Rape Crisis Shows No Sign of Abating." BBC, www.bbc.com/news/world-asia-india-43782471.

Black, Jeremy. *A Brief History of Slavery: A New Global History.* London: Constable and Robinson, 2011.

———. *Slavery.* London: Running Press, 2011.

Boge, Paul. *The True Story of Canadian Human Trafficking.* Canada: Castle Quay Books, 2018.

Bowley, Douglas, and Graeme Pitcher. "Motivation Behind Infant Rape in South Africa." *The Lancet* 359, no. 9314 (2002): 1352.

Boyer, Yvonne, and Judith Bartlett. "External Review: Tubal Ligation in the Saskatoon Health Region: The Lived Experience of Aboriginal Women." Canada: Health Region Saskatoon, 2017.

Brewster, Murray. "Key Allies Watching Closely to See How Canada Handles Sexual Misconduct Claims against Vance, McDonald." CBC News, https://www.cbc.ca/news/politics/vance-mcdonald-canadian-armed-forces-sexual-misconduct-1.5959563.

Brockbank, Nicole. "Dark Days at Camp." CBC News, https://newsinteractives.cbc.ca/longform/camp-wahanowin-abuse.

Brooks, Courtney, and Amina Umarova. "Despite Official Measures, Bride Kidnapping Endemic in Chechnya." Radio Free Europe/Radio Liberty, www.rferl.org/a/Despite_Official_Measures_Bride_Kidnapping_Endemic_In_Chechnya/2197575.html.

Budd, KM, and DM Bierie. "Victims of Sexual Assault Perpetrated by Female Youth: An Exploratory Study of Gender Differences." *Journal of Sexual Aggression* 24, no. 3 (2018): 274-93.

Burke, Ashley, and Kristen Everson. "Senior Military Commander under Investigation after Being Accused of Sexually Assaulting Subordinate." CBC, https://www.cbc.ca/news/politics/sexual-assault-allegations-vice-admiral-haydn-edmundson-1.5963430.

Burns, Judith. "MPs Seek Better Plan to Fight School Sexual Harassment." BBC News, http://www.bbc.com/news/education-37338712.

Butler, Colin. "Ex-Teacher Who Filmed Students with Spy Pen, Ontario School Board Named in $200k Civil Suit." CBC, https://www.cbc.ca/news/canada/london/ryan-jarvis-beal-voyeurism-civil-lawsuit-1.5996802.

Butler, Ed. "The Man Hired to Have Sex with Children." BBC News Malawi, www.bbc.com/news/magazine-36843769.

Cacho, Lydia. *Slavery Inc.: The Untold Story of International Sex Trafficking.* London: Portobello Books, 2012.

Calcasa. "Pedophiles and Child Molesters: The Differences." www.calcasa.org/wp-content/uploads/2007/11/pedophiles-and-child-molesters.doc

Canada's Human Rights History. "Duplessis Orphans." https://historyofrights.ca/encyclopaedia/main-events/duplessis-orphans/.

CBC. "40 Women in California Launch Lawsuit against Montreal-Based Parent Company of Pornhub." CBC, https://www.cbc.ca/news/canada/montreal/women-california-lawsuit-pornhub-1.5844705.

———. "Catholic Archdiocese of Vancouver Aware of 36 Cases of Clergy Sex Abuse since 1950s, CBC Learns." CBC News, www.cbc.ca/news/canada/fifth-estate-sexual-abuse-vancouver-catholic-diocese-1.5360493.

———. "Former Priest Pleads Guilty to 17 Sex Charges." CBC News, www.cbc.ca/news/canada/windsor/former-priest-pleads-guilty-to-17-sex-charges-1.999662.

———. "Maple Leafs Gardens Sex Offender Gordon Stuckless Dead, Lawyer Says." The Canadian Press, https://www.cbc.ca/news/canada/toronto/maple-leaf-garden-s-sex-offender-gordon-stuckless-dead-lawyer-1.5528992.

———. ""Prey": A Documentary by Windsor Director Shines a Light on Sexual Abuse by Priests." CBC www.cbc.ca/news/canada/windsor/prey-documentary-windsor-director-sexual-abuse-1.5097909.

———. "Supreme Court of Canada Rejects Catholic Archdiocese Appeal over Mount Cashel." CBC, https://www.cbc.ca/news/canada/newfoundland-labrador/mount-cashel-supreme-court-thursday-1.5871478.

———. "Supreme Court Upholds Sexual Assault Conviction in Case Involving Teens, Alcohol." CBC https://www.cbc.ca/news/politics/scc-youth-sexual-assault-1.6017773.

CBC Radio. "How a Sexual Assault Victim's Lawsuit Set a Precendent That Alarmed the Catholic Church." CBC Radio, www.cbc.ca/radio/thesundayedition/the-sunday-edition-for-april-14-2019-1.509537/.

———. "Indigenous Women Kept from Seeing Their Newborn Babies until Agreeing to Sterilization." www.cbc.ca/radio/thecurrent/the-current-for-november-13-2018-1.4902670/indigenous-women-kept-from-seeing-their-newborn-babies-until-agreeing-to-sterilization.

Chalmers, B, and K Omer-Hashi. *Female Genital Mutilation and Obstetric Care*. Vancouver, BC, Canada: Trafford Publishers, 2003.

Chalmers, Beverley. *Betrayed: Child Sex Abuse in the Holocaust*. UK: Grosvenor House Publishers, 2020

Charles River Editors. *The Rape of Nanking*. San Bernadino, California: Charles River Editors, 2016.

Chow, Emily. "Malaysians Outraged over Reports of Child Marriage." Reuters, www.reuters.com/article/us-malaysia-child-marriage/malaysians-outraged-over-reports-of-child-marriage-idUSKBN1JQ0R6.

Clementson, Linda, and Gillian Findlay. "'It's Overwhelming': Survivors Create Public List of Catholic Clerics Accused of Sexual Abuse." CBC News, www.cbc.ca/news/canada/catholic-sexual-abuse-london-diocese-1.5384217.

CNN. "157 Children Rescued from West Africa Trafficking Ring." CNN, www.cnn.com/2019/04/25/africa/dozens-of-human-trafficking-rescued-africa-intl/index.html.

———. "Boy Scouts Plan Fund with at Least $300 Million for Sex Abuse Victims, Court Documents Show." CNN, https://www.cnn.com/2021/03/02/us/boy-scouts-sexual-abuse-bankruptcy/index.html.

———. "Instagram Is Leading Social Media Platform for Child Grooming." CNN, www.cnn.com/2019/03/01/uk/nspcc-grooming-social-media-report-scli-gbr-intl/index.html.

Cole, Diane. *Kidnapped and Raped at Age 13, She's Finally Found Justice.* NPR News: USA, 2016.

Collins, R, V Strasburger, J Brown, E Donnerstein, A Lenhart, and I Ward. "Sexual Media and Childhood Well-Being and Health." *Pediatrics* 140, no. 5, Supp 2 (2017): S162-S66.

Cooke, Ryan. "Damning Decisions." CBC News, https://news interactives.cbc.ca/longform/mount-cashel.

Coping International. "Welcome to Coping International." Coping: Children of Priests International, www.copinginternational.com/.

Coren, Anna, Jessie Yeung, and Abdul Basir Bina. "She Was Sold to a Stranger So Her Family Could Eat as Afghanistan Crumbles." CNN, https://www.cnn.com/2021/11/01/asia/afghanistan-child-marriage-crisis-taliban-intl-hnk-dst/index.html.

Cousins, Sophie. "2.5 Million More Child Marriages Due to Covid-19 Pandemic." *The Lancet* Oct 10 (2020).

Crawford, Angus. "UK Paedophiles Pay to Watch Webcam Child Sex Abuse in Philippines." BBC, www.bbc.com/news/uk-25729140.

Dadrian, V. "Armenian Children Victims of Genocide." http://www.genocide-museum.am/eng/online_exhibition_3.php.

Damiana, Jessica, Kanupriya Kapoor, and Clarence Fernandez. "Indonesian Police Probe Foreign 'Orders' for Child Pornography." Reuters, www.reuters.com/article/us-indonesia-pornography/ indonesian-police-probe-foreign-orders-for-child-pornography- idUSKBN1EY10O.

Department of Justice Canada. "Criminal Code: Human Trafficking." Department of Justice Canada, https://www.justice.gc.ca/eng/cj-jp/ tp/legis-loi.html.

Dooley, Stacey. "Stacy Dooley Investigates: 'My Daughter Was Tormented by Spycam Sex Crime'." BBC, https://www.bbc. co.uk/bbcthree/article/63de169c-dfbb-4b22-9da3-b5f3a55 628a2.

Doria-Brown, Jessica. "Hidden History: Survivor Stories Fom the Indian Day School on Lennox Island, Located Just Off PEI's North Shore." CBC, https://newsinteractives.cbc.ca/longform/hidden- history.

Doyle, Thomas. *The 1962 Vatican Instruction: Crimen Sollicitationis: Promulgated on March 16, 1962.* April 1 2008.

Falder, Mathew. "Dark Web Paedophile Mathew Falder Jailed for 32 Years." BBC, www.bbc.com/news/uk-england-43114471.

Farley, M, J Lynne, and AL Cotton. "Prostitution in Vancouver: Violence and the Colonization of First Nations Women." *Transcultural Psychiatry* 42, no. 2 (2005): 242-71.

Farr, Kathryn. *Sex Trafficking: The Global Market in Women and Children.* New York: Worth Publishers, 2005.

Feleke, Bethlehem, Eliza Mackintosh, Gianluca Mezzofiore, Katie Polglase, Nima Elbagi, Barbara Arvanitidis, and Alex Plat. "Practically This Has Been a Genocide." CNN, https://www.cnn. com/2021/03/19/africa/ethiopia-tigray-rape-investigation-cmd- intl/index.html.

Fitzpatrick, Meagan. "Online Sexual Predators Eager to Take Advantage of Greater Access to Kids During Covid-19, Police Warn." CBC, https://www.cbc.ca/news/canada/sexual-predators- children-online-pandemic-1.5542166.

Flood, M. "The Harms of Pornography Exposure among Children and Young People." *Child Abuse Review* 18, no. 6 (2009): 384-400.

Fontaine, Theodore. *Broken Cicle: The Dark Legacy of Indian Residential Schools. A Memoir.* Canada: Heritage House Publishing Company, 2010.

Fournier, Suzanne, and Ernie Grey. *Stolen from Our Embrace: The Abduction of First Nations Children and the Restoration of Aboriginal Communities.* Vancouver: Douglas & McIntyre, 1997.

Fournier, Sylvie. "Black, Indigenous Mothers Say They Were Sterilized without Full Consent at Quebec Hospitals." CBC, https://www.cbc.ca/news/canada/montreal/quebec-hospital-sterilization-1.6188269.

Fox, Kara, and Antoine Crouin. "Men Are Suing Women Who Accuse Them of Harassment. Will It Stop Others from Speaking Out?" CNN, www.cnn.com/2019/06/05/europe/metoo-defamation-trials-sandra-muller-france-intl/index.html.

Frate, James, and Claudia Otto. "German Police Bust Child Sex Abuse Imagery Network with 400,000 Users." CNN, https://www.cnn.com/2021/05/03/europe/germany-child-sex-abuse-imagery-ring-intl/index.html.

Frears, Stephen. *Philomena.* 20th Century Fox 2013.

Furniss, Elizabeth. *Victims of Benevolence: The Dark Legacy of the Williams Lake Residential School.* Vancouver: Arsenal Pulp Press, 1992.

Galeana, Norma. "Mexico-Based Church Leader Charged with Sex Crimes Ordered Held on $90 Million Bail." Reuters, https://www.reuters.com/article/us-usa-mexico-church-court/mexico-based-church-leader-charged-with-sex-crimes-ordered-held-on-90-million-bail-idUSKCN2523FS.

Gallagher, Berhard. "The Extent and Nature of Known Cases of Institutional Child Sexual Abuse." *British Journal of Social Work* 30 (2003): 795-817.

Gallagher, Delia, Nadine Schmidt, and Kara Fox. "Top German Church Official Offers Resignation over 'Catastrophe of Sexual Abuse'." CNN, https://www.cnn.com/2021/06/04/europe/cardinal-marx-germany-resignation-pope-intl/index.html.

Gill, A. *Children of the Empire: The Shocking Story of Child Migration to Australia* UK: Random House, 1998.

Glass, Cathy. *Innocent.* London: Harper, 2019.

Global News. "25% of Human Trafficking Victims in Canada Are Children: StatsCan." Global News, https://globalnews.ca/news/4314916/25-of-human-trafficking-victims-in-canada-are-children-statscan/.

Goodwin, Jazmin. "Mastercard, Visa and Discover Cut Ties with Pornhub Following Allegations of Child Abuse." CNN, https://www.cnn.com/2020/12/14/business/mastercard-visa-discover-pornhub/index.html.

Government of Canada. "Child, Early and Forced Marriage." Government of Canada, https://www.international.gc.ca/world-monde/issues_development-enjeux_developpement/human_rights-droits_homme/child_marriage-mariages_enfants.aspx?lang=eng.

Grabe, S, JS Hyde, and SM Lindberg. "Body Objectification and Depression in Adolescents: The Role of Gender, Shame and Rumination." *Psychology of Women Quarterly* 31, no. 2 (2007): 164-75.

Grant, Meghan. "Victim of Alleged Child Sex Assault Says Interview with Lethbridge Office 'Like a Slap in the Face'." CBC News, https://www.cbc.ca/news/canada/calgary/lethbridge-police-historic-sexual-assault-complaint-1.6100895.

Greenfield, LA. "Sex Offences and Offenders: An Analysis of Data on Rape and Sexual Assault.". Washington DC: U S Department of Justice, 1997.

Grey, Rosemary. "Sexual Violence against Child Soldiers: The Limits and Potential of International Criminal Law." *International Feminist Journal of Politics* 16, no. 4 (2014): 601-21.

Gruenbaum, Oren. "Malawi: The Human Hyenas." *The Round Table: The Commonwealth Journal of International Affairs* September (2016).

Gupta, Swati. "Kathua Child Rape and Murder: Indian Court Finds Sex Guilty in Case That Outraged Nation." CNN, www.cnn.com/2019/06/10/asia/india-jammu-rape-trial-verdict=intl-hnk/index.html.

Gupta, Swati, and Jessie Yeung. "Dozens of Men Arrested in India Are Accused of Gang Raping a 15-Year-Old Girl Repeatedly." CNN, https://www.cnn.com/2021/09/24/india/india-gang-rape-mumbai-girl-intl-hnk/index.html.

Haque, Amber. "Breast Ironing Awareness 'Needed in School'." BBC, www.bbc.com/news/education-47695169.

Harris, Michael. *Unholy Orders: Tragedy at Mount Cashel.* Toronto: Penguin Books, 1990.

Harrison, Dr Nicholas J. "The Art of Precious Scars." In *Starwarssavedmylife,* 2019.

Harrison, Nicholas. "Dad's Day." Canada, 2019.

Harte, Alys. "A Man Tried to Choke Me During Sex without Warning." BBC Radio 5 Live Investigators Unit, www.bbc.com/news/uk-50546184.

Hay, Travis, Cindy Blackstock, and Michael Kirlew. "Dr Peter Bryce (1853-1932): Whistleblower on Residential Schools." *CMAJ* 192, no. 9 (2020): E223-E24.

Histrova, Bobby. "Families of Paul Bernardo's Victims File for Access to Records of Parole Hearing." CBC, https://www.cbc.ca/news/canada/hamilton/paul-bernardo-parole-files-1.5538586.

Holcombe, Madeline, and Lauren del Valle. "Lawsuit Alleges Past Culture of Sexual Abuse at University of North Carolina School of the Arts." CNN, https://www.cnn.com/2021/10/05/us/sexual-abuse-lawsuit-north-carolina-school-of-the-arts/index.html.

Hollington, Kris. *Unthinkable: The Shocking Scandal of the UK Sex Traffickers.* London: Simon and Schuster, 2013.

Hruby, Denise. "Where Survivors of Sexual Abuse Are Sued by the Perpetrators." CNN, www.cnn.com/2019/01/23/europe/austria-skiers-sexual-assault-int/index.html.

Huntley, Svetlana. "Russian Legislation on the Protection of Children against Sexual Abuse and Sexual Exploitation: A Review." https://www.icmec.org/wp-content/uploads/2015/10/Russian_Legislation_on_Protection_of_Children_Against_Sexual_Abuse_and_Exploitation_FINAL.pdf.

Independent Inquiry. "The Independent Inquiry into Child Sexual Abuse in Germany." Berlin, Germany: Aufarbeitungskommission, 2020.

Interpol. "Appropriate Terminology." UN, https://www.interpol.int/en/Crimes/Crimes-against-children/Appropriate-terminology.

———. "Crimes against Children." UN, https://www.interpol.int/Crimes/Crimes-against-children.

———. "International Child Sexual Exploitation Database." UN, https://www.interpol.int/en/Crimes/Crimes-against-children/ International-Child-Sexual-Exploitation-database.

———. "Interpol Annual Report." UN, INTERPOL_Annual Report 2019_EN (1).pdf.

Ireton, Julie. "'Far from Bankrupt': Catholic Order That Ran 48 Residential Schools Faces Criticism." CBC, https://www.cbc.ca/ news/canada/ottawa/oblates-complex-corporate-structure-protect-money-from-liabilities-residential-school-1.6259013.

Isely, Paul. "Child Sexual Abuse and the Catholic Church: An Historical and Contemporary Review." *Pastoral Psychology* 45, no. 4 (1997): 277-99.

James, E L. *Fifty Shades of Grey.* UK: Doubleday, 2013.

Jay, Alexis, Malcolm Evans, Ivor Frank, and Drusilla Sharpling. *Interim Report: A Summary: Independent Inquiry into Child Sexual Abuse.* UK: Crown, 2018.

Jones, Adele D, and Ena Trotman Jemmott. "Status, Privilege and Gender Inequality: Cultures of Male Impunity and Entitlement in the Sexual Abuse of Children: Perspectives from a Caribbean Study." *International Social Work* 59, no. 6 (2016): 836-49.

Jones, Celeste, Kristina Jones, and Juliana Buhring. *Not without My Sister.* London: Harper Element, 2007.

Kalvapalle, Rahul. "An Indian Train Passenger's Tweet Helped Save 25 Girls from Child Traffickers." Global News, www.globalnews. ca/news/4319117/india-girls-rescued-from-human-traffickers-tweet.

Kelly, Irene. *Sins of the Mother.* London: Pan Books, 2015.

Khan, M Ilyas. "Pakistan Zeinab Murder: New Law Aims to Catch Child Abusers." BBC, www.bbc.com/news/world-asia-51852381.

Knaul, Felecia Marie, Flavia Bustreo, and Richard Horton. "Countering the Pandemic of Gender-Based Violence and Maltreatment of Young People: The Lancet Commission." *The Lancet* (2019).

Kosovsky, Rena. "It's Time Schools Took Sexual Assault Seriously." JewishWomen'sArchive,https://jwa.org/blog/its-time-schools-took-sexual-assault-seriously.

Kraus, S, and B Russell. "Early Sexual Experiences: The Role of Internet Access and Sexually Explicit Material." *CyberPsychology and Behavior* 11, no. 2 (2008): 162-8.

Kristoff, Nicholas. "The Children of Pornhub: Why Does Canada Allow This Company to Profit Off Videos of Exploitation and Assault?" New York Times, https://www.nytimes.com/2020/12/04/opinion/sunday/pornhub-rape-trafficking.html?smid=em-share.

Krug, EG, JA Mercy, LL Dahlberg, and AB Zwi. *The World Report on Violence and Health.* Geneva: World Health Organization, 2002.

Laing, Aislinn. "Chile's National Prosecutor Requesting Vatican Sex Abuse Files." Reuters, www.reuters.com/article/us-chile-abuse-church/chiles-national-prosecutor-requesting-vatican-sex-abuse-files-idUSKBN1KM6BT.

Laser, Julie Anne. "Prevalence and Correlates of Enjo Kousai, School Girl and Boy Prostituion, in Japan." *Journal of Asian Research* 2, no. 1 (2018): 37.

Lesher, Michael. *Sexual Abuse, Shonda and Concealment in Orthodox Jewish Communities.* Jefferson, North Carolina: McFarland and Company, 2014.

Levenson, Eric, Sahar Akbarzai, and Taylor Romine. *No Prison Time for Man Who Pleaded Guilty to Rape and Sexual Assault of Four Teenage Girls.* USA: CNN, 2021.

Levinson-King, Robin. "The Brutal Secret of School Sport Initiations." BBC News, www.bbc.com/news/world-us-canada-46282988.

Lin, Mayuri Mei. "Malaysia Revised 'Victim-Shaming' School Text Book." BBC News, www.bbc.com/news/world-asia-46888332.

Loriggio, Paola. "Sexual Abuse Victims Tell of Lifelong Suffering from Gordon Stuckless." Macleans, https://www.macleans.ca/news/canada/sexual-abuse-victims-tell-of-lifelong-suffering-from-gordon-stuckless/.

Mabuza, Ernest. "Children Victims in 42% of All Rape Cases Recorded." Times Alive, www.timeslive.co.za/news/south-africa/2018-05-16-children-victims-in-42-of-all-rape-cases-recorded/.

Mackenzie, Tom. *The Last Foundling.* London: Pan Books, 2014.

Macleans, K E. "When You Have to Give Birth in Secret." Today's Parent, www.todaysparent.com/family/parenting/when-you-have-to-give-birth-in-secret.

Mandel, David, and David Pelcovitz. *Breaking the Silence: Sexual Abuse in the Jewish Community.* Jersey City, NJ, USA: Ktav Publishing House, Inc., 2011.

Mao, Frances. "Jeni Haynes: The Woman Who Created 2,500 Personalities to Survive." BBC, www.bbc.com/news/world-australia-49589160.

Marcotte, Alexandra S., Amanda N. Gesselman, Helen E. Fisher, and Justin R. Garcia. "Women's and Men's Reactions to Receiving Unsolicited Genital Images from Men." *The Journal of Sex Research* 58, no. 4 (2020): 512-21.

Mathews, Ben, and Delphine Collin-Vezine. "Child Sexual Abuse: Raising Awareness and Empathy Is Essential to Promote New Public Health Responses." *Journal of Public Health Policy* 37, no. 3 (2016): 304-14.

McCarthy, Tom. *Spotlight.* Open Road Films, 2015.

McClelland, Peter, Jennifer Coate, Bob Atkinson, Robert Fitzgerald, Helen Milroy, Andrew Murray, and Gail Furness. "Royal Commission into Institutional Responses to Child Sexual Abuse." Australia, 2017.

———. "Royal Commission into Institutional Responses to Child Sexual Abuse." edited by Australian Government. UK, 2017.

McDermott, Sarah. "My Father, the Catholic Priest Who Doesn't Want to Know Me." BBC, www.bbc.com/news/stories-42085065.

Meier, Eileen. "Child Rape in South Africa." *Paediatric Nursing* 28, no. 5 (2002): 1-5.

Menon, Malini. "Two Teenagers Gang Raped in India, One Commits Suicide." Reuters, www.reuters/com/article/us-india-rape/two-teenagers-gang-raped-in-india-one-commits-suicide-idUSK BN1I412J.

Menon, Praveen. "New Zealand Child Abuse Inquiry Finds Quarter of a Million Harmed in State and Faith-Based Care." Reuters, https://www.reuters.com/article/newzealand-abuse/new-zealand-inquiry-finds-quarter-of-a-million-abused-in-state-and-faith-based-care-idUSKBN28Q0C6.

299

Merdian, Hannah L., Derek E. Perkins, Stephen D. Webster, and Darragh McCashin. "Transnational Child Sexual Abuse: Outcomes from a Roundtable Discussion." *Environmental Research and Public Health* 16 (2019): 243.

Milloy, John S. *A National Crime: The Canadian Government and the Residential School System 1879-1986.* Manitoba: University of Manitoba Press, 1999.

Milotte, Mike. *Banished Babies: The Secret History of Ireland's Baby Export Business.* Dublin: New Island, 2012.

Ministry of Statistics and Programme implementation, UN "Sex Ratio of India." UN, http://statisticstimes.com/demographics/sex-ratio-of-india.php.

Ministry of the Attorney General. "Handouts: Child Sex Abuse." Ministry of the Attorney General, https://www.attorneygeneral.jus. gov.on.ca/inquiries/cornwall/en/hearings/exhibits/Peter_Jaffe/pdf/ Sports.pdf.

Mitchell, Alanna. "From the Survivors' Circle." *Canadian Geographic* 2017, 65-72.

Mitra, Esha, Rhea Mogu, Arpit Goel, and Manveena Suri. "Girl, 16, Says She Was Raped by Hundreds of Men in Western India." CNN, https://www.cnn.com/2021/11/16/india/india-girl-rape-hundreds-men-intl-hnk/index.html.

Mitra, Esha, Manveena Suri, Vedika Sud, and Rishabh Pratap. "Four Men Charged with Rape and Murder of 9-Year-Old Girl in India." CNN, https://www.cnn.com/2021/08/30/india/dalit-rape-men-charged-india-intl-hnk/index.html.

Moghe, Sonia. "NXIVM Founder Sentenced to the Remainder of His Life in Prison." CNN, https://www.cnn.com/2020/10/27/us/nxivm-keith-raniere-sentencing-supporters/index.html.

Mohan, Megha. "I Was Raped at 14, and the Video Ends up on a Porn Site." BBC, www.bbc.com/news/stories-51391981.

Moodysson, Lukas. *Lilya 4-Ever.* Metrodome Distribution and BBC Four, 2002.

Mullen, Peter. *The Magdalene Sisters.* Ireland: PEP Films, 2002.

Mullin, Malone. "Sending Nudes Can Have Dire Consequences. So Why Are N.L. Teens Still Doing It?" CBC News, https://www.cbc.

ca/news/canada/newfoundland-labrador/teen-sexting-nl-1.5483672.

Murata, Shakito. "Muta' Temporary Marriage in Islamic Law." Al Islam. org, https://www.al-islam.org/muta-temporary-marriage-islamic-law-sachiko-murata/permanent-marriage#iii-divorce-talaq.

Nagesh, Ashitha. "Does Denmark Have a 'Pervasive' Rape Problem." BBC www.bbc,com/news/world-europe-47470353.

Nakonechny, Simon. "As Catholic Church Balked at Paying Residential School Settlement, Quebec Nuns Sold Nearly $25m in Real Estate." CBC, https://www.cbc.ca/news/canada/montreal/residential-school-financial-settlements-quebec-catholic-church-1.6092215.

National Center for Education Statistics. "Student Access to Digital Learning Resources Outside of the Classroom." U.S. Department of Education, https://nces.ed.gov/fastfacts/display.asp?id=46.

National Crime Agency. "Man Sentenced over Some of the Worst Child Abuse Content NCA Investigators Have Ever Seen." National Crime Agency, https://www.nationalcrimeagency.gov.uk/news/man-sentenced-over-some-of-the-worst-child-abuse-content-nca-investigators-have-ever-seen.

Neustein, Amy. *Tempest in the Temple: Jewish Communities and Child Sex Scandals.* Lebanon, New Haven, USA: University Press of New England, 2009.

Nienaber, Michael. "German Police Make Arrests over Massive Child Pornography Website." Reuters, http://www.reuters.com/article/us-germany-sexcrimes-idUSKBN19R0VD.

O'Conner, J, J Cusana, S McMahon, and J Draper. "Students' Articulation of Subtle Rape Myths Surrounding Campus Sexual Assault.". *Journal of College Student Development* 59 (2018): 439-55.

O'Gorman, Colm. *Beyond Belief.* UK: Hodder and Stoughton, 2009.

O'Riordan, Steven, and Sue Leonard. *Whispering Hope: The True Story of the Magdalene Women* London: Orion, 2015.

Oakes, Bradlyn, and John Last. "Women on Arctic Mission Told Not to Wear Tight-Fitting Clothing." CBC, https://www.cbc.ca/news/canada/north/mosaic-dress-code-sexism-arctic-research-1.5739547.

Office of the High Commissioner of Human Rights. "Convention on the Rights of the Child." Geneva: United Nations, 1989.

Olaka, Musa Wakhungu. "Living a Genocide: Rape." USF Tampa Library, http://exhibits.lib.usf.edu/exhibits/show/darfur-genocide/modeofdestruction/rape.

Pandey, Geeta. "Abuse of Indian Children 'Common'." BBC, http://news.bbc.co.uk/2/hi/south_asia/6539027.stm.

———. "Why an MP Wants India to Talk About Child Sex Abuse." BBC, www.bbc.com/news/world-asia-india-34971791.

Panorama, BBC. "Pimps Caught Exploiting Women on Popular Classified Ads Website." BBC, https://www.bbc.com/news/uk-59219411.

Pathak, Priyanka. "India Catholic Cardinal Oswald Gracias 'Failed Abuse Victims'." BBC, www.bbc.com/news/world-asia-india-47302447.

Pauls, Karen. "New Rules on Removal of Illegal Online Content Could Help in Battle against Child Pornography." CBC, https://www.cbc.ca/news/canada/manitoba/canada-illegal-online-content-child-porn-1.5847695.

Pauls, Karen, and Cameron MacIntosh. "Woman Who Spent Years Scrubbing Explicit Video from Internet Urges Tech Firms to Make It Easier to Remove." CBC, https://www.cbc.ca/news/canada/manitoba/canada-internet-children-abuse-pornography-1.5822042.

Peter, J, and P Valkenburg. "Adolescents' Exposure to Sexually Explicit Internet Material and Sexual Satisfaction: A Longitudinal Study." *Human Communication Research* 35, no. 2 (2009): 171-94.

Peter, J, and PM Valkenburg. "Adolescents and Pornography: A Review of 20 Years of Research." *Journal of Sex Research* 53 (2016): 509-31.

Picard, André. "Cindy Blackstock: Advocate for First Nations Children." *The Lancet* (2018).

Plan International Canada. "Child Marriage." https://plancanada.ca/child-marriage.

Pressly, Linda. "The Community of 2000 People with 151 Cases of Sex Crimes." BBC, www.bbc.com/news/stories-43478396.

Proctor, Jason. "Instagram Evidence Convinces B.C. Judge Teen Was 'Set up' on Sexual Assault Charges." CBC News, https://www.cbc.

ca/news/canada/british-columbia/sexual-assault-instagram-teenager-1.5995282.

Pukall, Caroline. *Human Sexuality: A Contemporary Introduction.* Third ed. Canada: Oxford University Press, 2020.

———, ed. *Human Sexuality: A Contemporary Introduction.* 2nd ed. Don Mills, Ontario: Oxford University Press, 2017.

Pullella, Philip, and Scott Malone. "Vatican Voices: 'Shame and Sorrow' over Damning Sex Abuse Report." Boston, www.rreuters.com/article/us-pennsylvania-religion-mccarrick/vatican-voices-shame-and-sorrow-over-damning-sex-abuse-report-idUSKBN1L11W5.

Pullella, Philip, and Caroline Stauffer. "Key Cardinal Rebukes Pope over Abuse Comment in Rare Move." Reuters, www.reuters/com/article/us-pope-latum-abuse/key-cardinal-rebukes-pope-over-abuse-comment-in-rare-move-idUSKBN1F90ZH.

Quebec Ombudsman. "The "Children of Duplessis" a Time for Solidarity." In *Assemblee Nationale Quebec.* Quebec, January 22, 1997.

Raboch, J, H Cerna, and P Zemek. "Sexual Aggressivity and Androgens." *British Journal of Psychiatry* 151 (1987): 398-400.

Raftery, Mary, and Eoin O'Sullivan. *Suffer the Little Children: The inside Story of Ireland's Industrial Schools.* Dublin, Ireland: New Island Books, 1999.

Razzall, Kate. "Coronavirus: 'Worryingly Low Number' of at-Risk Children in School." BBC, https://www.bbc.com/news/uk-52228772.

Real Life News Life. "It's Hard to Believe That Bride Kidnapping Exists in 2017." Real Life News Life, /www.news.com.au/lifestyle/real-life/news-life/its-hard-to-believe-that-bride-kidnapping-exists-in-2017/news-story/9e7a445078231d94da67be33e3b b9157.

Reed, Jim, and Louis Lee Ray. *Lawn Tennis Association 'Missed Chances' to Stop Abuse.* UK: BBC, 2019.

Regan, Helen, and Sophia Saifi. "Pakistan's Most Populous Province Bans Virginity Tests for Rape Survivors in Landmark Ruling." CNN, https://www.cnn.com/2021/01/05/asia/pakistan-court-virginity-test-ban-intl-hnk/index.html.

Reissing, Elke, and Heather Armstrong. "Sexuality over the Lifespan." In *Human Sexuality: A Contemporary Introduction*, edited by Caroline Pukall. Canada: Oxford University Press, 2020.

Resnicoff, Steven H. "Jewish Law and the Tragedy of Sexual Abuse of Children: The Dilemma within the Orthodox Jewish Community ". *Rutgers Journal of Law and Religion* 13, no. 2 (2012): pp 4-6 (note 15).

Reuters. "Australian Police Arrests 14 Men on Child Abuse Charges." Reuters, https://www.reuters.com/article/australia-crime-int/australian-police-arrests-14-men-on-child-abuse-charges-idUSKBN27R05C.

———. "France Outlaws Sex with Children Aged under 15." Reuters, https://www.cnn.com/2021/04/16/europe/france-consent-age-intl/index.html.

———. "German Police Detain Man after Posting Child Abuse Victim's Photo." Reuters, www.reuters.com/article/us-germany-crime/german-police-detain-man-after-posting-child-abuse-victims-photo-idUSKBN1CF1F3.

———. "Gymnastics: U.S Governing Body Shocked over Death of Former Coach." Reuters, https://www.usnews.com/news/top-news/articles/2021-02-26/gymnastics-us-governing-body-shocked-over-death-of-former-coach.

———. "Macron Says France Will Tighten Legislation on Incest." Reuters, https://www.reuters.com/article/us-france-incest/macron-says-france-will-tighten-legislation-on-incest-idUSKBN 29S0KY.

———. "Mexican Judge Suspended after Outcry over Child Abuse Case." Reuters, https://www.reuters.com/article/us-mexico-crime/mexican-judge-suspended-after-outcry-over-child-abuse-case-idUSKCN25D067.

Rhodes, Blair. "Human Trafficking Charges Laid after N.B. Girl Rescued in N.S. Hotel Parking Lot." CBC, https://www.cbc.ca/news/canada/nova-scotia/human-trafficking-charges-laid-teen-found-hotel-1.6247021.

Rieger, Sarah. "Calgary Minor Hockey Club Probes 'Disturbing' Video That Shows Boy Passing out, Convulsing." CBC, https://www.cbc.ca/news/canada/calgary/calgary-hockey-seizure-video-1.5775894.

Robinson, Ben, and Michael Buchanan. "Bodies of 'Hundreds' of Children Buried in Mass Grave." BBC News, www.bbc.com/news/uk-41200949.

Rogers, Thomas. "A Major German Political Party Used to Support Pedophilia - and It's Coming Back to Haunt Them." https://newrepublic.com/article/120379/german-green-party-pedophilia-scandal.

Ronis, Scott, and Laura Kabbash. "Sexual Assault and Harassment." In *Human Sexuality: A Contemporary Introduction*, edited by Caroline Pukall, 392-419. Canada: Oxford University Press, 2020.

Rotenberg, C, and A Cotter. "Police Reported Sexual Assaults in Canada before and after #Metoo, 2016 and 2017." In *Juristat: Candian Centre for Justice Statistics*: Statistics Canada Catalogue no.85-002-x, 2018.

Rothbaum, BO, EB Foa, DS Riggs, T Murdock, and W Walsh. "A Prospective Examination of Post-Traumatic Stress Disorder in Rape Victims." *Journal of Traumatic Stress* 5 (1992): 455-73.

Rubino, Francesco, Rebecca M. Puhl, David E. Cummings, Robert H. Eckel, Donna H. Ryan, Jeffrey I. Mechanick, Joe Nadglowski, *et al.* "Joint International Consensus Statement for Ending Stigma of Obesity." *Nature Medicine* (2020).

Rush, Florence. *The Best-Kept Secret: Sexual Abuse of Children.* USA: McGraw Hill, 1980.

Russell, Diane. *The Secret Trauma: Incest in the Lives of Girls and Women.* New York: Basic Books Inc, 1986.

Ruston, Anna. *Secret Slave.* London: Blink Publishing, 2016.

Ruvugiro, Emmanuel Sehene. "Rwanda: The Gruesome Plight of Children During the Tutsi Genocide." Justiceinfo.net, www.justiceinfo.net/en/tribunals/ictr/34925-online-exhibition-pays-gruesome-tribute-to-child-suffering-in-rwandan-genocide.html.

Ryan, Justice. "The Commission to Enquire into Child Abuse Report." Ireland, 2009.

Sahara, Kento. "Japan Exhibition Puts Child Prostitution in the Limelight." Reuters, http://www.reuters.com/article/us-japan=prostitution-idUSKCN1180IT.

Sawa, Timothy. "Ontario Christian School Tells Court It Was Unaware Abuse Would Cause Emotional Damage." CBC News, https://

www.cbc.ca/news/canada/toronto/grenville-christian-college-lawsuit-appeal-1.6014135.

Schachter, Herschel. "Regarding Mesirah." The Torahweb Foundation, https://www.torahweb.org/torah/special/2007/rsch_mesirah.html.

Schmidt, Nadine, and Sheena McKenzie. *Two Men Convicted in One of Germany's Worst Child Sex Abuse Scandals*. USA: CNN, 2019.

Scotland. "Systematic Child Abuse Claims Published." www.bbc.news/uk-scotland-38566857.

Sekielski, Tomasz. *Tell No One*. Poland: YouTube, 2019.

———. *Tylko Nie Mów Nikomu (2019) (Tell No One)*. Poland: IMDb, 2019.

Sellars, Bev. *They Called Me Number One*. Vancouver: Talon Books, 2013.

Seo, Yoonjung. "Dozens of Young Women in South Korea Were Allegedly Forced into Sexual Slavery on an Encrypted Messaging App." CNN, https://www.cnn.com/2020/03/27/asia/south-korea-telegram-sex-rooms-intl-hnk/index.html

Sethi, A. " Domestic Sex Trafficking of Aboriginal Girls in Canada: Issues and Implications." *First Peoples Child & Family Review* 3, no. 3 (2007): 57-71.

Seymour-Jones, Carole. *A Dangerous Liaison: A Revelatory New Biography of Simone De Beauvoir and Jean-Paul Sartre* USA: Harry Abrams, 2009.

Shengold, Leonard. *Soul Murder Revisited* New Haven Conn: Yale University Press, 1999.

Shirbon, Estelle. "'#Metoo Movement' in British Schools as Teens Recount Sexual Abuse." Reuters, https://www.reuters.com/article/uk-britain-schools-sexual-abuse/metoo-movement-in-british-schools-as-teens-recount-sexual-abuse-idUSKBN2BM20L.

Shubert, Atika, Nadine Schmidt, and Claudia Otto. "Children and Parents Reported Sex Abuse for Years in Central Germany. Why Did No One Believe Them?" CNN, www.cnn.com/2019/04/05/europe/german-sex-abuse-michaela-andreas-v-intl/index.html.

Singh, Mannat Mohanjeet, Shradha S. Parsekar, and Sreekumaran N. Nair. "An Epidemiological Overview of Child Sexual Abuse." *Journal of Family Medicine and Primary Care*. 3, no. 4 (2014): 430-5.

Sini, Rozina. "How 'Metoo' Is Exposing the Scale of Sexual Abuse." BBC News, www.bbc.com/news/blogs-trending-41633857.

Sixsmith, Martin. *Philomena: A Mother, Her Son and a Fifty-Year Search.* London: Pan Books, 2010.

Skinner, E Benjamin. *A Crime So Monstrous: A Shocking Expose of Modern-Day Sex Slavery, Human Trafficking and Urban Child Markets.* Edinburgh: Mainstream Publishing, 2008.

Skylark, Kate, and Lucy Gilbert. *Daddy's Wicked Parties.* Bolton Ontario: Createspace, 2015.

Smith, John. *The Boys of St Vincent.* Frankfurt, Germany: Pro-Fun Media, 2011.

SNAP. "Snap SW Ontario Releases List of Credibly Accused Priests of the Roman Catholic Diocese of London (Ont)." SNAP Network, www.snapnetwork.org/list_of_credibly_accused_priests_diocese_of_london_ont_dec19.

Solomon, Dana. Personal Communication, 2020.

———. Personal Communication, 2021.

Solomon, Simon. 13 December 2017.

Spiegel, MC. "Survival and Recovery: Jewish Women Confront Abuse." In *Shine the Light: Sexual Abuse and Healing in the Jewish Community*, edited by R Lev, 146-61. Boston: Northwestern University Press, 2003.

Sport, BBC. "Simone Biles: Larry Nassar Abused Me, Says Four-Time Olympic Champion." BBC, www.bbc.com/sport/gymnastics/42697952.

Stanger-Hall, Kathrin F., and David W. Hall. "Abstinence-Only Education and Teen Pregnancy Rates: Why We Need Comprehensive Sex Education in the U.S." *PLOS-ONE* 6, no. 10 (2011): e24658.

Stark, Rodney, and Roger Finke. "Catholic Religious Vocations: Decline and Revival." *Review of Religious Research* 42, no. 2 (2000): 125-45.

StatsCan. "Sexual Misconduct in the Canadian Armed Forces Regular Force, 2018." StatsCan, https://www150.statcan.gc.ca/n1/pub/85-603-x/85-603-x2019002-eng.htm.

———. "Trafficking in Persons in Canada, 2018." Statistics Canada, https://www150.statcan.gc.ca/n1/pub/85-002-x/2020001/article/00006-eng.htm.

Stefanovich, Olivia. "NDP MP Calls on Lemetti to Preserve St Anne's Residential School Abuse Documents." CBC News, https://www.cbc.ca/news/politics/st-anne-documents-angus-lametti-letter-1.5839805.

Steven, Morris. "Revealed: Child Sex Abuse Gang 'with Tentacles That Go around the World'." The Guardian, www.theguardian.com/uk-news/2015/apr/22/child-sex-paedophile-abuse-gang-revealed-trial-two-convictions.

Stoltenborgh, Marije, Marinus H van Ijzendoorn, Eveline M Euser, and Marian J Bakermans-Kranenburg. "A Global Perspective on Child Sexual Abuse: Meta-Analysis of Prevalence around the World." *Child Maltreatment* 16, no. 2 (2011): 79-101.

Stroebel, SS, SI O'Keefe, KW Beard, SY Kuo, S Swindell, and W Stroupe. "Brother-Sister Incest: Data from Anonymous Computer Assisted Self Interviews.". *Journal of Child Sexual Abuse* 22 (2013): 255-76.

Sutton, Katherine, ed. *Variations in Sexual Behaviour*. Edited by Caroline Pukall. third ed, Human Sexuality: A Contemporary Introduction. Canada: Oxford University Press, 2020.

Sutton, Katherine, and Karen Blair. "Perspectives on Sexuality." In *Human Sexuality: A Contemporary Inroduction*, edited by Caroline Pukall. Canada: Oxford University Press, 2020.

Symonds, Tom. "The Child Abuse Scandal of the British Children Sent Abroad." BBC News, www,bbc.com/news/u7k-39078652.

Talaga, Tanya. *Seven Fallen Feathers: Racism, Death and Hard Truths in a Northern City.* Canada: Anansi Press, 2017.

Tasker, John Paul. "Senator Aims to Curb 'Violent' Porn, Pitches Mandatory Age Verification for Online Sites." CBC, https://www.cbc.ca/news/politics/senator-violent-porn-mandatory-age-pornhub-1.5810603.

The Economist. "Bully Pulpit." *The Economist*, June 25th 2016, 27.

———. "Hearts, Minds and Souls." *The Economist*, July 30th 2016, 47-48.

———. "The Sexualization of Children: Innocents and Experience." *The Economist*, July 21 2018, 45-46.

The History Place. "Stalin's Forced Famine: 1932-9133: 7,000,000 Deaths." The History Place, http://www.historyplace.com/worldhistory/genocide/stalin.htm.

The Lancet Editorial. "The Erosion of Women's Sexual and Reproductive Rights." *The Lancet* 393, no. 10183 (2019): 1-6.

The Stationary Office. "Lost in Care: Report of the Tribunal of Inquiry into the Abuse of Children in Care in the Former County Council Aras of Gwynedd and Clwyd since 1974.". Department of Health, Wales, 1999.

Thompson, Ann. *Say Sorry: A Harrowing Childhood in Catholic Orphanages*. Kindle, 2009.

Thompson, Elisabeth. "Child Sex Exploitation Is on the Rise in Canada During the Pandemic." CBC, https://www.cbc.ca/news/politics/pandemic-child-sexual-abuse-1.5645315.

Thomson, Mike. "Westeners 'Fuelling Phillipine Child Sex Video Rise'." BBC, www.bbc.com/news/world-asis-48517437.

Titheradge, Noel. "OnlyFans: How It Handles Illegal Sex Videos - BBC Investigation." BBC.

Titheradge, Noel, and Rianna Croxford. "The Children Selling Explicit Videos on OnlyFans." BBC, https://www.bbc.com/news/uk-57255983.

Torah Academy of Bergen County. "The Mesirah Dilemma by Rabbi Chaim Jachter." Torah Academy of Bergen County, https://www.koltorah.org/halachah/the-mesirah-dilemma-by-rabbi-chaim-jachter.

Trump, Donald. "Executive Order on Combating Human Trafficking and Online Child Exploitation in the United States." edited by Law and Justice. Washington, USA: The White House, January 2020.

Truth and Reconciliation Commission. *Honouring the Truth, Reconciling for the Future*. Canada: Government of Canada, 2015.

UN Gift. "Sex Trafficking of Minors in America." Global Initiative to fight Human Trafficking, www.ungift.org/2017/09/17/sex-trafficking-of-minors-in-america.

UNDATA. "Legal Age for Marriage." UN, https://data.un.org/DocumentData.aspx?id=336.

UNICEF-UNFPA. "Global Programme to End Child Marriage." UNICEF-UNFPA, https://www.unicef.org/protection/unfpa-unicef-global-programme-end-child-marriage.

UNICEF. "Child Marriage: Latest Trends and Future Perspectives." UNICEF, www.data.unicef.org/wp-content/uploads/2018/06/Child-marriage-data-brief.pdf

———. "Children under Attack: Six Grave Violations against Children in Times of War." UNICEF, https://www.unicef.org/stories/children-under-attack-six-grave-violations-against-children-times-war.

———. "Sexual Violence against Children." UNICEF.

———. "Together for Girls: Sexual Violence Fact Sheet." UNICEF, www.unicef.org/protection/files/Together-for-Girls-Sexual-Violence-Fact-Sheet-July2012.pdf.

United Nations Commission on Human Rights. "Culture of Abduction, Rape and Forced Marriage Violates Women's Rights in Kyrgyzstan, UN Experts Find." United Nations Commission on Human Rights, www.ohchr.org/EN/NewsEvents/Pages/DisplayNews.aspx?NewsID=23583&LangID-E.

United to End Genocide. "The Cambodian Genocide." United to End Genocide, http://endgenocide.org/learn/past-genocides/the-cambodian-genocide/.

University of Alberta. "University of Alberta: Hazing Information." University of Alberta, https://www.ualberta.ca/current-students/student-groups/hazing/index.html.

Valsan, Lucian. "Simone De Baeuvoir: A Nazi, a Pedophile, and a Misogynist." http://www.avoiceformen/feminism/simone-de-beauvoir-a-nazi-a-pedophile-and-a-misogynist.

Vandoorne, Saskya, Simon Bouvier, and Sam Bradpiece. "More Than 200,000 Children Sexually Abused by French Catholic Clergy, Damning Report Finds." CNN, https://www.cnn.com/2021/10/05/europe/france-catholic-church-abuse-report-intl/index.html.

Vienneau, R. Collusion: The Dark History of the Duplessis Orphans. Canada: Kindle, 2010.

Walter Laqueur, Richard Breitman. Breaking the Silence. Hanover: Brandeis University Press, 1986.

Warick, Jason. "Critics Blast Catholic Church for Spending after Commitment to Residential School Survivors Went Unmet." CBC News, https://www.cbc.ca/news/canada/saskatoon/critics-blast-catholic-church-1.6086030.

Warick, Jason, and Justin Li. "Catholic Bishops Pledge $30m for Residential School Survivors, AFN Expresses Skepticism." CBC, https://www.cbc.ca/news/canada/catholic-bishops-30-million-1.6191677.

Wen, Philip, and Adam Jourdan. "China Kindergarten Sex Abuse and 'Needlemark' Claims Prompt Police Probe." Reuters, www.reuters.com/article/us-ryb-education-china/china-kindergarten-sex-abuse-and-needlemarks-claims-prompt-police-probe-idUSKBN1DO01D.

Wesbrook, Tom. "Australian Report into Child Sex Abuse Wants to Break Confessional Seal." Reuters, www.reuters.com/article/us-australia-abuse-idUSKCN1AU0R7.

Westbrook, Tom. "Australian Police File Hundreds of Sex Abuse Charges against Seven People." Reuters, www.reuters.com/article/us-australia-sexabuse/australian-police-file-hundreds-of-sex-abuse-charges-against-seven-people-idUSKBN1FS17L.

Whewell, Tim. "Norway's Hidden Scandal." BBC, www.bbc.co.uk/news/resources/idt-sh/norways_hidden_scandal.

Whitehead, John W. "The Essence of Evil: Sex with Children Has Become Big Business in America." *Global Research* April 24 (2019): 1-4.

WHO. "WHO Horrified over Sexual Exploitation by Aid Workers in DR Congo." BBC, https://www.bbc.com/news/world-africa-58710200.

Williamson, Lucy. "Olivier Duhamel: French Incest Allegations Prompt Victims to Speak Out." BBC, https://www.bbc.com/news/world-europe-55707613.

Wolf, Dick. *Angels, Law and Order Special Victims Unit 4th Year*. USA: Universal Studios, 2007.

———. *Pandora, Law and Order Special Victims Unit 3rd Year*. USA: Universal Studios, 2007.

World Health Organization. "Global Status Report on Preventing Violence against Children." World Health Organization.

Ybarra, M, and K Mitchell. "Exposure to Internet Pornography among Children and Adolescents: A National Survey." *CyberPsychology and Behaviour* 8, no. 5 (2005): 473-83.

Ybarra, M, K Mitchell, M Hamburger, M Diener-West, and P Leaf. "X-Rated Material and Perpetration of Sexually Aggressive Behaviour among Children and Adolescents: Is There a Link?". *Aggressive Behaviour* 37, no. 1 (2011): 1-18.

Yehuda, R, M Friedman, TY Rosenbaum, E Labinsky, and J Schmeidler. "History of Past Sexual Abuse in Married Observant Jewish Women." *American Journal of Psychiatry* 164 (2007): 1700-6.

Zaugg, Julie. "These North Korean Defectors Were Sold into China as Cybersex Slaves. Then They Escaped." CNN, www.cnn.com/2019/06/09/asia/north-korea-defectors-intl-hnk/index.html.

Zurbriggen, EL, RL Collins, S Lamb, TA Roberts, DL Tolman, LM Ward, and J Blake. "Report of the APA Task Force on the Sexualization of Girls." Washington DC: American Psychological Association, 2007.

Index